THE RELIGION OF NEGRO PROTESTANTS

The Religion of Negro Protestants

CHANGING RELIGIOUS ATTITUDES AND PRACTICES

RUBY FUNCHESS JOHNSTON

PHILOSOPHICAL LIBRARY
NEW YORK

PRINTED IN THE UNITED STATES OF AMERICA

To

The Reverend and Mrs. S. A. Funchess,
Elizabeth, Mayme, Clementine,
Emma Louise, and Juanita

Preface

The conceptual scheme (which is simply a plan or way of presenting material) the author is making use of to present observations, ideas, and conclusions to the reader is only a matter of choice. That is, the facts of the study could have been presented by using other terms. The important thing is to consider with thought the information which is being presented regardless of the use of language. This is essential in order clearly to comprehend the changes which are occurring in religion today. Some writers select certain terms or use a particular style of writing while presenting information to readers; others make use of some other form of language to present their observations. Whatever style is used might depend upon any number of considerations, such as the experiences of the writer, his education (the nature and extent of), his occupation (whether a scientist, a clergyman, a laborer, a humanitarian, etc.), his objectives, etc. Actually it makes no difference as far as the validity of a work is concerned what terminology is selected. The important consideration is not to disregard the merit of scientific findings regardless of one's penchant for a particular style of writing or terminology.

The author makes use of the "action plan or schema," which shows man acting in a situation with ends or objectives in view according to a norm, which regulates the choice of ends and prescribes what procedure is appropriate in acting or seeking to attain goals. That is, definite principles are formulated to regulate action, so that one is expected to govern action by a certain system of rules to which there is a sense of obligation to conform. Obviously, these rules arise through social interaction; as one associates with one's fellows, values are absorbed during the process of social relationships. Particular norms are important to the individual according to the society in which he develops; for example, a man who lives under a democratic system of government would in all probability have a different point of view from a man who has lived in and has been educated under an autocratic state. It is necessary, however, not to discount man himself, the role of the individual in action. Since man is not a machine but is a thinking being, he does not unquestionably absorb everything from his social midst. His reflection, his original nature, and his social experiences interplay to condition and determine his actions.

It is significant to understand that not all individuals and groups are motivated by the same norms or rules although there is a general system of norms to which value is attached in any organized society. Values are significant according to one's position, etc., and therefore the dominant or ruling group has some values which are entirely different from those of the subordinate group; the laborer's ends are not identical with those of the promoter of industry, and so on. Since this is true, one's probability of realizing objectives or of attaining ends is conditioned by the goals of others. Man's action is related to the actions of others; the means one employs to realize ends inevitably depend upon the goals of others in the action process.

Correspondingly, concession and adjustment are indispensable elements in peaceful or harmonious social relationships. To minimize conflict in a social system it is necessary to put forth effort and to act concertedly to harmonize opposing points of view or contrasting positions.

This study illustrates the importance of blending varied positions; it shows that there has been dissatisfaction and maladjustment in the Protestant church (with particular reference to Negro Protestants) as religious values were changing while relatively new goals were being sought, with minimization of interest in after-life; and it establishes the observation that tension subsides with recognition and consideration of the objectives of diverse groups. It, in the meantime, clearly emphasizes the importance of the PRINCIPLE OF BROTHERHOOD in social relationships.

Although there are types of Negro Protestants, each type regarding certain values as being of especial significance, there is a common point of view which characterizes the Negro Protestant group as a unit. To some persons, action related to other-worldly (transcendental, supersensory, non-empirical, non-experimental) values is primary; this type is sometimes referred to as the traditionalist or transcendentalist, who tenaciously clings to conservative ideas of religion and staunchly affirms the reality of God. To other persons, both temporal and spiritual values are important; there is a tendency, nevertheless, to depart from a pronounced expression of emotion during church worship. To another group, values of this world (empirical, experimental, sensory) are outstanding; other-worldly elements are not prominent to this type, which is not particularly concerned about "eternal salvation" or Heaven. This type, which is sometimes referred to as the empiricist, does not welcome nor tolerate an overt expression of emotion in an emphatic manner. Irrespective of different types of churchmen, there is a common system of values among Negro Protestants.

A statement of the normative principle (norm) to which reference is made in this study of Negro Protestants is as follows. There should be a moderate or subdued form of worship, with no exaggerated expression of emotion; a religion related to living and improvement of the social midst through application of the principle of brotherhood is essential. Men should employ techniques or go through procedures (means) which ensure realization of an abundant life in terms of the principles of Christianity.

R. F. J.

Contents

ACKNOWLEDGMENTS

THE ASSISTANCE of all persons who aided in the development of this study is appreciated.

Clergymen and laymen were generously cooperative. Although it is not possible to enumerate all persons who assisted the writer, cognizance must be taken of a few who helped in innumerable ways and spent considerable time answering questions. The ministers whose churches were intensively studied each spent more than twenty hours discussing religion with the writer. Among those assisting the writer are the Reverend and Mrs. S. A. Funchess, whose cooperation facilitated the South Carolina phase of this study, the Reverend and Mrs. Richard M. Owens, Reverends Samuel L. Laviscount and Oddous Barber, Doctors W. Frederic Fisher and Charles B. Copher, Doctor and Mrs. Julian E. Grant, and Mr. Oscar Fitzallen.

The writer acknowledges suggestions made by Doctors Carle C. Zimmerman, Albert N. Cousins and Kirkland W. Green.

Libraries which the writer appreciates having had the advantage of using for research are as follows: Widener Library and the Library of the Department of Social Relations, Harvard University, Cambridge, Massachusetts, the Congregational Library, the Theological Library, and the Boston Public Library, Boston, Massachusetts, and the South Carolina State College Library, Orangeburg, South Carolina.

RUBY FUNCHESS JOHNSTON

List of Protestant Types

List of Tables

Introduction

Scientific Conceptualization

This study aims to show the changing system of beliefs and practices of Negro Protestants. This is an analysis of religion mainly in terms of the action schema, with utilization of those features of action which are adequate or pragmatic for this particular study. There is a generalized use of the action schema on the concrete and the analytical levels. Although some attention is here given to the conceptual scheme, technical details are not given because conceptualization can be grasped as the analysis proceeds.

In the process of conceptualization, phenomena are divided into units or parts. The basic unit of the conceptual scheme is "the unit act," which consists of these elements: actor, end, means, conditions, and norms. The unit act in relation to other units constitutes systems of action.[1]

An act, which is a process in time, involves, first, an agent or actor, the person initiating the action. Second, an act must have an end, a future goal toward which action is oriented. The end implies a state which is not in existence and which would not occur without the intervention of the actors; if, however, the desired state is already in existence, it would not remain unchanged, without effort on the part of the actor. Thus an end is a desired future state of affairs toward which action is oriented; it differs in important respects from the state which the actor would expect to occur without his intervention. An end, on the analytical level, is the difference between the anticipated state and that which it could have been predicted would develop without the active intervention of the agent. In the process of action, the actor visualizes his end and attempts to attain, realize, or achieve it.[2]

Action does not take place separately but occurs in a series of interrelated chains; hence, what is from one point of view an end to which means are applied may be from another a means to a further end, and it may be a link in both directions in the series of acts. Ac-

[1] Parsons, Talcott, *The Structure of Social Action,* McGraw-Hill Book Company, Incorporated, New York, 1937, pp. 43–45.

[2] *Ibid.*, 45, 49, 75, 229–230, 457.

tion may be oriented to higher ends in the same chain or group of related ends, and it may also be directed to ends in other chains as well. Each act in the chain is a means to some further end, and similarly, a given end might be served by many means while action is progressively oriented toward an ultimate end.[1]

The ultimate end is a clear guiding principle of action which does not fall in the intrinsic immediate end sector of the means-end relationship, because the ultimate end is non-empirical (for example, in this study, the orienting of action toward the attainment of "Heaven"). This is a non-scientific sector of the means-end schema; one cannot tell whether the means employed are efficacious to the end. The appropriateness or suitability of means to end cannot be determined empirically, inasmuch as these non-experimental entities are outside the range of science. The ultimate end and the selective choice of means in pursuit of the anticipated future state of affairs, as well as the explanation of why the ends should be pursued, are the manifestation of a sentiment.[2] This "value attitude," which expresses itself in transcendental ends, is without the domain of observation and experience, and hence action in the pursuit of non-empirical ends is non-logical or non-experimental.[3] There is no criterion to determine experimentally the coincidence of means and ends. The theories, which motivate the actions, are non-experimental or non-scientific, and therefore the scientific standard of rationality is not applicable in this sense.

The third element in "the unit act" is "the situation" of action. The act takes place in a situation, of which the "trends of development" differ in some respects from the anticipated state of affairs, the end. The situation is analyzable into two parts: conditions, and means. Conditional elements are those over which the actor has no control and cannot alter in his efforts to realize his end. They limit and restrict action. Means are those elements in the situation which can be altered or controlled by the actor in conformity with his goal.[4] In the system of action of the Negro collectivity, means will refer to those elements over which the actor has an appreciable degree of control in the pursuit of his end.

The fourth element in "the unit act" is "the guiding norm." Within the area of control of the actor, means employed are determined by a selective factor. Action is oriented to a normative principle. In so far as the situation allows alternatives, the actor chooses means which he considers effective toward the achievement of his end. The norm consists of a clear guiding principle toward which action is

[1] *Ibid.*, p. 457.
[2] *Ibid.*, pp. 456–457.
[3] *Ibid.*, pp. 256–257.
[4] *Ibid.*, pp. 44–49.

oriented. The norm is an ideal prescription of what action should be; with the statement of the course of action deemed desirable goes the injunction that future actions should conform to the norm. The normative element is the manifestation of a sentiment attributable to one or more actors in the system of action that an end is of itself desirable irrespective of its status as a means to some further end for some of the members of the collectivity or for the collectivity itself.[1]

In the system of action of the collectivity, action culminates in an ultimate end in a system of common ultimate ends. Action is oriented toward a normative element in the adaption of means to ends.[2]

There are subjective categories in relation to the theory of action. The element of choice as regards ends and means in relation to the normative concept involves the possibility of error, failure to realize ends or to apply the proper means to obtain the end.[3] Objectively, the action would be categorized as unscientific since the operations are not logically united to the end.[4] In subjective motivation during the process of action, phenomena are being considered as they appear from the actor's point of view. Aspects or elements in "the state of mind" of the actor are being analyzed. From the subjective point of view, the action may be logical; that is, the actor considers his action logical. There is appropriateness of means to the end, as the actor conceives it. But from the point of view of the scientific observer, the objective, the action may be illogical, involving error. There is ineffectiveness of means to end, failure of the two elements of action to correspond.[5]

Empirical science is concerned with understanding "the phenomena of the external world." And the facts are, to the scientist, facts of the external world, objective.[6] A fact is a "receptor experience" in terms of a conceptual scheme. A "receptor experience" is observation in terms of sensory perception. Sensory experiences are classified in terms of a conceptual frame of reference.[7] The scientist observes important uniformities in fact and constructs theories by logical reasoning from facts. By a process of resubmitting, retesting and verification, experimental theories are developed. The criterion of the truth of these theories is fact, rather than sentiment.[8] Homans and Curtis use the terminology "experimental" for Pareto's "logico-experimental theories."

1 *Ibid.*, pp. 45, 49, 75, 251.
2 *Ibid.*, pp. 45–46.
3 *Ibid.*, p. 254.
4 *Ibid.*, p. 256.
5 *Ibid.*, pp. 46–47, 82.
6 *Loc. cit.*
7 Homans, George C., and Curtis, Charles P., Jr., *An Introduction to Pareto,* Alfred A. Knopf, New York, 1934, pp. 51–52.
8 *Ibid.*, p. 53.

Whenever a significant uniformity in fact is observed over a period of time and its regularity is so conspicuous that the observer can predict its application under given conditions in the future, "scientific laws" arise.

While the social scientist seeks uniformities in the external world, he is concerned with the minds of the persons whose actions he studies. In the social sciences, "the phenomena being studied have a scientifically relevant subjective aspect."[1] Men construct "non-experimental" or "nonlogico-experimental" theories about their actions. These theories, which are based upon sentiment in terms of moral or religious principles rather than upon fact, are immensely common among men. The criterion of the truth of these non-experimental theories rests upon sentiment rather than observation.[2] The ends of action are pursued in terms of these theories to a considerable extent. Since action is classified by its end, nonlogical or non-experimental action is prevalent in society.[3] Pareto terms the constant nonlogical actions of men "residues." These actions are manifestations of sentiments. To the observer, the actions are without the range of scientific competence, but from the subjective point of view the beliefs and their manifestations in action are a reality and are experimental or logical. There is inveterate firmness in the strength of the beliefs.

A further consequence of the subjective category of the theory of action results from the actor, "ego," or "self." The body of the actor is for him as much a part of the situation of action as the external environment, which is important in influencing action. Hence, as a result of the subjectivity, his action is subject to conditions relating to his body; his mind and the powers of his body are "the most important means at his disposal."[4]

Another important consideration in the use of the action schema on an analytical level is the effect of the ends of others upon the actor in the process of social interaction. Not only are the ends of the actor related to each other so as to constitute a system, but they are related to the ends of other actors in the total system of action. The concrete actor is pursuing concrete ends in a concrete situation of action. In the situation of action, the present and anticipated actions of others upon the concrete actor may be related as means and conditions. In the total system of action, discrimination of the role of normative and non-normative elements is important. For the non-normative means and conditions of one actor are partly explainable "only in

[1] Parsons, *loc. cit.*

[2] Homans and Curtis, *op. cit.*, pp. 53–54.

[3] *Ibid.*, pp. 70–82.

[4] Parsons, *op. cit.*, p. 47.

terms of the normative elements of the action of others in the system."[1] In an analysis of action, the problem of the relation of the action of a concrete individual "in a concrete, partly social environment, and that of a total action system including a plurality of actors" is extraordinarily significant.[2] The ends of the actor, who constitutes a unit in the total system of action, are conditioned by the role of the normative elements of the collectivity as a unit.

In spite of some differences in individual ends in the system of action, there is an approach to the normative principle as a guide for action. A process of change proceeds toward an "increase in the value of the property of rationality."[3] The mutual orienting of acts and action systems of different individuals to each other constitutes social relationships.[4]

The smallest unit in the action schema is the unit act, with its elements—ends, means, conditions, and norms. These elements are part of an act; there is an actor or "personality" who initiates the action.[5] Action is thought of as a series of acts of one or more persons.[6] The unit act must be considered in relation to other acts or type parts in the system of action.[7]

Within the frame of reference, it is possible to construct historical individuals, subdivide these and combine the units. In employing "the relationship schema," which provides a convenient, comparative method for describing facts in a condensed manner, it is not necessary to observe all the attitudes and acts of the individuals in a relationship. There can be classification of types into the descriptive frame of reference. To understand action, it is necessary to know whose act it is and the relationship the schema of one type of actor bears to the actions of other types in the system. Thus it is possible to group acts according to type of actor.[8] In this study of religion, the type concept of classifying men motivated by similar ends is a technique which provides a shorthand method of presenting facts.

The concept of individual or "personality" arises in grouping units of action according to the actor. "In this sense a personality is nothing but the totality of observable unit acts described in their context of relation to a single actor."[9] This organic system of action has emergent properties not deducible from atomistic unit acts.[10] In employing "the personality schema," another descriptive schema of action, it is only necessary to observe enough unit acts of the person

1 *Ibid.*, p. 50.
2 *Ibid.*, pp. 50–51.
3 *Ibid.*, p. 751.
4 *Ibid.*, p. 744.
5 *Ibid.*, p. 738.
6 *Ibid.*, p. 745.
7 *Ibid.*, p. 743.
8 *Ibid.*, p. 745.
9 *Ibid.*, p. 746.
10 *Loc. cit.*

"to identify him as a given theoretically relevant kind of person."[1] Objectively, these identifying features may be regarded as "character traits"; subjectively, as "attitudes."[2] A system of unit acts with reference to the same actor arises.[3]

The "group schema" develops from carrying the process of aggregation further. Actions of a plurality of actors in the system may be characterized as groups. The persons motivated by similar expectations become identified in a particular group. There can be description and classification of groups without presenting all the character traits and attitudes of the individual members. There are emergent properties not derivable from characteristics of members in isolation from their group.[4]

The aggregations of relationship, personality, and group schemata are units of the religious system which is in turn a unit of the social system. Religion gives expression to ultimate common value attitudes of society.

As is true of the emergent properties of aggregates on an analytical level in the other unit or type parts, the identification and classification of the various actors in the religious system into one unit, designated as the Negro religious collectivity, abstraction involves the development of emergent properties not deducible from the groups in conceptual isolation.

With precautions, generalizations of unit or part concepts on these analytical levels can produce empirical generalizations adequate for various facts.[5]

The Diminution of Non-Experimental Elements of Action and Emotionalism

Negro religion is increasingly falling within the category of experimental action.

In order to ascertain the changing status of ends among Protestants, beliefs and actions of churchmen were studied. Techniques of investigation consisted of observation and interview, with a standardized questionnaire as the basis of information.

Evidence of the trend of change can be seen in the relation between men's beliefs or theories and their actions, and the normative choice of means in terms of end. The progressive trend toward this-worldly action is seen in the type of ends pursued and the gradual coincidence of means and end. Empirical ends are becoming important. Action is progressively falling within the logical intermedi-

[1] *Loc. cit.*
[2] *Loc. cit.*
[3] *Loc. cit.*
[4] *Loc. cit.*
[5] *Ibid.*, p. 747.

ate sector of the intrinsic means-end schema irrespective of the ultimate non-empirical end.

This statement does not imply, however, that all religious action precisely meets the logical standard. Ends are pursued in terms of non-experimental and experimental theories. Sentiments play an important role in motivating action in regard to empirical and non-empirical ends. At the same time, men in the religious collectivity are greatly interested in pursuing experimental ends.

The inconspicuous role of transcendental ends as compared with empirical is reflected in men's attitudes toward the Deity. Concomitant with the changing attitudes toward the Supernatural is a changing type of religion as demonstrated in sermons, conversion, and church programs. Attitudes toward the Deity are influencing the type of religious action. The trend from transcendentalism and emotionalism is accompanied by a more rational religion, not entirely logical, but there is an approach to rationality. Further evidence of the trend will be seen in succeeding chapters as an analysis of the attitudes and actions of the subjects is presented.

The changing attitudes and practices constitute a problem. With the diminution of non-experimental action, those persons seeking traditional values find their ends obscured. The presence of normative elements in the system of religious action constitutes non-normative means and conditions in the situation of action for the "old type" of religionist.

Negro religion is in a process of arriving at or attaining a "new" state of equilibrium. In this process of change, new values and forms of expression are being introduced and substituted for old; some traditional forms are being altered, while old modes of action are being retained by some groups. This trend is conspicuous as regards the decline in emotional action accompanying sentiments.

In order to appreciate this thesis, it is necessary to give an explanation of the concept "equilibrium." Equilibrium takes two forms: first, the static, balanced type, and second, the accelerated, progressive type, which is set in motion by the introduction of new elements into the system.[1] Forces set the system in action and change the equilibrium either temporarily or permanently.[2] In this religious system, new elements are contributing to the establishment of the progressive type of equilibrium, with changes of a permanent nature.

This equilibrium is dynamic rather than static. In the static form of equilibrium, which was prevalent in the past, transcendental ends

[1] Homans and Curtis, *op. cit.*, pp. 271–273.
[2] *Ibid.*, pp. 274–275.

and emotionalism were characteristic. But non-experimental action is diminishing in the transitional process. A group accustomed to a regular mode of existence and of expression experiences a disturbance by modifications being introduced into the system; thus the introduction of normative elements in the system of action necessitates adjustment.

In order adequately to picture the change, it is important to examine present attitudes of churchmen to the Divine since beliefs regarding the Supreme constitute a focal point of the Christian religion, and since these attitudes are reflected in action and partly determine other religious functions and aspects of social life. At the same time, the social character of religious ideas and action is apparent. Religious ideas reflect ultimate values of society. And attitudes toward the Deity greatly condition whether or not an empirical or a non-empirical religion will predominate.

For the group studied, the predominance of transcendental values, reflected in emphasis upon after-life and exaggerated emotional action, meant a non-experimental religion. As transcendental ends among churchmen are diminishing in importance, action is becoming more experimental and logical.

This study aims to show the relation between the Negro's religious ideas and actions, and the interdependence between these religious ideas and ultimate common ends of the Negro collectivity.

Explanation Regarding the Manner of Designating Churches

As has been indicated, the type-concept provides a precise and succinct manner of categorizing religious action with regard to men and churches. It facilitates a more exact measurement of attitudes and practices than specifically referring to churches by name; the material can be handled more adequately by employment of the type-concept. And consequently, churches were referred to by numeral and letter. Furthermore, pastors were identified in the same manner so that the relationship between the leader and his church could be readily visible. If there is concentration upon names, important implications might be disregarded.

Although the method used to present the data might detract from interest, it is justifiable because it promotes a convenient and scientific manner of presenting information.

In addition, there are other considerations which contributed to a degree of anonymity irrespective of authenticity.

For the convenience of the reader the following summary of types is presented to be referred to from time to time during examination of the material.

Church Type One	Unemotional, practical action important, elevated social classes numerous in the church.
Church Type Two	Semi-restrained, somewhat conservative in departing from traditional standards, action directed to this world and the other world, persons of various levels though middle-income groups tend to predominate.
Church Type Three	Emotional, the supernatural outstanding in action, persons of low income and meager formal education numerous.

Although denomination as such is not the primary and sole determinant of type of religious action since all types of churches might be found in one denomination (for example, the three types are found in the Methodist and the Baptist church), the denominations of the churches are presented since the reader might be interested in this information.

Boston Churches

Church One	Congregational
Church Two	Baptist
Church Three	Holiness background

South Carolina Churches (All Methodist)

Church A	Landless, impecunious persons of meager education predominant. Sharecroppers numerous. Not extremely emotional but exuberant feeling sometimes expressed. Comparable in some respects with Church Three.
Church B	Some landowners, school teachers and college graduates and a few sharecroppers. Feeling generally subdued. Comparable in some respects with Church Two.
Church C	Some landowners, school teachers and college graduates; some sharecroppers. Feeling generally restrained. Comparable in attitude with Church One in some respects.
Church D	Landless membership of very modest education. Spontaneous feeling sometimes manifested; ardent reliance upon God.

There was no effort precisely to fit the rural churches studied in the type-concept analysis although some comparisons are made with Boston churches and although the relationship between type of religion and social conditions under which communicants live is not obscured. Not any of the rural churches specifically studied are extremely emotional.[1] All of the churches are on the same charge (under the direction of the same pastor) and constitute a unit.

[1] See pages 139–140, 143.

Part I

Religious Theories

CHAPTER I

The Decline in Traditional Religion

O for a faith that will not shrink,
Tho' pressed by every foe,
That will not tremble on the brink
Of any earthly woe![1]

DOES THE Negro churchman have this inveterate faith today? Has there been a modification of his attitudes toward religion? Is there still a staunch adherence to traditional religious practices? What is the present course of the Negro's faith? Has there been a transmutation of action of the Negro?

By carefully examining the chapters comprising this study one can grasp with clarity the Negro's present religious attitudes.

ATTITUDES TOWARD THE SUPREME BEING

Beliefs in the Supernatural.—Both transcendental and empirical ends are found in Negro religion. That is, the religious man motivates his behavior, to some extent, in terms of ends which are not scientifically verifiable. And at the same time, some of his ends and the means by which he seeks to realize them are scientifically demonstrable.

The conviction that the visible world is a part of the spiritual universe which gives significance to life motivates man to enter a voluntary relation with God. Man's ends are to realize a harmonious relation or unity with "the higher universe."[2]

The religious man enters a relationship with the Supernatural Being and hence in his speculation invades a world which surpasses the limits of sensory knowledge, a world of the mysterious and unknowable. Believing that the existence of the world is a mystery calling for explanation, man accounts for the inscrutable elements in terms of an omnipotent creator and director of the universe. "The sentiment of mystery" has varied remarkably in different ages and sometimes is relegated to a subordinate place among Christians.[3]

[1] William H. Bathurst and Thomas A. Arne, "O For A Faith," *The Methodist Hymnal*, The Methodist Book Concern, New York, 1935, p. 270.

[2] James, William, *The Varieties of Religious Experience*, Random House, New York, 1902, p. 475.

[3] Durkheim, Émile, *The Elementary Forms of the Religious Life*, The Macmillan Company, New York, 1926, pp. 24–25.

The religious man still seeks non-empirical ends as seen in his concepts of the Deity. Almost all informants believe in the divine order of the universe. Although transcendental ends are still found in Negro religion as seen in beliefs in God, Heaven, Hell, and prayer, the churchmen's conceptions of these non-empirical aspects have changed remarkably. The modification of attitudes is reflected in the significance of these concepts for action. Beliefs in God, and in the efficacy of prayer are stronger than beliefs in Heaven and in Hell. The sentiment of fear, which has operated as a constrainer of action, is decreasing. Fear of God and of Hell are declining as conditioners of action among the group studied.

The Efficacy of Prayer.—Not from fear, as much as from a feeling of dependency and inadequacy, man enters a relationship with God, the controlling power of the universe, to whom petitional and adorational prayers are addressed. Man seeks the help of the Almighty whose powers are superior to his, and strives to persuade and to act upon the Deity by psychological processes with the aid of words, prayers, offerings, and sacrifices.[1]

There is a firm belief among Negro informants that God answers the prayer of the sincere; and this attitude is demonstrated in the fervency of the prayer of the deeply religious. Some Christians feel the presence and active influence of the Almighty upon whom they lean for support and guidance.[2]

Prayer is communion or conversation with the Deity. "Petitional prayer" (asking God to grant requests or favors), as well as adorational prayer, is found among Negro religious men. Sometimes a soul in distress enters into intercourse with the Supreme, upon whom the individual feels dependent. By the act of prayer man comes in intimate, personal relation with God and clings to the Supreme Being from whom life is drawn. Through prayerful consciousness, ends of salvation are sought in this life and in after-life.[3] Through prayer or "inner communion" with the Spirit of God, man receives spiritual energy which vitalizes him and causes psychological and material accomplishments "within the phenomenal world."[4]

It is true that the churchman still believes in the efficacy of prayer and thus seeks to achieve his ends by the means of addressing and imploring the Almighty. The strength of the idea is demonstrated in his action. Nevertheless, it is also true that there has been some diminution of this value attitude. This is seen in the fact that the frequency and the length of the prayer have declined with other tran-

[1] *Ibid.*, pp. 29–30.
[2] James, *op. cit.*, p. 461.
[3] *Ibid.*, pp. 453–455.
[4] *Ibid.*, p. 475.

scendental values while man strives to realize his ends in an empirical frame of reference.

The Principle of Retribution as Seen in Beliefs in God, Heaven and Hell as Constraining Forces.—As experimental ends gain ascendancy over non-experimental, the decline in the sentiment of fear is seen in regard to changing conceptions of God, Heaven, and Hell as motivators of men's actions. The churchmen's beliefs regarding these non-experimental elements are undergoing a change to the extent that action is not so greatly influenced by these transcendental values in terms of constraint today as in the past. In other words, most of the informants believe in some form of Heaven and Hell, but attitudes regarding the idea of punishment and reward are declining in importance. For some, the concepts "Heaven" and "Hell" have an empirical reference.

Religion is idealistic as well as realistic. Elements of good and evil in religion are manifested in men's attitudes toward God, Heaven, and Hell. Society as it is and operates is the basis of religion.[1] Society is imperfect; it contains two opposing forces—good and evil, justice and injustice, truth and error. Yet it inspires sentiments of love and abnegation required by religion of its followers. Men strive to attain noble aspirations which come from the depths of their being, and they strive to move toward the ideal in which good, justice, and light overbalance evil, injustice, and darkness.[2] These sentiments are expressed in religious action. Since an ideal state of society is not realizable, is not an empirically observable fact, men seek final attainment of this end in Heaven, a place of harmony, balance, peace, happiness, justice, where the faithful are rewarded for their worldly pursuit of Christian ends. While pursuing these ends, men seek to conform their actions, though they may fall short of this in their deviations, according to the principles of God, the tenets of which are of social origin.

With this idealistic side of religion goes a realistic aspect. This is seen in men's ideas of a demon and of Hell. "Thus religion, far from ignoring the real society and making abstraction of it, is in its image; it reflects all its aspects, even the most vulgar and the most repulsive."[3] The spirit of evil is given a place in Christian mythology. Satan, a part of the Christian system, is given extended powers, though he is subordinate and inferior.[4]

Certainly ideas of Heaven and Hell are significant today. But the trend is from non-experimental action as regards Hell. That is, Hell is a transcendental value attitude; the means which are employed

[1] Durkheim, *op. cit.*, pp. 420–421.
[2] *Loc. cit.*
[3] *Loc. cit.*
[4] *Loc. cit.*

to avoid escape from its horrors are not scientifically demonstrable. One cannot factually state that the means are efficacious to the end. Derivations in the form of tabus are increasingly becoming ineffective in religion today. Man is exhorted to act because of certain reasons. Pareto's third class of derivations shows that man is persuaded to act in accord with sentiments or principles. "These derivations persuade a man to act in a certain way, to believe in a certain statement because such action, such belief, is either with his own sentiments or those of others. The residues used to derive are most frequently those of Sociability or of the Persistent Aggregates."[1]

In attempting to persuade a man to regulate his conduct according to group sentiments, and by so doing to increase social solidarity, a means of approach is that of individual interest. Derivations of individual interest take the form of urging a man to act in accord with sentiments, first, by urging conforming with or refraining from violating group codes in terms of personal advantage, and second, by admonishing the application of sanctions against the non-conformer. A tabu is a derivation when the sanction or tabu is unreal—non-experimental.[2] A tabu in the form of a derivation—that is, admonishing the individual to pursue a certain course because of a desire for salvation in terms of realization of an ulterior end, Heaven, or urging a man to follow a certain course of action because of the desire to escape the consequences of the act in the form of punishment in after-life—has diminished in importance in the pursuit of a Christian life. As men seek to attain the ideal in terms of the empirical, religious sanctions diminish in importance.

There is a decrease in the role of non-experimental sanctions in action. The idea of sin and Hell has been conspicuous in Negro religion. However, there is a rapid decline in the emphasis upon sin, fear, and Hell today. This trend is seen in the beliefs and the actions of Negro churchmen. The cultivation of an optimistic, cheerful religious attitude, which emphasizes surmounting impediments or obstructions, has resulted in minimization of the evil aspects of existence and the principle of retribution.[3] Thus religious action is moving toward subordination of the pathological. Becoming free from repentant, remorseful, and sombre states, which incapacitate rational action, the agent is seeking experimental ends, with religious action directed toward attainment of the ideal in society.

What was formerly a non-empirical or transcendental end is becoming an empirical end. The concept of Heaven is changing in

[1] Homans and Curtis, *op. cit.*, pp. 194–195.
[2] *Ibid.*, pp. 198–199.
[3] James, *op. cit.*, pp. 89, 125–126, 128–129.

terms of sensory experiences in this world. Thus realization of the ideal state is being conceived as a possible receptor experience. Formation of the ideal—something adduced to and placed beyond the real—occurs in group life by assimilating the ideals of society. "Systematic idealization" is expressed in religious action.[1] Idealization proceeds in religious action in terms of non-experimental and experimental ends. With diminution and elimination of the emphasis upon sin and repentance, there is an increasing tendency for "the good life" to be conceived in terms of experimental action. Thus develops a changing type of religion. Increasingly, the Negro strives to achieve ideal ends in a mundane rather than a celestial society. The attempt to substitute for the real world a world to which men transport themselves by psychological processes has some significance. Men still conceive the ideal—the triumph of righteousness—in terms of an other-worldly Heaven. Yet their action is motivated mainly in terms of moving toward a this-worldly state in which "beauty" prevails. The "newer" type (experimental action) of ideal is gaining in importance over the traditional type.

Conversion.—The decline in sentiments of sorrow, evil and retribution is seen in men's attitudes toward conversion and the change in conversion forms today. The process and type of conversion show the status of transcendental ends and the values men attach to them, since conversion is a means of attaining an ultimate end, which may be pleasing the Almighty by living according to his will and commandments, or which may be attaining entrance to Heaven or avoiding Hell. Conversion may also relate to man's existence in this world in that it may promote inner peace and harmony; it may be a means of self-mastery and success in achieving personal ends, or it may be regarded from a social point of view as a means of promoting group harmony, a means of re-strengthening the mores of the group, of reaffirming social values.

Conversion may be a means of revitalizing collective sentiments through religious experience. Inasmuch as collective sentiments are in terms of empirical values to a great extent, the ideal is regarded in terms of "real" rather than "imaginary" ends. The changing attitude of the churchman toward conversion is indicative of changing social values, which are reflected in religion. The former attitude of emphasizing transcendental ends is rapidly giving ground to a more practical attitude toward "salvation."

The rites[2] of spiritual transformation—passage from the world

[1] Durkheim, *op. cit.*, pp. 420–423.

[2] Ceremonies or acts in regard to "the sacred," characterized by attitudes of "respect" and "apartness."

of "the profane" into that of "the sacred"—are less ceremonious today than in the past in Negro religion. They are also less symbolic and literal in the sense of revitalizing and restimulating traditional religious sentiments. The differences between the world of "the sacred" and the world of "the profane" are not so great; that is, the meaning of the two is not as distinct as formerly as far as conversion or spiritual metamorphosis is concerned.

In belief and in practice, the two worlds are not so far apart as formerly. Informants' replies to questions regarding "activities in which a Christian should not engage" indicate this, inasmuch as for many the factors determining whether one should or should not refrain from secular activities are more personal than religious. Also, many churchmen's beliefs and practices show that a Christian may participate in "worldly or temporal pleasures."

The decline in ritual conversion today is symbolic of changing religious beliefs and sentiments. In the group studied, there has been considerable variation from the ceremonious type of conversion. Ritual conversion as seen in initiation ceremonies is longest retained by either educationally retarded or isolated groups.

To depict further these changing values, let us go into further elaboration of the meaning and the process of conversion.

To pass from "the profane" to "the sacred" world, regeneration is necessary. This change is demonstrated by initiation rites, consisting of "a long series of ceremonies with the object of introducing the young man into the religious life."[1] By the process of leaving "the profane world" and entering "the sacred world," there has been transformation of his being, spiritual rebirth.[2]

Men who are conscious of the evil aspects of existence deem it necessary to go through a process of transmutation, which represents a triumph of "good and righteousness" over "sin and iniquity," a supremacy of "higher principles over lower." To the traditional Christian, this redemption comes through the forgiving mercy of Jesus, the Deliverer from "sin," and the Bestower of harmony.

Conversion denotes a gradual or sudden process by which the conflicting, discordant personality struggling to achieve unity between "the higher" and "the lower self" secures peace, balance, equilibrium through transfiguration as a result of a firmer grip upon "religious realities." Religion serves as a means of securing inner unification.[3]

Thus man, who is conscious of the two opposing principles of life, regards religion as a manner of achieving harmony representative

[1] *Ibid.*, p. 39.
[2] *Loc. cit.*
[3] James, *op. cit.*, pp. 172–173, 186.

of supremacy of those forces tending to accelerate individual and social well-being.

To attain "the state of grace," some men believe that sensational methods and emotional behavior are necessary. Those who maximize evil, or for whom the dark aspects of life are significant, strongly express sentiments of sadness, unhappiness, wretchedness, desperation, pain, fear, and human helplessness. They are conscious of the vanity of earthly things, the sense of sin, and are fearful and weary of life.[1] The traditional religionist looks to God as a means of alleviating distress in this life, and he concentrates upon a non-empirical value, where light and happiness will prevail. Conversion provides a means of attaining this goal. In the process of becoming converted, or escaping the consciousness of evil as a pervasive element of the world, this type usually undergoes the crisis type of conversion, which is accompanied by miracles, revivals, and emotionalism. In other words, emotional action predominates in the traditional form of conversion, with its emphasis upon non-empirical ends. Religion is related to remote hopes and values, and life is more satisfying as a result of these anticipations.

At the present, however, there is a marked tendency from this form of conversion so that there is prevalent the gradual form of decision, termed "lysis."[2]

With the passage of the conservative form of conversion and religion, emotional action is in the process of modification and elimination. This change is accompanying the trend from transcendental ends as there is a tendency to express empirical values. Religion is becoming more logical.

Since man is seeking to attain the ideal state in this life, as exemplified in changed conceptions of religious functions, the declining importance of ritual conversion is understandable. While discussing the relation between the elements of religion as a unified system of beliefs and actions regarding "the sacred," Durkheim shows that men do not "celebrate ceremonies for which they see no reason."[3] Men's systems of ideas or theories which aim to explain the world and in turn to regulate action, systematically change with the diminution of non-experimental action.

Religion as a Norm.—Religion is conceived as a norm of action in this life. The conceptions that the persons in this study have of religion show that the ends of action are sought in terms of the principles of Christianity. Thus religion is "a guide for living," "a pattern of conduct," "a harmony of belief and action according to

[1] *Ibid.*, pp. 128, 158–159. [2] *Ibid.*, p. 180.

[3] Durkheim, *op. cit.*, pp. 430–431.

Christian precepts," "a system of action in which ends are pursued in a Christlike manner."

Religious beliefs are reflected in action. Churchmen regard the basic principle motivating their conduct as the tenets of Christianity. Their replies regarding "the principles determining their social relationships" show the importance of religion "par excellence" as a norm of conduct. For the informants, the philosophy of treating others with kindness, consideration, and of exhibiting those attitudes which they should like for others to manifest toward them is of cardinal importance.

The social character of religious beliefs is reflected in action. Thus religion is "a means of making men live." Religion is action.[1] Religion is a social force influencing the morals of the group. Religion puts spiritual powers into play and acts upon the moral life.[2]

Religion as a means of facilitating individual and social harmony and growth has, to some extent, operated in Negro religion in the past. But previously there was considerable limitation of this expression of religion inasmuch as religion emphasized non-experimental values. The central expression was directed toward living in a manner acceptable to God and of attaining happiness in an eternal home. Salvation was central. But today there is a changing conception of religion; the old type is giving way to a new form, and consequently religion is regarded not as an end in itself but as a means of attainment of an abundant life in this world realizable in terms of the Christian ideal. Religion is becoming more meaningful and systematic.

Also, in connection with the diminishing form of traditional values, the further appearance of the social aspect of religion is seen in men's beliefs regarding the source of the principle governing their conduct. Certainly the basis of Christianity is the precept to which informants ascribe their actions. However, there is not agreement among the informants regarding the source of this norm. In response to the basis of this value, informants answered variously. Some (usually traditional religionists) imputed the source of this principle to the Christian religion or Jesus Christ; some said they arrived at this rule from personal reflection, or it consists of their philosophy of life; others attributed its adoption by them to the influence of social institutions, as the family, the school, the state; and others regarded this principle as a combination of two of these institutional influences. It is obvious that multiple factors are responsible for inculcation of this norm. At the same time, the failure of churchmen to impute the source of the belief predominantly to

[1] *Ibid.*, p. 429. [2] *Ibid.*, p. 420.

the Christian religion shows the importance of other values to them. This verifies the essence of Durkheim's theory of society as the source of religion.[1] Durkheim did not, however, discount the role of beliefs as influencing religious action. Men's actions are influenced by society, and normative rules are in turn responsive to the individual's beliefs, or, in other words, the legality of the norm is conditioned by the attitudes men have toward it.

This analysis does not contradict the previous statement of religion as a norm; it does not discount the influence of the Supernatural upon men's beliefs and actions. But it does show that non-empirical values are increasingly becoming less conspicuous in the system of action. Men's interests are directing their actions in different channels. Values are changing. Though Christianity is valid, the attitudes men take toward religion are changing. Value elements in the Negro collectivity are influencing the change in the Protestant system of action. There are mutual relations of value attitudes and ideas of the Supernatural.[2]

The Waning Influence of Sacred Norms in Regulating Conduct in the Pursuit of Pleasurable Ends.— There is a wane in the authority of God as a sanction of conduct as knowledge is perceived in terms of sensory experiences. The traditionalized system of sacred norms is not so important in regulating conduct today as in the past. Men are less inclined to conform to the ethical norms of Jesus Christ; at present, the norm does not greatly condition action in the pursuit of ends. Men take various attitudes toward living according to the Ten Commandments in the pursuit of their objectives. There is a variation in orienting actions to the norm. Some manifest neutral attitudes; some accept it, while others combat and reject it.[3] Living according to the ethical norm in pursuit of transcendental ends is diminishing in the system of action as a unit. The present norm is an empirical religion, with the presence of some "imaginary" or non-experimental values. What in Negro religion was once "the legitimate order," living according to the Ten Commandments in the pursuit of non-experimental ends, or a norm of action regarded by the group as morally binding, is modified. The norm is a practical religion with little emphasis upon transcendental values. The traditionalized system of sacred norms is becoming de-traditionalized to the extent that the action of the churchman is not oriented toward this normative element as much as in past years. Man does not observe this norm so rigidly. Attitudes toward the source of legality are changing.

The authority of the Divinity is waning as a source of moral rules

[1] *Loc. cit.* [2] Parsons, *op. cit.*, p. 717. [3] *Ibid.*, p. 251.

for personal conduct. The derivation offering justification for personal codes of conduct is increasingly among Negro churchmen deriving its sanction from the individual or the collectivity. Observance of codes of conduct as regards pleasurable activities in which the church goer participates is not rationalized in terms of the sentiment of the authority of the Divinity for many persons; regulation of ends according to the ethical norm is diminishing.

As individuals in the collectivity are becoming more rational and logical in their processes of thinking and acting, many are regarding codes from a socio-religious point of view, with some consideration of observance of the codes in terms of social values and group integration. Some persons are not considering the religious factor at all. Although elements of non-experimental theories indicate a degree of existing relationship between "moral" action and the teachings of Jesus as far as some church members are concerned, elements of logical analysis are becoming prominent in terms of the relation between what men say and do.

Concomitant with the diminishing authority of the Deity is an increase of individualistic standards. The religious ideas of Negroes influence their secular activities; the disappearance of fear of God is accompanied by an increasing trend toward personal standards of conduct. Christianity has always stressed the individualistic factor (and this is especially true of the Protestant religion). With the Protestant, salvation is a personal matter, a relation between man and God, with no intermediary influence. With the lapse of time, individualism became more acute in Christianity.[1] Today, the emphasis upon individualism is striking; this is observed in social relationships, and it is seen in the religious attitudes of churchmen. The Negro religious man is motivated by these attitudes in his secular activities.

Secularization trends are seen in the churchmen's attitudes toward "activities in which a Christian should not engage." Religious beliefs and practices show that for many "the sacred" as isolated and set apart from "the profane" is losing in importance. The distance between the two categories has shortened considerably. Attitudes toward "sacred things" in relation to profane activities show variation among Protestants. There is a high degree of integration relative to the importance of Christianity as a norm in the Negro church, but as pertains to secular activities from which the Christian should isolate himself, the solidarity is not conspicuous. There is departure from traditional norms according to type of church, location, type of man, and age. The traditionalist recognizes the

[1] *Ibid.*, pp. 106–107, 109–110.

norm of the Ten Commandments as binding, and hence there is conformity with it. The liberalist considers this norm as not alone important; other elements in the system of action bear consideration. Traditionalistic standards of conduct are giving way to other standards.

Changing religious values are reflected not only in personal ethical standards of conduct. Individualism is apparent in the position of the church, in correspondence with the beliefs and the interests of the communicants. The role of religious ideas on secular activities is manifested in "tolerant" attitudes toward pleasurable pursuits. Doctrines of the church change in accord with the attitudes of society. Weber did not disregard the influence of the religious attitudes of the masses on the direction which the Protestant ethic took, although he emphasized the role of the Protestant ethic itself as influencing secular acquisitive tendencies. He did not discount the importance of the religious ideas of church leaders and followers as effecting the change leaning toward the extension of religious ideas into practical affairs. Although Weber's primary interest was in the congruence of the Protestant ethic and the spirit of capitalism, the implications of his theory are valid for other considerations of the role of ideas in the motivation of different or various secular actions. As, according to Weber, the religious "interests" of the individual directed his action in acquisitive activities, so do present interests of the churchman motivate him to participate in activities not designated religious but secular in the pursuit of his ends.[1] As non-empirical or transcendental values diminish with the wane of the authority of the Divinity as a source of sacred norms, the churchman increasingly derives his values from the individual or the collectivity in the pursuit of secular ends. The implication of this theory is that with a continued decline in supernatural values, individual and social values will predominate and churchmen's ends will increasingly fall within the empirical frame of reference.

Emotionalism

Emotion in Religion.—Extreme demonstrativeness accompanying emotion diminishes with a decline in transcendental values. Manifestation of emotion was prevalent during the period of transcendental intensity. With the shift of emphasis from non-empirical ends, the churchman's attitude toward exhibition of religious sentiments of fear, sorrow, and joy concomitantly changes.

Emotion is usually accompanied by physical changes, organic

[1] *Ibid.*, pp. 251, 512, 531–534.

disturbances, and action.[1] Under emotional stimulation, an aspect of irrational action, the individual is "helplessly carried along by forces" beyond his control as he unrestrainedly yields to the feeling aroused under the stimulus of religious objects.[2] Religious sentiments are manifested in action.[3] Sentiments of joy may be aroused by adoration of, submission to, and dependence upon the Deity; the triumph of "the higher" over "the lower self," blending of the discordant personality; and anticipation of the final victory of good over evil, peace over turmoil, and harmony over disharmony in an everlasting home. The emotion of sorrow may be aroused as a result of personal perplexities, sympathy for mankind, or lament over the agonies of Jesus. These emotions may find an outlet in religious experiences and may be accompanied by action, vocal exclamation, and bodily movement. These emotions may manifest themselves in extreme action, and they may also be expressed in a subdued or moderate manner. Extreme emotional stimulation incapacitates rational thinking.

Although there are sentiments other than the above which are expressed in religion, attention is directed to these sentiments inasmuch as they are the main emotions manifested by those whose interest is chiefly upon transcendental ends.

Conditions of Action for the Traditionalist.—The fact that Negro religion is arriving at a new state of equilibrium or is undergoing a process of transformation constitutes a problem. For those accustomed or favorably disposed to "the old religion," the introduction of new conditions or elements into the religious system necessitates adjustment. For those preferring an empirical religion, action is *somewhat* hampered by the presence of "the old type of Christian," who is adjusted to the static form of equilibrium and maladjusted to the progressive, dynamic form, in the situation of action.

The trend from transcendental values is a significant problem for the traditional religionist. Although the predominant "transitional religionist" is limited to some extent in achieving his empirical ends because of the presence of "the vanishing traditionalist" in the church, the former makes a few concessions (mainly because of the influence of the pastor) and continues to seek realization of his goal. This type of man is "taking over" control of the church and submerging the traditionalist. The changing religion, regarded from the subjective point of view, is a barrier for the traditionalist. There

[1] Edman, Irwin, *Human Traits and Their Social Significance,* Houghton Mifflin Company, Boston, 1920, pp. 40–44.
[2] Parsons, *op. cit.,* pp. 584–585.
[3] Homans and Curtis, *op. cit.,* pp. 133, 136.

are factors in the situation of action, over which he has no control, conditioning his expression. These conditions (features of action which he cannot appreciably control) prevent the traditionalist from using certain means to attain his end.

For the traditionalist, the situation is that of action occurring in a trend of development—unemotionalism and empirical values—different from the end toward which his action is oriented, transcendentalism. Being unable to alter greatly this trend, because of features in the situation which he cannot control, his overt expression of non-empirical ends is suppressed. The conditional factor in the system of action, for the traditionalist, can be seen in the application of "the unemotional norm" resulting from changed and changing attitudes toward transcendental values and non-experimental action. The changing conception is reflected in the status of forms of expression, such as conversion, revivals, testimonies, accompanying non-experimental values.

The presence of normative elements in the system of action as a whole constitutes non-normative means and conditions for the traditional Christian. However, there are some limited methods which the traditionalist may employ partly to achieve his ends. These are as follows: contemplation, prayer and communion with the Divine in a subdued manner, limited expression on certain occasions, and withdrawal from the group whose norm is counter to his interests.

In the system of action, what will be the result of the presence of normative elements upon those whose mode of expression is not compatible with them? Application of the guiding principles of action may have these effects: withdrawal, accommodation, formation of new religions, expression in extra-religious channels.

In the Protestant collectivity, what will be the over-all effects of rapid submergence of emotion and the manifestation of religious sentiments in non-experimental action? There will be a decline of religion and church membership. Unless satisfactory channels are provided to facilitate adjustment, there will be either a "dead church" failing to maintain its grip upon many, or a type of religion attractive to all will develop.[1] The choice of alternative courses as far as the leaders of the Protestant church are concerned involves re-integration of ends of all types of churchmen in the religious system or ignorement of the varied ends of the groups in the system of action.

[1] The writer is indebted to The Reverend S. A. Funchess for this idea.

CHAPTER II

The Goals of Negro Protestants

Ain' got nowhere, Lord,
Ain' got nowhere, Lord,
Ain' got nowhere to lay my head.
But on the other side of Jordan
Jesus' makin' up my dyin' bed.

THIS SPIRITUAL (as well as related melodies with respect to anticipation of a "celestial home" as a means of assuaging trouble, conflict, and perplexity) is heard today on some occasions and in some areas. Does it, however, reflect the goals of Negro Protestants as a group? Does the doleful melody, which is sometimes accompanied by psycho-dramatic performances, represent the essential features of religious Protestant action?

How important is empirical action to Negro Protestants? Examination of the religious objectives of types of churchmen and types of churches succinctly reveals the status of non-empirical ends today.

OBJECTIVES OF THE CHURCH

Ends of the Negro Collectivity.—The ultimate ends of different types of religious men are related so as to constitute a coherent system. In the means-end schema of the Negro church, there is relation of the ends of the different types (transcendentalist, moderate religionist, and empiricist) of religious men. In logical action, "the total action system of an individual must be related in some degree to a coherent system of ultimate ends."[1] There is relation of the ends of types of church members to the ends of the collectivity. In regard to the ultimate end systems of types of religious men, there is some degree of integration of ultimate ends into the system of the religious collectivity.[2] The ends of the types of churchmen do not vary at random but constitute a relationship to the common system of ends.

In the ultimate end of the collectivity (that is, the Christian

[1] Parsons, *op. cit.*, p. 232.

[2] *Ibid.*, p. 238.

should strive to attain heaven, an ideal society), the churchmen choose the pursuit of this state in terms of alternative ends.[1] The selective factor, as far as the individuals are concerned, involves different attitudes. The types of churchmen conceive reality or knowledge differently. One type regards fact primarily in terms of intuitive or spiritual insight or revelation; the empirical is subordinate to the spiritual realm. Another considers both the spiritual and the empirical important, with the latter sometimes relegated to a somewhat subordinate place. A third type emphasizes cognition essentially in terms of sensory experiences. The selection of one alternative rather than the other also depends upon differences in the conception of the ideal and the manner in which it should be pursued. The traditional religionist seeks a transcendental Heaven, while the moderate or modern religionist seeks establishment of the Kingdom of God primarily in this world. These ends and their expression in action may be regarded as either a traditional religion or a somewhat empirical religion. To the traditional group, eternal values are important and central; to the other, social values are significant. The ends of the traditionalist are primarily (though not entirely) non-experimental, but the ends of the modern religionist are essentially empirical. The contrasting types are, to some extent, guided by different norms in the pursuit of their ends.

Although there is some degree of integration of the system of ends of the Negro collectivity, the ends are not perfectly integrated. The common value system is not the source of all ends of the different types of religious men. There is a general tendency to seek to attain "near" ends instead of "remote" (pursuing empirical values rather than emphasizing transcendental values). The decline in non-empirical ends is seen in the ultimate common value schema of Negroes. Though it is true that there is an approach to the logical criterion, it is not maintained that the religious action precisely meets the logico-experimental standard; but it is *approaching* rationality, with the motivation of action according to the system of normative rules.

For the group as a whole, the schema of the Protestant collectivity is representative. However, "the old-time religionist" finds his ends obscured by the prevalence of experimentalism. Conflict has resulted from imperfect integration of the ultimate ends of action systems of groups in the church. The nature of this conflict will be brought out under a discussion of "the unemotional norm." In order to visualize the importance of this occurrence, it is necessary to note the means-end schema of the Negro church, which constitutes the

[1] *Ibid.*, p. 231.

focal point around which the ends of the various types and groups of men coalesce.

The Means and Ends of the Negro Protestant Church

	End	Means	Norm
I.	Alteration of traditional Negro religion	1. Changing attitudes toward the meaning of religion	Religion should be related with living.
II.	Elimination of the stereotyped idea of the Negro as emotional	1. Submerging emotion 2. Eliminating extreme manifestations of emotion 3. Focussing attention on religious functions other than emotion	There should be subordination of emotion in religion.
III.	Extirpation of extreme emotional action accompanying sentiment	1. Minimization of emphasis upon transcendental values especially as regards sin and retribution 2. Ridicule of demonstrativeness 3. Sublimation of emotion 4. Redirecting interests 5. Providing entertainment and instruction (speeches, plays, recitals, etc.)	Religion should make man conscious of empirical values.
IV.	Educational, intellectual, and religious development	1. Providing discussion groups, scholarships, and concerts 2. Maintenance and improvement of colleges, establishment of nurseries and Bible schools	Man should be aided in the development of his mental and moral faculties.
V.	A practical religion	1. Emphasizing thought rather than emotion 2. Providing intellectual, instructive sermons 3. Providing channels for empirical action	Religion should prepare man to meet the situations of life.

THE MEANS AND ENDS OF THE NEGRO PROTESTANT CHURCH (*cont.*)

VI. End	Means	Norm
To make life profitable and happy	1. Promotion of economic activity and business 2. Sponsoring charitable and community betterment programs 3. Providing recreational opportunities	Religion should aid man in his quest for an abundant life.
VII. Ultimate End	**Ultimate Means**	**Norm**
Attainment of an ideal state	1. Living according to the Golden Rule 2. Exhibiting a spirit of unselfishness in intimate face-to-face or primary relationships 3. Demonstration of brotherliness in group relationships 4. Achieving harmonious inter- and intra-racial relationships 5. Aiding man in making his life productive	Man should strive to achieve final victory of the positive principles over the negative.

TYPES OF CHURCH MEMBERS

Ends of Churchmen According to Type.—Within a church there are various types of men seeking to fulfill their ends. (However, some churches are unified as far as ends are concerned.) Since there is usually diversity, it is necessary to give attention to "the type concept" in order to reveal the relation of types of ends to the Negro church. For this study, the immediate end sector was worked out in the churches in terms of various types of groups pursuing their immediate ends, for example, the gospel chorus, the regular choir, and the dramatic or the discussion societies, etc. In the system of action, types were classified in terms of concrete ends of individual action systems. These types show the ends of various groups of individuals in the church and represent these groups typically. Not all ends of the individual churchmen could be included; for each type, some persons in the group vary in their ends, some being more radical or conservative in their departure. The type concept is used for convenience; it is a compact way of handling a mass of material.

This procedure of "breaking down" into type parts and combining the units is not necessary for Church One in Boston since the persons in this church converge around one type, "the empirical"; this is mainly a unified, undiversified system of action. The ultimate ends of the congregation are almost identical.

The procedure of "breaking down" is primarily necessary because the three types are generally found in Negro churches, and because the church-type concept, which will be given subsequently, is not in some respects adequate for the rural groups studied, even though there is some similarity between Churches Two and Three in Boston and the rural groups.

The following schemata show the attitudes of the three types. "The empiricist" concentrates upon experimental values; "the moderate religionist" considers spiritual and temporal values; "the transcendentalist" feels the need of overt emotional expression while some experimental ends are being pursued.

Empirical and non-empirical elements of action are involved. There is a combination of experimental and non-experimental theories as a basis of action. There is no clear-cut transcendental end which is completely independent of some empirical ends (as seen in desires and efforts to improve life here), although the non-empirical end is the ultimate objective. Sometimes a sentiment is the basis for pursuit of experimental ends.

Action is experimental to the extent that it is possible to ascertain whether or not the means employed will result in the anticipated state of affairs (the end). In logical action, the means and end coincide. For example, one can empirically determine whether establishing and maintaining educational institutions, sponsoring lectures, discussions, etc., accelerate the intellectual development of a group and stimulate thought instead of emotion. On the other hand, action is non-logical or non-experimental to the extent that it is not scientifically possible to predict whether or not the means applied to realization of the end will produce the desired result. For example, the traditionalist believes that salvation can be attained by conversion, baptism, church membership, prayer, support of the program of the church, and pious living; and on the basis of his belief, he orientates his action to the sacred norm. But it is not possible to determine whether the means he employs are efficacious to the end since this transcendental value is beyond the range of scientific competence. Though this is true, for the person exhibiting the belief and action, Heaven is a reality. From the subjective point of view (that of the actor), the action is experimental. But from the objective point of view (that of the scientific observer), the action is non-experimental. In logical action, subjective and objective ends correspond. In logical or experimental action, means and end coincide; that is, the individual applies techniques and goes through procedures which lead to realization of his goal.

Examination of the schemata shows that the traditionalist concentrates upon non-experimental ends; and his beliefs in the divine order of the universe and in the principle of retribution are sometimes accompanied by emotional outbursts. On the other hand, the empiricist or liberalist is not primarily concerned with salvation "beyond the grave" and does not manifest overt emotion accompanying his religious sentiments; his primary concern is with what religion does to contribute to the attainment of the ideal in society.

The following schemata illustrate differences in religious attitudes of types of church members.

Means and Ends of Types of Religious Men

THE EMPIRICIST

I. End	Means	Norm
Elimination of emotionalism	1. Discouragement or ridicule of the demonstrative 2. Concentrating upon activities of this world rather than upon an afterworld	Irrational actions should be extirpated and supplanted by rational action.
Situation There are some members who like to express their emotion overtly and some preachers who appeal to feeling rather than thought.	3. Presentation of instructive, intellectual sermons rather than emotional 4. Submergence of the spiritual (in the truly religious sense) 5. Dissemination of a changed conception of religion 6. Offering a varied program of action in the church	
II. End	**Means**	**Norm**
A practical religion	1. Exhibiting religion in living 2. Offering moral and financial support to the unfortunate 3. Adjusting the program of the church to present needs and trends, and making it attractive	The church should teach man how to live and should aid him in developing potentialities for wholesome living.

MEANS AND ENDS OF TYPES OF RELIGIOUS MEN (CONT.)

Situation Many churches continue to function on the basis of "the old program."	4. Offering a religion that inspires and helps man to live, to overcome difficulties and to adjust himself to perplexing problems or situations 5. Sponsoring discussions, speeches, and clinics 6. Providing recreational or community centers 7. Establishment and maintenance of nurseries and higher educational institutions	
III. Ultimate End	Ultimate Means	Norm
Realization of the ideal	1. Re-direction of the program of the church 2. Making religion a guide for living 3. Living according to the Golden Rule	For religion to be really effective, man must demonstrate the principle of charity in living.

THE MODERATE RELIGIONIST

I. End	Means	Norm
Gradual departure from traditional religion	1. Teaching and instructing the members and nonmembers on the meaning of religion 2. Maintenance of warmth and spirituality in the church service 3. Offering a variety of church programs and organizations 4. Provision for a full program or a weekday activity schedule	Since extreme emotionalism is undesirable, the members should be given something to do.
Situation "The old-time religionist" is often isolated and no provision is made for his needs.		
II. End	**Means**	**Norm**
Sponsoring educational and social welfare programs	1. Offering spiritual, physical and financial aid to those in need of it	The church should help man to make his life happy and meaningful.

MEANS AND ENDS OF TYPES OF RELIGIOUS MEN (CONT.)

	2. Providing religious education in the church by means of weekly classes and Bible schools	
Situation There has been dilatoriness in the assumption of these functions by the church.	3. Promoting nurseries, kindergartens and maintaining higher educational institutions 4. Offering teas, concerts, lectures 5. Providing a community center	
III. Ultimate End	Ultimate Means	Norm
Heaven	1. Support of the program of the church 2. Worship and praise of the Lord 3. Regarding the rights and well-being of others 4. Exhibiting charity 5. Integrating religion with life 6. Living according to the ethical norm	It is indispensable that the Christian demonstrate "good work."

THE TRANSCENDENTALIST

I. End	Means	Norm
Inspiration from church service Condition There is a tendency on the part of many members to seek a formal service devoid of emotional stimulation.	1. Participation in the program of the church 2. Communion with the Deity through song and prayer 3. Hearing a spiritually stimulating "gospel sermon" 4. "Making a joyful noise unto the Lord" 5. Receiving sympathetic response from co-worshipers; enjoying the fellowship of a community of Christians	There should be maintenance of spiritual warmth and fellowship in the church.

MEANS AND ENDS OF TYPES OF RELIGIOUS MEN (CONT.)

II. End	Means	Norm
A church interested in the welfare of its members[2] Situation The program of the church sometimes goes no farther than the Sunday service; local communicants desire and feel the need of more frequent contact with church leaders.[2]	1. Visiting and aiding the sick, "needy," and aged financially and spiritually 2. Having more frequent church services[1] 3. Sponsoring more church organizations[2] 4. Sponsoring recreational and social activities[3] 5. Provision of instruction on "how to live"; that is, informing the people concerning means of meeting local problems, and improving community life[2]	The church should exhibit more interest in the community.[2]
III. Ultimate End	**Ultimate Means**	**Norm**
Heaven Ultimate Conditions There is a general tendency to disregard the conservative principles of religion, the observance of which the traditional religionist considers essential.	1. Regeneration through conversion, baptism, and church membership 2. Faithfulness to the program of the church 3. "Serving the Lord" (through prayer, etc.) 4. "Doing the will of the Lord" 5. Living by the Golden Rule 6. Living according to the Ten Commandments 7. Evangelism, with "salvation of souls" as the prime objective	It is necessary for the Christian to "glorify thy Father who art in Heaven," and to live according to the sacred norms.

[1] Particularly true of the rural groups, some of which have church services only once or twice a month.

[2] This applies especially to rural groups, where the need is greatest, from the subjective and the objective points of view.

[3] Not of a secular or mundane type.

CHAPTER III

The Goals of Negro Protestants (*Continued*)

THE PROTESTANT clergy plays an important role in shaping the policy of the church and in directing the interests of communicants. The minister's actions are not restricted to the church; the influence of the clergyman extends into the community.

The pulpit might be a more effective instrument in influencing public opinion and in directing action outside of the church irrespective of the increasing prominence of secular agencies and institutions.

Some ministers seem unaware of their potential strength in regard to diverting changes which are occurring in the Protestant church. Indeed some do not grasp the full import of change in various directions.

TYPES OF MINISTERIAL LEADERS AND THE CHURCHES THEY DIRECT

Type of Clergyman and Type of Church.—In order to show the relation of ends of church leaders and followers, there was a division of the church into three groups, which are typical of the types of churches (not denominations) found among Negroes. Attention is not centered upon denomination because emphasis is upon the essential features of the Negro church. The types of churches are restrained, semi-restrained, and emotional. All of these types may be found in one denomination (for example, either the Baptist or the Methodist). Emotionalism does not depend primarily upon denomination, although there are some influences.[1] Education and economic status are important factors. There is a correlation between emotionalism and class. There is a direct relationship between the types of ends sought by each church, and the socio-economic status of its members.[2] This is true in urban and rural groups.

The type-concept as applied to the Negro collectivity is valid; Protestant Christianity comprises the basic unit of this study inasmuch as Negroes are preponderantly Protestant.

The attitudes of leaders of the church are conspicuous in shap-

[1] See p. 38.

[2] This relationship will be brought out later.

ing the policy of the churches they direct. For that reason, Negro clergymen were divided into three groups, based upon the kind of end pursued and the means applied to achieve realization of "the anticipated state of affairs." The examples of types in terms of Boston clergymen are legitimate devices since these samples are representative of the Negro Protestant clergy. The material was arranged to show the pastor of Church One in one means-end schema, the pastor of Church Two in another, and the pastor of Church Three in an additional chain, with some degree of integration of the various relationships. Each pastor uses means to attain his end, and the ultimate end of each is related. This is especially striking in regard to the pastors of Churches One and Three; social work and a practical religion are the ultimate ends of action for these two leaders. One link in the means-end relationship of the three leaders has as its end either subordination or elimination of pronounced emotional action accompanying religious sentiment.

As changes occur in a collectivity, there is mutuality and dependence; the interdependent relationship is seen in the reconciling of opposing interests of types of persons in the unit. Changes in a collectivity accrue as a result of the operation of forces from two sides, each influencing the other. The process of action is retarded or "slowed up" by the necessity of adjustment of the two forces in an effort to secure balance and harmony. As the religious attitudes of one group change, a response from the other side is necessary. This is a reciprocal relationship. A gradual process is seen in the reactions of various leaders to other leaders whose points of view are in some respects different from theirs. And it is also seen in the adjustment of ideas and actions of the leaders and of the followers. The attitudes of the leaders are certainly important; those of the members are also an important point of consideration.

In a religious system of action, the attitudes of the clergy are instrumental in determining the ends which churches pursue. Each pastor influences the beliefs of his followers and directs the program of the church according to his ideas and according to the situation of his particular group. The leaders play an important role in redirecting the interests of the group with which they work, and the ideas of the pastors are incorporated in their churches. Note the similarity in belief and action of the preacher and of the church he leads.

Although this is true, the churches retain some of their independent characteristics; that is, the church is in a changing process, and therefore, the pastors of the conservative type of churches cannot depart abruptly from "interests" of the members.[1] Also, they must satisfy the different types of religious men found in their churches; consequently the changing system of beliefs and action does not proceed as rapidly as the pastor himself desires.[2] Also, the ideas of the clergyman are usually more advanced than those of his church as a body. The clerical leader generally has a wider perspective and a more clarified perception of objectives than his congregation as a unit. Observe, for instance, the attitudes and actions of the director of Church Three in Boston.

Instead of placing the personality and group schemata here, they will be placed with the discussion of "the unemotional norm" because the ends of the leaders and of the followers will there reflect their situation in the action schema.

The Unemotional Norm.—As action becomes empirical and transcendental values decline, extreme emotional actions tend to diminish and disappear. At one time, manifestation of sentiment in overt emotional action enjoyed moral authority in religion. Motivation by transcendental values was expected of churchmen. In the established religion, uniformities of action in terms of non-experimental ends were inculcated. However, as religion becomes more highly organized, there is a decrease in the intensity of emotion. Though the manifestation of emotion has remained relatively constant for a few church members, the wane of emotional behavior is conspicuous at present. The tendency to impose uniformity of conduct by defining appropriate standards of behavior while pursuing ends is applied in terms of unemotionalism and rationality as a norm in Negro religion.

The role of value elements (attitudes accompanying religious ideas) has influenced the change in religion. These value elements are seen in terms of orientation of action to norms. Members have sentiments regarding appropriate behavior during the church service. In terms of "interest," uniformities are understood in terms of the "orientation of the actors to similar expectations."[3] In terms of "interest," means are adapted to ends.[4]

There is a system of rules, sometimes explicit and sometimes implicit, regarding decorum in church. Preponderantly, this normative concept has increased in importance among churchmen so that it has not only functioned to insure conformity with rules, but this

[1] See pages 39–40, 46–49.

[2] Note, for example, the hesitancy necessary on the part of the director of Church Three in order actually to execute his long-range objectives.

[3] Parsons, *op. cit.*, p. 650.

[4] *Ibid.*, p. 653.

value element has become an important sector of the means-end schema for many persons. It exists as a norm irrespective of its status as a means to a further end. Since the value element embodied in a system of normative principles regulating conduct (that is, church service should be devoid of manifestation of sentiment in pronounced vocal and bodily action) enjoys moral or institutional authority in the religious society, sanctions are applied against those who fail to conform to the standard. The element of constraint is effective in that some traditional members who have not fully accepted this principle restrain their emotions after persons motivated by the selective standard request or demand adherence to the norm. Violators are ridiculed, suppressed, and coerced. Through application of the norm, rules are enforced.

Thus there is evidence of Durkheim's quality of "moral obligation," the property of the order which defines and conditions action in the pursuit of ends, and Weber's "legitimacy," which signifies the idea on the part of men of the existence of an order as a norm.[1] Church members are diligent in pursuing ends according to the norm, which circumscribes and limits the manner in which ends may be pursued. Durkheim's modified version of constraint viewed in terms of sanctions attached to selective principles, which reflect ultimate common value attitudes, is effective in the religious system of action.[2]

Some Effects of Application of "the Unemotional Norm."—In a system of change, disharmony results from the operation of opposing forces; this is followed by a phase of balance of diametrical interests.

Though there is a legitimate order defining and restricting the modes and conditions under which ends are to be pursued, the system of ends of the collectivity is imperfectly integrated. The interests of one group are seen in terms of rational adaptation of means to end (in terms of empirical values). Action is oriented to the norm in the pursuit of goals; the individuals are motivated by similar expectations (this is typical of Church One). However, the traditional group finds its action curtailed by the application of the norm; this constitutes a "conditional element" in the system of ends of this type of churchman. To the traditionalist, "interests" are being suppressed and expectations are being unfulfilled. There is a clash of interests and a state of tension between the normative and the conditional elements of action.[3] This conflict of interest results

[1] *Ibid.*, pp. 75, 150, 400, 463, 650. [2] *Loc. cit.* [3] *Ibid.*, p. 732.

from different attitudes toward non-empirical ends. Sentiments motivating the transcendentalist are reflected in action. This type of person conceives the manifestation of sentiment in overt emotional behavior as desirable. Consequently, some of "the old-time religionists" resist and combat the normative rule.

Disregard of the common system of rules has important effects in action. The disagreement and the hostility in Methodist and Baptist churches over transcendentalism and emotionalism have these results: (1) withdrawal and expulsion, (2) establishment of new faiths and churches, (3) competition and rivalry between the old church and the new, and (4) accommodation, and reintegration. Although it is preferable not to elaborate on these processes at this point since they will be revealed in "the attitudes and the reactions to the norm," a brief explanation is in order.

New religions develop from conflict in the action system. The group finding its action too greatly hampered or restricted seeks a different kind of religion.[1] First, there is the voluntary form of withdrawal as seen in the case of Protestants seeking the Catholic faith *partly* because of the quiet form of worship. Then there is the case of members of Protestant churches being attracted to cults, which provide emotional expression in an exaggerated manner; there is voluntary withdrawal in this instance also. On the other hand, there is coercion applied to the extent that the demonstrative are either isolated or expelled from the church. As a result of differences in ends of groups in the Protestant church, there is a departure of the very emotional to apostolic churches. And there is a departure of those who find the presence of some remaining emotional members in Methodist and Baptist churches extremely obnoxious, to Episcopal or Catholic churches.

Second, some leaders seize upon the disparity, clashes of interests, and conflict of ends of various types of men in the Protestant collectivity as an opportunity to establish new churches. This attraction and inclusion is accomplished by two methods—little or no effort to integrate the periphery groups in the Protestant collectivity, and attempt or effort to integrate these groups in the established church. The ends of the leader may be (1) selfish or exploitative, (2) altruistic, and (3) humanitarian and utilitarian combined. Under the first method, the leaders make little or no effort to integrate individuals maladjusted to the system of norms into the ultimate common system of religious ends. This is seen in the prevalence of "store front" churches and cults in metropolitan areas

[1] See pages 48–49.

and in their existence, though to a lesser degree, in villages, and small cities (especially in the South). Exploitation has in some cases been the purpose of these leaders. These leaders might be compared with Hobbes' sovereign in whom authority is posited as a means of security for the members whose ends clashed with those of other men in the religious body. After receiving this power to restore order by bringing into a system of action those whose interests are identical or nearly so, the sovereign usurps privileges for his own benefit while sometimes partially supplying some needs of a material and religious nature as a means of attracting, appeasing, placating, and retaining.

Under the second method, the leader seeks to sublimate and redirect interests through training and activity. Some leaders, for example, the director of Church Three, take the type of men motivated by "old principles" and attempt to direct the group gradually to common ultimate ends of Negro religion, while at the same time they consciously give some realization to the individual ends of the members of their group.[1]

If, in the future, the Protestant collectivity does not give more consideration to the ends of the transcendentalist in the church, and does not attempt to provide for the expression of his ends, there will be an increasing departure of its communicants to other faiths. Also, if the ends of the three types of church goers are not considered in planning the program of the church so as to provide a partial means of realization of ends of all types, the church will continually lose its members. Some will either follow other religions or will refrain from church participation and membership.

The third effect of application of "the unemotional norm" is that rivalry and hostility have arisen as a result of competing churches. This competition is seen among the "regular" or established Protestant churches which are motivated by somewhat different ends; it is seen in terms of the Catholic church and the Protestant church; and it is seen in terms of the established Protestant church and the cults or "new religions." In the Boston and South Carolina churches, motivated in terms of types or particular systems of action, there is competition resulting from the pursuit of different ends. There is rivalry and hostility as a result of the imperfectly integrated common system of ends; this is especially true in regard to the established and the recently developed Protestant churches, and these attitudes are reflected by both leaders and followers of the various types of churches. Thus, the presence of the three types of persons in the

[1] See pages 47–49, 160–162.

system of action evolves into churches essentially characterized by the predominance of one type of communicant; and competition results from the various elements in the religious collectivity.

Fourth, there are some efforts to achieve a significant degree of integration or re-integration of the ends of the Protestant collectivity as a result of the imperfect integration in the system. Among the various action systems, there is some cooperation, accommodation, and adjustment, a gradual approach to re-integration of ends in spite of some differences in various end systems. This is seen in an attempt to become more tolerant of "newer faiths." And it is seen in an approach to the problem of harmonizing ends of various types of members in some of the established Protestant churches. There is some provision of opportunity for various types of individuals to pursue their ends. For example, this is true in Church Two in Boston.

The situation is somewhat different in rural churches, though there is an inclination gradually to follow the norm of urban churches. In some rural churches, there is a tendency to let the members pursue their discrete ends while gradually leading them to the common ultimate system of ends. For some leaders, this common system has not been formulated theoretically; for others, there is partial consciousness or realization of it; for the majority, some actions are oriented to the norm. The rural clergy are not as conscious of the normative principle and generally do not as precisely formulate their ends as the leaders in metropolitan areas.

Various Approaches to Emotionalism and Reactions to the Norm According to Type of Clergyman and Church.—In a system of action, groups manifest various attitudes toward the normative system of rules; those who urge precise adherence, and for whom the sentiments motivate empirical actions, tend to dominate in the action system. At the same time, the attitudes and actions of this group are counterbalanced by a more temperate religionist who "levels off" the disturbance in the system by giving some consideration to both transcendental and empirical ends.

There are three types of clergymen and churches, the followers being greatly influenced by the leader. They are as follows: (1) Group of men advocating elimination of sentiment in overt emotional action; this group favors a rigid application of and assiduous conformity with the system of selective rules. (2) Advocators of semi-restrained emotion and transcendental ends; this group inclines toward a mild application of the norm. (3) The group favoring manifestation of sentiment in non-experimental action; emotionalism is desirable.

Attitudes toward transcendental ends are based upon sentiments of the members. These attitudes are reflected in action. Pareto calls these sentiments residues, which form the basis for the construction of theories of action.[1] The individual is exhorted to accomplish an act; this exhortation is the "residue-in-chief." Then he is told the reason he should strive for or pursue the end in terms of "the will of God," "the fulfillment of the principle of group well-being," etc. This is the "residue used to derive," or the derivation, which offers justification for or rationalization of the pursuit of the desired end.[2] The residues operate together. The derivations strengthen, vitalize, and re-enforce the residues by clarifying sentiments and bringing them to "the focus of consciousness."[3] The derivation rationalizes the residue-in-chief.[4]

It has been shown that sentiments regarding non-experimental entities (those which cannot be observed by the senses, and cannot be scientifically tested and verified) have occupied a conspicuous place in Negro religion. At present, however, attitudes toward the manner (whether in terms of primarily empirical or non-empirical forms) in which the ideal should be pursued vary. And the reasons or justifications (derivations) for the pursuit of the end in a particular way are changing. Men construct theories of action in terms of their interests. For many, "interests" do not relate to transcendental sentiments accompanied by emotional action. Though some beliefs and actions regarding the end and the principle regulating the mode of action are non-scientific, there is a combination of non-experimental and experimental actions. It has been shown that the churchman who attempts to orient his action according to scientific standards is also motivated by sentiment. In other words, experimental and non-experimental values are expressed in action.

Being motivated by transcendental and empirical values, the churchman is seeking effectively to realize his ends by means which it is believed will result in the desired state of things. In some instances, the means applied do not actually produce the end, and hence the action is not logical from the objective point of view, though from the subjective point of view the means are efficacious to the end. But for some persons the means and ends coincide or correspond, and the action is logical. Both of these types of action occur among the subjects of this study. However, action is increasingly falling within the experimental realm in the group as a whole. This increase in empirical action is concomitant with the decline in

[1] Homans and Curtis, *op. cit.*, pp. 88–89. [2] *Ibid.*, pp. 89, 175, 240, 243–244.
[3] *Ibid.*, pp. 96, 117, 132, 137, 244–245, 247–249, 268. [4] *Ibid.*, p. 176.

transcendental ends and emotionalism and non-rational action.[1] This trend is seen in a variety of ways. And under certain conditions, which will be later presented, there is an increase of rationality.

Experimental actions are those which men make whenever they are seeking an effective means of realizing their end. Pareto terms these actions "interests," those things men pursue in an effort to make life profitable, enjoyable, and abundant, and in an effort to acquire esteem and honor. These actions are usually rationalized. Men seek these ends in a variety of channels.[2] This is true of the Negro, but it is also true that this group greatly expresses these ends in religion.

Religious ideas are significant in action.[3] The religious ideas and actions of the Negro reflect the "interests" of the collectivity. There is a close relation between the common value attitudes of the group and religious ideas. Religious beliefs and actions not only reflect common value attitudes of this group, but these attitudes canalize the direction of interests in the pursuit of ends. Man's active attitudes toward the non-empirical play an important role in action.[4] The religious ideas of the Negro are a combination of transcendental ends and ultimate value attitudes in terms of the "interests" of the Negro group.

Most informants believe in the principle of divine control. But their attitudes toward the Deity have changed. The degree of dependence upon the Supreme is not so great as formerly; the idea of "waiting upon the Lord" is subordinate. Consequently, man is not so passive as active. There is still trust in the Divine Providence, to some extent. But this faith is a basis for action. Man seeks to change the existing state of things, and this action finds an outlet in the church and in the community. Anticipation is not mainly in terms of eternal values (in the hereafter) but in terms of earthly values. The present is more important than the future for the modern or "reformed" or transformed religionist.

Action being guided or motivated by the belief that emotional action accompanying religious sentiment is undesirable, two groups of men in whom this belief is strong wish to impose uniformity in the collectivity through the normative concept. Thinking in terms of "interests," these groups wish to inculcate this principle in the group

[1] From the scientific point of view, action is characterized as non-rational whenever means are adapted to non-experimental ends, and it is impossible to state whether the means are appropriate to the end inasmuch as action is directed to entities outside the domain of experience and observation.

[2] Homans and Curtis, *op. cit.*, pp. 77–78.

[3] Parsons, *op. cit.*, pp. 73–74.

[4] *Ibid.*, p. 154.

tending to adhere to "the old order." Men express non-scientific (philosophical) ideas about their motives for acting.[1] Though this is true to some extent of all the types of churchmen herein analyzed, the conservative religionist is to a great extent motivated to act in terms of beliefs in a controlling Divinity, and in retribution. Therefore, the "empirical man" (prevalent in Church One) seeks to impose the norm upon the traditionalist, while the type of member found in Church Two is inclined to seek a gradual inculcation of the norm under the influence of the pastor.

In the religious system of action, groups recommending changes are motivated by the belief that the collectivity will derive advantages from a transition from the present order of things.

This brings us to further consideration of the first group of men, those proposing elimination of emotionalism. This is basically the type of person in Church One in Boston. There is conspicuous absence of sentiment in overt emotional action in this church. The pastor and the members regard emotionalism as undesirable. And there is harmony of belief and action in this group. The pastor consciously seeks the elimination of emotionalism in the Negro collectivity.

The group advocating a departure from the emphasis upon transcendental ends and emotionalism is motivated mainly by these ends: (1) removal of overt emotional elements so that the churchman will be logical in his thinking and will proceed to make life abundant in terms of empirical values, and (2) restoration or protection of group integrity. Considering the integrity of the Negro damaged as a result of being regarded emotional, this group wishes to dissociate manifestation of overt emotion from religion. Removal of the stigma is to be performed by operations upon the subject so that there will no longer be manifestation of exaggerated action accompanying religious emotions.

Within this group are strong proponents of unemotionalism. Many persons advocate total submergence of emotion; they are extremely hostile to a display of feeling and vociferously state their condemnation. Opposition and antagonism to, as well as intolerance of, pronounced emotional action is characteristic of Protestant clergy and laity.

Although some non-experimental values remain in this group, motivation is mainly in terms of scientific standards. The importance of empirical values is seen in the program of the church.

[1] *Ibid.*, pp. 11–12.

THE ROLE OF THE PASTOR OF CHURCH ONE

I. End	Means	Norm
A *decided* alteration of traditional Negro religion	1. Presentation of information on the meaning of religion 2. Ridicule and condemnation of emotionalism 3. Emphasis upon the importance of living in *this* world rather than concentrating upon "laying up treasures in Heaven"	The Negro should strive for empirical ends.

II. End	Means	Norm
Extirpation of emotionalism Situation Some churches continue to offer mainly the traditional type of religion.	1. Promotion of education 2. Provision of practical channels of action by the church	Man should seek to be logical in his thinking and acting.

III. End	Means	Norm
Offering a practical, attractive religion by the church Situation The church has not offered a program that keeps pace with rapid social changes.	1. Christian education 2. Intellectual programs 3. Interdenominational, recreational, and community programs	The church must adjust its program to the present needs of its members.

IV. End	Means	Norm
Consciousness of the necessity of working for the peace, happi-	1. An appreciation of the dignity of man 2. Provision of programs that promote understanding, sympathy, and co-	A religion that has merit must give consideration to the welfare of *all* people.

The Role of The Pastor of Church One (*cont.*)

End	Means	Norm
ness, and prosperity of mankind	operation of races, creeds, and governments	
Situation Many churchmen have been mainly interested in local programs affecting their particular church.		
V. Ultimate End Heaven[1]	Ultimate Means 1. Provision for the intellectual, economic, and social needs of man 2. Provision of opportunities for the individual to develop his potentialities so as to promote a productive life	Norm Religious men must govern their conduct by the principle of sympathy, love, and assistance that Christ demonstrated.

THE UNEMOTIONAL GROUP

Means and Ends of Church One[2]

I. End	Means	Norm
Alteration of traditional Negro religion	1. Disparagement and ridicule of emotionalism 2. Provision of channels of action	Emotionalism is undesirable since it retards action on a reflective level.
Situation Some persons in the Protestant collectivity manifest emotion overtly.		

[1] The "Heaven" sought by this clergyman is decidedly of an empirical nature. Not considering the "old type of religion" feasible, he directs his church into primarily practical channels. He is interested in the social aspect of religion.

[2] It is unnecessary to subdivide this group further since the vast majority of the men in this church are motivated by similar ends. In addition to unity and unanimity of belief, attitudes and actions tend to correspond.

MEANS AND ENDS OF CHURCH ONE (*cont.*)

II. End	Means	Norm
Promotion of education	1. Sponsoring lectures, group discussions, concerts, dramas, clinics, nurseries, kindergartens, and collegiate institutions	Education should be promulgated because enlightenment facilitates advancement.
Situation		
Some persons in the collectivity manifest little interest in activities other than those of the "purely religious type."		
III. End	Means	Norm
Sponsoring activities of a social nature	1. Engaging in local and foreign missionary work 2. Providing a social worker, and crime prevention bureaus, promoting centers of recreation, and providing opportunities for leadership and for participation in community programs 3. Investigation of employment and business opportunities, and creation of church employment agencies and establishment of business enterprises 4. Dissemination of information on civic responsibilities	The church should seek practical ends and concentrate upon "the near" rather than upon "the remote."
Situation		
The collectivity has been dilatory in promulgating a practical religion and sponsoring a program of action in terms of empirical standards.		
IV. Ultimate End	Ultimate Means	Norm
Attainment of Heaven[1]	1. Demonstrating charitableness and brotherliness 2. Promoting the intellectual and social faculties of man	It is essential to apply "the Golden Rule" in social relationships.

[1] Although this group believes in a transcendental Heaven, the emphasis is upon an "empirical heaven."

In the action system, as action is oriented toward the normative concept, the group responding somewhat slowly to the change from non-experimental action is inclined to consider the interests of various types of persons in the religious unit.

The second type of clergyman and church tend to advocate semi-restrained emotion and a mild application of the normative concept. The members of Church Two vary in their beliefs, however. Some attempt a forcible imposition of the norm, while others favor a gradual application of it; and, on the other hand, some desire an inclusion of opportunities for emotional expression in the church. This church is undergoing a process of change and represents a decaying rural or semi-rural institution. It is somewhat conservative and is changing from the traditional to the modern type. Aside from rural influences resulting from migration, there are other features in the situation of action tending to retard change.

It is maintained that denomination is not the primary influence regarding emotionalism. There is, nevertheless, some influence. This is a Baptist church, and it is true that the popular Protestant churches, holding the vast majority of Negro memberships in the United States, were in the past emotional. However, for many years the Baptist and the Methodist denominations have had within their jurisdiction the three types of churches (subdued, semi-emotional, and emotional). And since the emphasis is upon type of church rather than upon denomination, what is being stated about this particular church is true of the same type in other denominations.[1] This is a typical conservative church in a stage of transition. A far more important factor than denomination is education. Later, the correlation between transcendentalism and class status will be made. In spite of this, however, the Negro church as a unit is changing, irrespective of education.

Some members of church-type-two so strongly adhere to the norm that there is application of pressure to non-conformers, or the extremely emotional. Ridicule or censure is the chief method employed; however, some of the churches of this type (this is especially marked in the urban church) have expelled those who do not govern their actions according to the guiding rule.

Notwithstanding the fact that there is some hostility in Church Two to manifestation of sentiment in emotional action, some op-

[1] This is especially emphasized because some students of religion have failed to give ample consideration to the type-concept in their studies of religion. They have overemphasized the present status of emotion in terms of denomination rather than in regard to other very important factors. Thus they erroneously interpret the popular Protestant churches and characterize them as emotional.

portunities are provided for various types of members to express their interests and ends. This is true in the rural church of a similar type. The type-concept is valid for rural churches also; they fit into the three kinds of churches, with some distinctions.

The role of the pastor in shaping the policy of the church has been pointed out. He influences, restrains, and directs the followers, some of whom would go to the extreme in either direction were it not for his guidance. Over a period of years, the pastors of the Boston churches have exerted their influence over the members' pursuit of ends and the manner in which they were pursued. It is significantly true that the leaders of the urban churches have sought the attainment of ends in terms of their local church, surrounding churches, and in terms of the Negro church as a unit. They are applying means which they consider efficacious to the end in terms of a selective standard.

The pastor of Church Two occupies a "middle ground," not being extreme in either direction. In order to provide a degree of satisfaction of various types of individuals having different interests and ends, he compares the utilities of the various groups in his congregation and seeks to regulate his church program so as to provide the maximum of utility for the congregation as a body. He strives to satisfy the diverse ends of the groups (emotional, intellectual, etc.) by reducing heterogeneous ends to a common denominator. While providing a degree of satisfaction for the worshippers in his church, he is *leaning* toward unemotionalism as a norm. Though he considers provision for semi-restrained emotion essential, he is strongly opposed to extreme emotional action and is *inclined* to ignore and restrain "the very demonstrative." However there should be a retention of warmth in the service; a too sudden departure from the traditional manner of worship is not practicable. Correspondingly, this leader does not verbally express his unfavorable attitude toward emotionalism to the congregation; he quietly, cautiously, and conservatively attempts to remold members' attitudes. While action is oriented to the norm, distant objectives are planned.

Nevertheless, pastors' attitudes and actions are also influenced by those of the members. Some pastors are responding to the demands of the modern religionist; yet some leaders have failed to seek changes in keeping with the interests of a militant few. Some have failed to visualize and grasp the present trend. And as a result there is some confusion and maladjustment. Therefore the modern religionist is sometimes impatient and disgusted over the slow rate of change, from the subjective point of view. He is inclined to be disrespectful and intolerant of the attitudes and policies of the leader, whose beliefs are sometimes more retarded than his, and whose capacity is sometimes not on the level of that of some of the members. There are some preachers, nevertheless, who have some realization of the trend; but they hesitate to inaugurate change because of fear of criticism, and fear of condemnation by their superior church officials, and because of lack of interest and willingness actually to take the time to plan a program other than the regular one of preaching, singing, and collecting money.

Since there are some centrifugal interests escaping control and resulting in a state of tension or relative *anomie,* some persons have withdrawn from the established Protestant church and have sought an environment more favorable to the expression of their sentiments in non-experimental and emotional action.

The Role of The Pastor of Church Two

I. End	Means	Norm
Provision of maximum utility for the Negro church	1. Inclusion of elements in the church to satisfy a diversity of interests	The church should seek a degree of fulfillment of the ends of different types of persons in the collectivity.
Situation		
Since this congregation, as well as the Negro collectivity, comprises various classes, consideration of the interest of only one type would be unsatisfactory to the different types.		
II. End	Means A	Norm A
A gradual departure from (a) emotionalism, and (b) archaic rules	1. Recognition of the "old elements" in the church 2. Provision of many organizations so as to insure channels of satisfaction and action for all	It is desirable that the church provide some expression of traditional religious ends and continue to satisfy some emo-

THE ROLE OF THE PASTOR OF CHURCH TWO (CONT.)

	3. Specific clubs or groups, such as "the gospel chorus" and quartettes, for "the demonstrative" 4. Permitting emotional persons to express their feelings on infrequent or inconspicuous occasions, as the mid-week prayer service, revivals, and the New Year's Eve service	tional needs, though irrational action should be discouraged.
Situation A The traditionalists, who demand expression of their attitudes, conflict in point of view with young, modern groups in the church.	5. Offering an atmosphere of reverence, warmth, and fellowship 6. Redirection of interest of traditionalists 7. Conducting classes of instruction on the meaning of religion, and the responsibilities of a Christian in keeping with present trends and needs	
Situation B	Means B	Norm B
Since the congregation includes traditional religionists, a sudden re-vamping of laws and practices would be opposed by those who urge rigid adherence to the Ten Commandments.	1. A sympathetic, tolerant, helpful attitude rather than a disdainful, condemnatory one with respect to deviators or violators of ethical norms 2. Retaining non-conformers in the church and wielding them into the religious system 3. Not delving too closely into the personal lives of members 4. Educating traditional members to the need of changes in rules and practices in keeping with present values and trends	There should be reexamination of the rules of the church; outmoded laws should be discarded in favor of those suited to the present time.

THE ROLE OF THE PASTOR OF CHURCH TWO (CONT.)

III. End	Means	Norm
Coordination of religion with life Situation The group has been primarily interested in a stereotyped religious program rather than a varied one with practical ends.	1. Calling attention to the role of religion in the past, and its present potentialities 2. Presenting lectures, discussions, concerts, and scholarships 3. Maintenance of educational institutions 4. Sponsoring and supporting local and foreign missionary work 5. Presenting vital issues which affect the lives of the wage-earning class, such as housing and employment 6. Cooperating with truant officers and the juvenile court by aiding in rehabilitation of offenders 7. Working with interdenominational and interracial groups	The church should act to promote harmony in family, school, and other associational relationships, and it should be instrumental in promoting the "Kingdom of God" on earth.
IV. Ultimate End	**Ultimate Means**	**Norm**
Heaven	1. Faithfulness to the program of the church 2. Sincerity and fairness in personal and group relationships 3. Participation in community programs 4. Exhibiting Christian precepts in living	The Christian must continually strive to follow the unselfish, humanitarian example of Jesus in integrating religion with life.

THE SEMI-RESTRAINED GROUP

Means and Ends of Church Two[1]

I. End	Means	Norm
Modification of traditional Negro religion Situation Numerous persons in this church are "the old-type of Christian."	1. Discouragement of extreme emotionalism 2. Provision for semi-restrained emotional expression 3. Introduction of a variety of programs in order to satisfy desires of various types of church members	The Negro should not manifest extreme action accompanying religious emotions.

II. End	Means	Norm
Re-direction of interest in Negro religion with some regard to spiritual and eternal values	1. Offering a spiritually stimulating service, one that "satisfies the soul" 2. Provision for the really religious needs (awe, communion, inspiration, and dependence of man upon the Deity) 3. Calling attention to spiritual, emotional, moral, intellectual, and social needs	Transcendental ends should not be exclusively pursued.

III. End	Means	Norm
Provision for practical action Situation Since this congregation consists of a motley group, a program strikingly depart-	1. Sponsoring local and foreign missionary work 2. Maintenance of higher educational institutions 3. Providing lectures, concerts, scholarships, choral societies, sewing circles, floral clubs, community centers, and participation in crime-prevention programs	The church should promote religious, moral, and social development.

[1] Although this is a Baptist church, the ends are given according to type and not denomination inasmuch as Baptist churches of the three types are found in Boston and elsewhere. The ends of Church Two are approaching those of Church One in some respects and are similar to those of Church Three in some ways. Church Two is the typical conservative type, occupying a middle position between types one and three.

The Semi-Restrained Group (cont.)

ing from really religious features would be objectionable, although some progressive practices are inculcated and promulgated.		
IV. Ultimate End	Ultimate Means	Norm
Heaven Situation The church has not fully demonstrated the Christian principle.	1. Piety, reverence, and support of the church and "its cause" 2. Demonstration of neighborliness, charity, and fellowship in all relationships 3. Promotion of activities that facilitate moral, intellectual, and social growth, and lead to establishment of "the Kingdom of God on this earth"	The Christian should live according to "the ethical norm" and treat his fellowman with respect and consideration.

In the system of action, there is first resistance to the trend from non-experimental action followed by a process of accommodation.

Finally, the third group or type of church regards emotionalism desirable. However, there are differences between the attitudes and ends of the director and those of the followers, although the leader is gradually directing the group to ends he has perceived.

Effort to impose uniformity in religion in terms of the normative concept has significant effects in action. Normative structures are important in action in relation to impeding factors.[1] The norm is only one structural element in concrete action. Since there is resistance to its attainment, the failure of action to conform with the norm does not indicate that the principle is not important; there are other important elements in action. Resistance, and even its partial overcoming, implies another significant element, effort.[2]

The presence of a variety of men in the collectivity has important results in action. Conflict has resulted from the different ends of the

[1] Parsons, *op. cit.*, p. 251.

[2] *Loc. cit.*

types of persons in the system. Resistance, which is an obstacle in the attainment of one's ends, results from failure to consider the interests of others in action.[1] In the Protestant collectivity, the emotional group has failed to get maximum satisfaction from the religious services because of the trend from concentrating upon transcendental values and manifesting emotional actions. Since the ends of the traditionalist are different from those who regard a departure from emotionalism desirable, the change in the type of service has affected the interest of persons for whom the authority of custom is strong. Since certain changes affect the interests of different groups in different directions, the groups whose interests are disregarded have sentiments opposing alterations in the established procedure. Thus the traditionalists resist threats to their individual and group integrities, since the modernists disfavor emotionalism and have expressed disdain by curbing extreme manifestation of emotion.

Those seeking primarily non-experimental ends consider opposition a challenge to "freedom of expression."[2] They regard promulgation or establishment of a form of equilibrium to which they are not adjusted either with disfavor or hostility. Those who hesitate to express verbally their desire to retain the stable equilibrium to which they are adjusted regard the trend from the established order as inimical to their interests. For most people, equilibrium represents the present state of things or a society changing in a manner which they approve.[3] Thus the types of religious men have different attitudes toward equilibrium. The traditional group considers equilibrium a static process, whereas the other groups consider it a dynamic one. For the latter groups, equilibrium consists of either subordination or elimination of extreme emotional action, a religious system moving toward the prevalence of logical action according to the norm. In approaching this desired state, antithetical tendencies of the groups result in various reactions.

The traditional group regards emotionalism as characteristic of a

[1] *Ibid.*, p. 650.

[2] It might appear upon casual observation that the writer uses the words "non-experimental" and "emotionalism" interchangeably. Though there is a difference in meaning between the words, they sometimes occur together in this study because of the close relationship with respect to religious action. Persons whose ends are to a great extent supersensory manifest feelings of jubilance, exhilaration, and depression under the stimulus of religious objects. They sometimes weep with joyful anticipation of Heaven and proclaim their elation and comfort over the protection and guidance of God. They also act in a manner (praying, being observant of the Ten Commandments, attending church, adoring the Deity, etc.) to influence God to grant their requests and heed their entreaties.

[3] Homans and Curtis, *op. cit.*, p. 156.

stable, customary order of procedure in the church service. The persons in this group regard with skepticism those by whom the authority of tradition and custom has been questioned. The religion of the past which sufficed for their ancestors is in some respects adequate for them. These men desire "that old religion" and resist changes not consistent with their interests. Some in this group are recalcitrant to innovations coming to disturb uniformity. Hence motivated by the sentiment of neophobia, they resist threats to their integrity by forming combinations, "putting together" elements previously dissociated.[1] This is seen in the formation of cults to provide emotional outlets being denied in the regular Protestant church. While some withdrawals are voluntary, others are compulsory. Reference has been made to the attitudes of the dominant groups as reflected in ridicule, subordination, and accommodation (in the form of permitting emotionalism on certain rare occasions and providing special groups, such as gospel choruses, for the very demonstrative), and expulsion while orienting action to the norm.

In relation to the group which prefers maintenance of the established form of worship, the leader or director of Church Three plays a role of primary importance to the interests of the traditionalists.

Isolated in their withdrawal or expulsion, and regarded with disdain or contempt, the "old religionists" continue unintegrated in the general religious system. They fall under the leadership of those who are of their opinion, or those who seek to further their own interests by permitting an unhampered expression of exuberance. Some cult leaders employ highly sensational methods further to captivate the emotional, who are waiting for some form of guidance or a "place" in religion; some add some practical features, and some emphasize ostensible economic values. There is another type of leader who can contribute to the general well-being of this group.

A strong leader can aid those maladjusted to the new equilibrium to achieve ends in terms of the general religious system. Though motivated by a somewhat different point of view as regards the normative concept, he can direct the group and promote or facilitate gradual reintegration. Thus he can lead confusion out of disorder, clarify concepts, and provide satisfaction and status while pursuing his ultimate end.

In the general religious system, action is in a state in which there are experimental and non-experimental elements. Action is moving toward empirical values in terms of the normative concept; nevertheless, there is resistance to the guiding principle of action, and

[1] *Ibid.*, pp. 98, 141.

consequently the influence of the director of Church Three is of cardinal importance in the action system. He perceives ends which the collectivity "should pursue" and formulates normative aspects of action "in abstraction from the resistant and non-normative aspects."[1] The non-normative factors consist of the sentiments and conditions of action of the traditional group in terms of the religious unit. The actions of the traditionalists are restricted by the predominance of those seeking to eliminate emotionalism. The director of this church perceives values in terms of achieving a religion which would emphasize empirical actions of a nature to aid man in his present adjustment to society. A practical religion is desired; however there should be retention of restrained or semi-restrained emotion. Emotion is subsidiary to action. His objective is to achieve his end in terms of the normative standard particularly in relation to the groups which are finding their place vanishing or vanished in religion. He seeks to work with the group which is retarded as far as the general system of religious action is concerned and which experiences some other handicaps. His goal in terms of the general religious system is foremost in his mind, although he does not suddenly make it apparent to his followers.

He acts in a situation. For him, the situation of action consists of the educational and emotional level of the persons in his church. He selects norms to achieve his end. He acts in terms of superposed normative elements. Though motivated by the general norm, he is also motivated by the principle that the emotional group of men in the religious system should not be neglected, but aided. Since the latter norm is somewhat subsidiary to the former, he first applies means gradually to overcome resistance. Achieving this immediate end will be a means of realizing progressive ends in the means-end schema. The Director must first alter the situation in which he acts in order to attain his end. To do this, he utilizes certain methods, notably sublimation and education. In other words, this leader considers the ends of the traditional group of men and means at their disposal for realizing goals, as related to the subjective category of action. He gives thought to the minds and bodies of the subjects and is aware of the element of error involved in the choice of means to attain the ideal. But the Director goes further; he considers the ends of various groups in his church and in the community and integrates these into a system of action to which he applies a norm by regarding ultimate ends beneficial in a group system of action. That is, he attempts to relate the ends of the types and groups of

[1] Parsons, *op. cit.*, p. 252.

men to each other and thereby to further harmony or balance in the Protestant collectivity. Integration of ends in a system of action is his central objective.

Since there is disharmony in the religious system resulting from imperfectly integrated ends, and since there is resistance to the normative concept, he seeks to overcome this resistance by first appealing to sentiments. Since he is dealing with a group disposed to manifest sentiment in exaggerated action, he offsets rejection of his end by not formally and logically offering it instantaneously unsupported by an appeal to values in terms of the manner in which the traditional religionist conceives them. Thus he approaches potential refractoriness by a recourse to the sentiments of his followers. An immediate end is to capture "the old time religionist" who is either dissatisfied in or expelled from the established Protestant church, by emotion, evangelism, and supernaturalism. The leader possesses spiritualistic powers as a result of special contact with the Deity. By divine insight or revelation, he was led to direct the group in Boston and to spread the Gospel and the Kingdom of God throughout the country. There is, therefore, a strong appeal to transcendental values.

As a result of changes in the Protestant collectivity not consistent with the interests of the traditionalist, followers are attracted to a religion which appears to them to satisfy their needs by the use of non-empirical beliefs, and ceremony, and ritual actions. The charismatic leader can invoke special blessings upon the followers. He uses these sensational methods as a means of attaining a further end —sublimation of emotion. This leads to a superposed end—a practical religion. Although non-experimental elements are apparent, a system of logical action is developing while action is oriented toward the normative principle. Believing a gradual application of the norm feasible, the leader uses methods he regards advisable in the situation of action. Believing that religion is not all emotion, he aims to direct his group to betterment of their local community. And his ultimate end partakes of a mundane character. The importance of empiricism to him is seen in the name he applies to his religion, "The Church of Personal Experience." The religion is related to the lives of the followers. Values in terms of this world are pursued in business and social welfare.

The group of followers whose subjective ends are consolidated in a new religion, which welcomes all groups irrespective of status, or limitations, manifest attitudes of respect and reverence toward their leader. To some extent, he is a symbolic representation of the Supernatural. An element of sacredness adheres about him and the acts he performs. There has been acquirement of the charismatic quality. The action of the leader of Church Three is approaching the experimental standard. Logical action is significant in his adaption of means to end. By addressing the sentiments of his subjects, he directs them to ends he has perceived. He utilizes the means at his disposal by considering the situation in which both he and his followers act. He seeks to achieve a kind of harmony between diametrical ends by concession and adjustment. And at the same time, he applies other means which he believes will achieve realization of his immediate and long range objectives. His action definitely leans toward the empirical, although he is partly motivated by sentiment.

For the most part, he employs means which are appropriate to the end.[1] Then in terms of Homans and Curtis' revamped criterion of Pareto's logico-experimental standard, the Director's actions are experimental. This leader's action is experimental to both doer and observer in that his act is an "efficacious means toward its immediate purpose."[2]

THE ROLE OF THE DIRECTOR OF CHURCH THREE

I. End	Means	Norm
Gradual modification of traditional Negro religion Situation This group consists of members, with a Protestant and with a cult background, who were generally emotional in the past.	1. Provision of instruction on the meaning of religion 2. Providing some services and clubs which offer emotional outlets 3. Guiding the group from irrational action by offering practical channels of action in and out of the church	There should be a departure from extreme emotional behavior in the Negro church, and at the same time there should be redirection of the traditional religionist.

[1] This does not relate to non-experimental ends and non-empirical actions previously explained.

[2] Homans and Curtis, *op. cit.*, pp. 72, 77–78.

THE ROLE OF THE DIRECTOR OF CHURCH THREE (CONT.)

II. End	Means	Norm
Integration of ends of various types of religious men	1. Providing a program that satisfies diverse groups 2. Promoting understanding of, sympathy with, and tolerance of the ideas and actions of others 3. Gradual sublimation of emotion by offering an inclusive, varied seven-day program	The church should sponsor a program including attractive features to the emotional, the semi-restrained, and the restrained.

III. End	Means	Norm
A non-sectarian, interracial church Situation The persons served by this church have an insecure place in "the outer community" and are generally overlooked by groups occupying a more favorable educational and economic status, and by churches serving the needs of the other groups.	1. Local and national evangelistic programs to attract attention to this religion, and to the importance of spiritual reawakening 2. Extending an invitation to Protestants, Catholics, etc., to become communicants of this church 3. Incorporation of ideas and actions that attract the devout, the demonstrative, the serene, the educated, the uneducated, the impecunious, and the favorably situated economic groups 4. Promulgating policies and programs that promote charity, goodwill, brotherhood, and cooperation 5. Offering assistance to submerged groups in need of leadership in the community 6. Interdenominational cooperation through exchange and interchange of speakers, clubs, etc., in the city, and the state	The church should follow the Christian ideal and should welcome all groups into its fellowship.

THE ROLE OF THE DIRECTOR OF CHURCH THREE (CONT.)

	7. Providing opportunities for spiritual growth and communication with the Divine	

IV. End	Means	Norm
A church that is a vital part of the community Situation The members of this church are mainly unskilled laborers.	1. Going into the community, identifying one's self with the people, becoming acquainted with their problems, and helping them to live abundantly 2. Giving encouragement and advice to "the depressed and downhearted" 3. Offering help in legal, business, and domestic matters through personal consultation 4. Sponsoring social service programs 5. Helping the people to acquire skills, techniques and experiences that lead to employment in the community 6. Sponsorship and ownership of business enterprises	In pursuit of transcendental values, the church must not lose sight of the necessity of promoting the "Kingdom of God" on earth.

V. End	Means	Norm
Heaven[1]	1. Manifesting attitudes of sincerity, devoutness, sacrifice, and charity 2. Aiding man to adjust himself to the situations of life 3. Integrating religion with life	The church must not lose sight of spiritual values while adjusting its program to the community.

[1] For this leader, a transcendental heaven has some significance; however, efforts to attain a nonempirical ideal state must not be paramount. Realization of heaven in this life is essential.

THE TRADITIONAL GROUP

Means and Ends of Church Three

	Means	Norm
I. End Emotional satisfaction Situation Some of the members of this church were dismissed from churches being guided by "the unemotional norm."	1. Hearing spiritually strengthening sermons 2. Communication with the Divine through prayer and song 3. Giving personal testimony of the help and power of God	The church should satisfy the emotional needs of its members.
II. End A church that offers a full program designed to satisfy a multiplicity of ends	1. Sponsoring classes in Christian education, and promoting growth in the knowledge and reality of God 2. Giving weekly church dinners to provide opportunities for fellowship 3. Demonstrating piety, beauty, and harmony in living 4. Aiding the sick and distressed morally and financially 5. Sponsoring missionary work in the form of evangelism, and education 6. Meeting the spiritual, economic, and social needs of its members	The church should offer a medium for Christian fellowship, and inspiration in helping its members to meet the difficulties of life.
III. Ultimate End Heaven	Ultimate Means 1. Being prayerful, sincere, and holy 2. Offering comfort and help to others	Norm The Christian should follow Christ's example of encouragement and help to all.

MEANS AND ENDS OF CHURCH THREE (*cont.*)

3. Living according to the Golden Rule
4. Being tolerant of the beliefs and actions of others
5. Cooperating with the Director, who exemplifies the Christian principle in living.

Adjustment to the Unemotional Norm.—Changing religious attitudes and practices in terms of a normative standard, with emphasis upon logical aspects of action, eventually leads to integration of ends of the collectivity in spite of the presence of conflict, especially marked in the early stages of application of the norm. Irrespective of some resistance to the normative concept, there is increasing reintegration of ends in the religious system. There is a degree of acceptance of and adjustment to the guiding principle of action, which is promoting change. It has been shown that the group motivated by sentiments reflected in emotional action considered the trend from transcendentalism a threat to their group integrity. Some individuals remain of this opinion. Some have acquiesced in a position of silent "acceptance." However, some of the persons in the traditional group have begun to assume a more experimental attitude and manner of acting with the passage of time and thus have begun to consider the effects of the proposal to eliminate manifestations of extreme emotional action upon the total action schema of Negro religion.[1] Therefore they are orienting their actions to the change.

While various types of men are reacting to the proposal to submerge emotion, some proponents of the change have begun to facilitate adjustment by giving some consideration to the interests of different types of persons in the system. That is, some suggest a type of service which provides opportunities for experimental and non-experimental actions. Another form of adjustment is that of gradual direction of non-experimental action into practical channels.

The approach to integration of ends of the collectivity can be observed in the similarity in belief and practice of Churches One and Three in spite of some differences. For example, the leaders of both of these groups are directing their followers to experimental ends through a different manner of approach. One method is sudden and

[1] This position is indeed influenced by skillful leadership.

open; the other is gradual and veiled. Both leaders have almost identical ultimate ends. The director of Church Three is leading his group in the direction of the state already attained by Church One. However, some differences between the methods of the two leaders are likely to remain inasmuch as Clergyman One approaches his group in terms of primarily scientific standards. On the other hand, Clergyman Three gives considerable attention to the motivation of man by sentiment. In addition, the levels of the two congregations are different. Clergyman Two occupies a middle position between the other two leaders, and in many respects is "the conservative" between two extreme or relatively contrasting positions.[1] There is some degree of integration of ends of the three types of leaders.

The changing role of ends in Negro religion in terms of a selective standard, which circumscribes the action of churchmen within the religious system, is leading to a closer degree of integration in terms of the common, ultimate religious value. Non-empirical elements and emotional hysteria are being displaced by practical approaches to religion. The norm is being applied and realized in terms of the leaders (clergy and lay) of Negro action systems formulating "the ends churchmen should pursue" in terms of coalescence with a common system of values. These ends are being formulated and expressed in social programs to aid and relieve the handicapped, and in terms of recreation, and civic work. This transition of ends for the Negro religious community bears out Durkheim's conception of the social factor as a system of common rules governing the actions of men at the same time that men themselves consciously seek modification of these norms in harmony with common ultimate value attitudes. While Negro religion is achieving a greater degree of integration, it is becoming more logical with application of the unemotional norm.

Leaders' Approach to the Scientific Standard.—Is the action of the pastors logical?[2] It is necessary to bear in mind that this can be answered only in terms of empirical standards. Non-empirical ends exist side by side with empirical. For the non-experimental ends, no answer can be given as they are outside the range of science. But the question can be answered with respect to the coincidence of means and ends as far as the church program is concerned.

The pastors are approaching the situation and are in a process of applying means which are effective to bring about realization of their ends. Their beliefs and their actions are coinciding. This can be seen in regard to the programs in operation in their churches. Not all

[1] His attitudes characterize those of the pastor of the rural churches studied.
[2] Considerable attention has been given this.

clergy, however, are as scientific as these urban leaders. The norm of rationality is not applicable to some (this is true in urban and in rural areas). For some, ends are somewhat random; principles have not been precisely formulated. There is not a clear determination of ends and a precise approximation of standards for all. Action is somewhat haphazard; means are not always appropriate to the end. Some leaders are more retarded than these three in terms of the logical standard. These pastors are highly trained.

However, irrespective of training and location, the trend is one of approaching rationality. Even those who have not so clearly perceived their ends are moving toward a program which subordinates emotional action. Leaders are acting in the situation according to the norm. In spite of some differences in attitudes toward emotional and transcendental actions, there is a preponderance of those who are leading their groups to a practical program. A survey was made of the beliefs and practices of rural and urban pastors. The clergy are orienting their actions to "the unemotional norm," though their attitudes regarding the manner of applying it, and their methods, vary.

As non-empirical and emotional elements of action decline in religion, religion becomes more reflective and practical.

CHAPTER IV

Types of Programs Pursued

As HAS been indicated, there is a relationship between the type of program churches promulgate and attitudes toward God, Heaven, and Hell. As the intensity of feeling with respect to God subdues, the church tends to become more closely related to the community in diverse ways.

The Relation Between Ideas and Actions with Specific Regard to Church Programs.—Religious ends increasingly fall within the empirical or experimental sphere as transcendental ends lose their ascendant position. When transcendental religion, with its emphasis upon the Supreme, predominated, practical programs were impeded. The changing religion, with more consideration being given to empirical ends, is seen in a more reflective sermon and a more practical church program integrated with the community. Thus religion becomes more rational with continuous application of the normative concept. Changing ends in the Negro collectivity result from changing conceptions of religion. The system of rules guiding conduct emphasizes action rather than emotion. There is increase in the rationality of action during the process of change, with motivation according to the norm, which enjoys institutional authority.[1]

There is a direct relationship between men's conceptions of the meaning of the world and the direction of religious interests. Men's ultimate value interests are inextricably bound with their conceptions of the Supernatural. When the Negro concentrated upon the omnipotent, omnipresent, omniscient Creator who would rectify undesirable features of existence, and who would reward "the righteous" and punish "the offender," salvation was pursued in terms of non-experimental values. At the same time, great emotion was displayed in regard to these non-empirical values. However, with changing conceptions of the Supernatural (as previously shown), men's interests are not primarily in terms of ascertainment of "the state of grace" in the hereafter. Since religious ideas canalize interests, and since the religious beliefs are themselves responding to changes in the common ultimate value system, salvation is being pursued in this

[1] Parsons, *op. cit.*, p. 751.

world. As a religion emphasizes the power of the Creator and dependence upon him, ends are centered chiefly around the Supreme. As there is wane in the authority of the Divinity as the person conceives it, the prominence of non-experimental values is less evident. Interests are different, and actions correspond with changing conceptions. Religious ideas of the Negro are important in directing or canalizing interests and actions, and the ultimate common value attitudes of the Negro group are instrumental in influencing changing religious conceptions. Differences in interests and the pursuit of them is seen in the type of program instituted in the church. In the system of action, those still concentrating upon and clinging to transcendental values follow the traditional type of church program. Those inclining toward experimental values inaugurate a program which penetrates community life. Although non-experimental theories are important to conservative types, experimental theories exist also in religion; and non-experimental beliefs are progressively being used as motivators of experimental actions.

The direction of religious interests in relation to men's conceptions of the Supernatural can be seen in terms of the meaning of religion to the individual and the manner in which he desires his church to function. Religious interests define actions and the objectives men hope to realize by virtue of the acts.[1] There is a complex process of interaction. The reciprocal relationship is seen in that men attempt a cognitive understanding of the non-empirical by virtue of religious ideas; these ideas are partly determined by and partly determine common ultimate value attitudes.[2] The religion of the Negro is related to the common ultimate value attitudes of the Negro group. The sociological significance of religious ideas is seen in their relation to the moral community. There is a process of interaction between religion and society. Religious ideas, ultimate value attitudes, and action are in a state of mutual interdependence.[3] The significance of the role of ideas in a religious system is that they direct religious interests into practical action. Ideas determine the manner in which interests are pursued.[4]

Ideas are effective in motivating action. The present interests of the Negro are mainly in terms of empirical, observable ends; consequently action is falling within the logical sphere, with the direction of action according to the norm, which is regarded as binding upon the persons in the system. The role of the rationality of norms is seen in the conception of ends to the individual. To a great extent, all types of religious men believe that there should be integration of the

[1] Parsons, *op. cit.*, p. 666.

[2] *Ibid.*, pp. 425–426.

[3] *Loc. cit.*

[4] *Ibid.*, p. 572.

church with the community. Religion should help man to adjust himself to society. It should lead man to a full, productive life by pursuit of action in terms of Christian principles reflected in meeting social, economic, intellectual, and moral needs. To do this, the church should promote educational, civic, recreational, and rehabilitational programs. Thus religion is greatly regarded in terms of empirical values.

There is gradual coincidence of means and ends. The Negro church is sponsoring activities of an empirical nature. Steadily a practical program is being inaugurated. And as the traditional religionist further accepts experimental standards, the church will further assume leadership and guidance in the designated type of action.

To conclude this section of the analysis, action is being motivated by experimental values according to a norm of rationality. That is, action becomes more logical with the direction of religious ends according to observable, demonstrable standards. In spite of some resistance, there is general adherence to and respect for the norm. In the process of change, there is gradual acceptance of and compliance with the norm, the intrinsic value of which increases with the progression of action.

Also, some transcendental values exist in connection with the trend toward empirical standards inasmuch as sentiments partly motivate action. Nevertheless, the diminution of non-experimental ends is seen in present attitudes toward the Deity, and the principle of retribution. With the decline of objectives in accord with non-empirical standards, emotional action accompanying sentiments decreases.

In addition, the changing status of ends is reflected in the type of church program sought and executed. The increasing value of church functions in terms of the community attests the emphasis upon values of this world. And means are being applied to bring about the desired or anticipated end. Ends are pursued in terms of the interests of the Negro collectivity, and in terms of common ultimate values.

This changing system of action can be interpreted basically as functions of urbanization and of education.

CHAPTER V

Factors in the Wane of Traditional Religion

SINCE THERE has been a change in men's religious actions, what are the factors in the subordination of non-experimental action and emotion? Will there be an increasing trend from the supersensory? What groups respond more slowly to social change and longest retain traditional religious practices?

URBANIZATION AND AGE

With urbanization, there is an increase of church organization, and rationality of action. There is a more logical orientation of action toward the norm in the adaptation of means to end.

In the system of action, urbanization and education are important in determining the types of ends pursued. As man comes under the influence of city life, his religious attitudes and practices are greatly influenced by the variety of contacts and experiences in the urban midst. The individual encounters a motley group with diverse backgrounds, ideas, interests, and experiences. Becoming acquainted with these differences and variations, the city dweller forms new attitudes, and the strength of former beliefs is weakened. Old values are questioned and attacked. New needs are conceived, and new interests are developed; hence there arises a different type of religion, one in terms of the urban environment. As a result of the stimulations of the urban surroundings, the traditional forms of religious expression fall into disuse and disrepute. And in connection with this, a variety of forms of religious expression is found. This diversity has been demonstrated in the analysis of types of churches; it will be further interpreted with regard to religion and class.

Traditional religion is more common in the country than in the city.[1] This is reflected in the greater frequency of emotional action

[1] The factor of rural life might be considered less important than that of education and economics; nevertheless, multiple causation is obvious, and there is interrelation between the factors of education, age, and urbanization inasmuch as youths who go to urban areas to be educated are subject to city influences and manifest city attitudes after returning to the country. Those migrants who fail to return for permanent resumption of rural life are in contact (by visit or correspondence) with country relatives or associates and influence their beliefs and actions.

accompanying sentiment, and in the interest in salvation and eternal life in rural sections. Religious beliefs tend to express themselves in non-empirical values. Correspondingly, actions in rural communities are not so greatly motivated in terms of social programs as in the city. This occurrence cannot, however, be interpreted solely in regard to locality because other factors, such as the quality of clerical leadership, retarded education, and economic inadequacy, are indeed significant.

Further Comparison of Rural and Urban Religion as Regards the Supernatural, the Sacred Norms, and Emotional Action.—The ends of rural men are greatly conceived in terms of an Omnipotent Ruler. Rural churchmen assert stronger beliefs in the existence of a Supreme Being than urban men; and there is a closer, more direct relationship with God. Although this is generally true of the rural group, there is marked similarity of attitudes of the persons in Church Three, and the elderly persons in Churches Two and One in comparison with rural churchmen. The aged as a whole are *emphatic* in their knowledge of the existence of God. In other words, age is an important consideration in the degree of strength of the belief. Truth is in terms of religious and moral sentiments, and not in terms of science; it is not in terms of actual sense perception. Although reference is being made to the firm conviction of the aged and the similarity of belief irrespective of locality, the force of the idea is generally stronger in the country than in the city. In the urban setting, those groups (as in Church Three) which tend to preserve the old religion, in some important respects, express a firm knowledge of the existence of a Controlling Power.

Nevertheless, generally in the Negro collectivity churchmen believe in the divine order of things. However, there is generally a mild form of acceptance and expression among the middle-aged and young persons; hence there tends to be correspondence of belief among these groups in rural and in urban areas. In the country, the young people's ideas are closely related to those of city people. Age level and educational level have much to do with the persistence and strength of the belief.

These differences are seen in the emphasis upon and choice of words (such as, I know there is a God, etc.) during the interview. And they are seen in the degree of intensity of expression during the church service. In prayer and in other types of action, the urban worshipper is more restrained than the rural. In the country, the elderly worshipper lengthily describes the Venerable Supreme and expresses his adoration in prayer; he devoutly beseeches and pleads for the mercy of God. Tears of joy and dependence often accompany this action.[1] Not all persons of advanced age in the country are emotional. Generally, however, the rural groups are far more expressive in this respect than the urban.

The informants of this study believe in the efficacy of prayer, and the same general conclusions can be reached regarding their belief that God answers prayer and their belief in the existence of a Supreme Being.

Also, the principle of retribution has more value for rural and elderly groups than for urban and youthful. Nevertheless, there is a change in the manner in which the belief influences action. Generally in Negro religion, ends are not greatly perceived in the non-experimental entities, Heaven and Hell. To a great extent, actions are not in terms of these frames of reference.

As action moves toward the norm and rationality increases, all forms of traditionalism undergo a change. Attitudes toward the Supernatural, and the principle of retribution are reflected in the type of sermon desired and heard. The rural groups are inclined to accept the authority of the Scripture and generally prefer (and hear) a Biblical or religious sermon. They are less critical of sermons than urban churchmen. The urban groups generally prefer either a "combination religious and practical type" in which Christian principles are related to life, or a "practical type" that does not necessarily make reference to Biblical stories but emphasizes current social problems and stimulates thought. Generally in the Negro church, however, the members are leaning from the conservative or "old type of sermon." And the comparison made of urban types of churches and rural churches in other respects is valid as far as the type of sermon is concerned.

The general unpopularity of the "Hell-fire sermon" shows the striking departure from traditionalism and transcendentalism. In many instances, rural groups do not respond favorably to the Heaven and Hell sermon, which seeks to stimulate emotion. The other-worldly sermon is usually ridiculed by groups of all levels of education. A change in the system of action occurs gradually, and some forms of expression are discarded earlier than others. The most emotional and obviously illogical forms first undergo change. For example, the other-worldly sermon accompanied by emotional action is first held in disrepute; yet a Biblical sermon still enjoys authority. And with an increase of guidance of ends by the normative principle

[1] This emotional act is more prevalent among persons who feel strong economic pressures, and in churches situated among people of the poverty level than among the economically favored.

Biblical or religious sermons will continually give way to sermons which aim to aid man in adjustment to situations of life.

In regard to attitudes toward the Deity, there are differences in adherence to the Sacred Norms according to urban or rural areas. The traditional approach, and the accompanying authority of the Deity and the Ten Commandments, is stronger in the country than in the city. The strength of moral beliefs is seen in terms of "right" and "wrong" in the rural area, which offers a smaller variety of beliefs and standards than the urban environment. There is more homogeneity in belief and action, in all important respects, in the rural area than in the urban. The rural churchman is inclined to have greater respect for the Sabbath and hesitates to participate in secular activities (Sunday baseball games, for example) on this day. However, the youthful groups who have gone to the city to receive their training and who partly reside in the city and in the country are influenced by city pursuits and therefore manifest less reverent attitudes toward the Sacred Day than their elders.

Conservatism of rural churchmen is seen in their attitudes toward amusement. They generally believe that a Christian should not participate in sensuous activities or "things of the flesh rather than the spirit," and they more greatly refrain from diversions such as dancing and playing cards than urban church goers. In enumerating activities in which a Christian should not engage, the rural group believes that there should be conformity with the ethical norms of Jesus, and there is greater frequency of prohibitive responses among rural than among urban informants.

In a comparison of rural and urban attitudes of reverence and sacredness, factors other than those designated (urban heterogeneity, age groupings—migration of rural youths to urban areas—education, and occupational status) are important. The rural group is in closer relation with nature than the urban and for this reason more strongly believes in a Creator and feels a greater dependence upon the Supreme. Also, Negro religion had its beginning in this natural setting; hence conservatism remains longer in the rural environment.

However, with increased communication and interchange of ideas, changes in all groups occur. The rural church changes and responds to urban influences. The rate of change proceeds faster in rural areas having a close relationship with urban centers than in remote areas, where contacts with the city are fewer. Distance from the center of dominance is an important factor in change.

The manifestation of sentiment in exaggerated emotional action is everywhere falling into decadence. Even in the country, emotionalism is waning to the extent of disparagement of it and manifestation of it on special occasions and in special forms, as the singing of the spiritual, for example.[1] And extreme emotional actions are condemned. Nevertheless, the rural group is somewhat more tolerant of emotionalism than the urban group.[2]

There is a decline of emotionalism; yet the urban and rural informants are emotionally satisfied. Subjectively, emotional needs are different from those of the past. And forms of religious expression change with altered attitudes. The present trend from transcendental values in the Negro church is outstanding. However, it is not maintained that the Negro is not religious; religious interests are different from those of past years, and hence the change in religious action.

The slower rate of change in the rural church as compared with the urban is reflected in the type of programs in these areas. The rural church does not penetrate the community as much as the urban; the program is more religious (in the sense of worship) and less practical. Aside from other interpretations given, this difference can be accounted for in these ways: the residence of the rural pastor in an urban area, distance of the communicants from the rural church, and lack of information on means of improving rural life. The city dweller is widely acquainted with institutional programs and seeks to help the community through the church. The church is the center of life of the rural churchman, and few rural groups belong to organizations other than the church.

Although rural churchmen are prone to think that the church should satisfy spiritual needs mainly, some needs for community help and guidance are being expressed. Urban groups are more conscious of experimental needs, however.

The underlying thesis of the change in the functional emphasis of the church is substantiated by a decrease in one of the past major forms of expression—emotionalism—and a rapid expansion into other spheres of interest, especially apparent in the urban church.

In conclusion, a change in religious beliefs and actions proceeds more rapidly in urban than in rural areas, and there is greater variety in religious forms and expressions in the former than in the latter. Traditional religion is proceedingly and increasingly modified among all Protestant denominations and among all socio-economic groups; the modification is more marked and accelerated among those of high educational, economic, and social accomplishment. Since this level is found among urban populations, it is in the city that wider divergence is found, while in the country are found more orthodox

[1] Even the spiritual is falling in disrepute.

[2] The groups whose situations are comparable with those during the static form of equilibrium tend to be tolerant of a variety of religious actions.

beliefs and practices. At the same time, the city, with its various economic and educational levels, offers contrasts, and therefore it contains some persons whose ends are conceived in a transcendental religion. Those in the city who, for some reason, retain or adopt orthodox practices are generally regarded with disfavor; and they find their position in the system of action challenged. With an increasing pursuit of ends according to the normative standard, there is progressive integration in the collectivity. The rural church in response to the normative principle changes, but its rate of modification is less accelerated than that of the urban church.

Education and Class

As religion falls within the experimental sphere of action, rationality increases with educational and occupational advancement. Although sentiments are conspicuous in action for all groups, they are more outstanding and prevalent among those of meager education and of low income. Sentiments especially motivate action and determine ends for uneducated classes. Non-experimental theories (based upon moral and religious sentiments) are longer retained by uncultivated groups, and correspondingly there is an increase of experimental action with cultural advancement.

As education permeates a collectivity, transcendental sentiments expressed in emotional action decrease. With an increase in the extent and quality of education, action proceeds in the direction of approach to the normative element, more or less regarded as binding upon the persons in the system.

However, reference has been made to the tendency of some churchmen to resist the change in religion. As the new equilibrium (unemotionalism and experimentalism) is being reached, some of the conditions of the old religion remain. Disturbance of the former equilibrium results in a reaction to retain the original state. During the predominance of the "old religion," most of the religious men were uneducated; and lack of knowledge greatly facilitated emotional and non-empirical action. The relationship between uneducation and the type of person who strives to safeguard the relatively "static equilibrium" can be seen in this respect: Clamoring for the old or former religion is mainly characteristic of the aged, the "uneducated," and the impoverished, although there are some noteworthy exceptions. That is, there is a degree of similarity between the level of persons who struggle to regain the original state and the former conditions. Thus those whose present situation of action is analogous to the general uncultivation of the collectivity during the form of "static equilibrium" tend first to react negatively to forces acting to constrain them in the new system. Since the educational level of the collectivity has changed so remarkably, the new equilibrium will not return to its former state; action will proceed according to the system of norms.

Imperfect integration increasingly is succeeded by a fairly good degree of harmony in the general system of action, with ends guided by the unemotional norm. Attention has been called to the present approach to re-integration of ends of the various types in the collectivity.

Educated groups tend to lead and to promote change in the system of action. Those directing the trend toward rationality of belief and action are mainly the cultivated persons whose training and experiences in urban centers prompt them to minimize non-experimental values. And the uncultivated groups tend to follow the dominant groups. There is a tendency to react positively to the leadership and guidance of the groups advocating change.

Since action is approaching the norm and empirical ends and unemotionalism have not been fully achieved, variation of religious ideas and practices still exists.[1] There is a correlation between education and experimental religion.[2] Logical actions increase with economic and educational development. The professional and semi-professional and business classes emphasize experimental actions and seek to achieve ends in terms of this world. The religious beliefs of these groups do not rigidly adhere to traditionalism. Emotionalism is discouraged, and programs of a practical nature are encouraged. It follows that a church consisting of dominance (either in numbers or leadership) of these occupational groups, who generally have had advantages of a high school, a college, or a university education, conceives religion as a guide for living. Consequently, emotional action accompanying sentiment is absent, and there is prevalence of intellectual programs, recreational, and social activities. The church really "moves into" community life.

Further Comparison of Types of Churches According to Class.— Church One in this study is representative of the type just discussed. The presence of the "empirical type of man" is general in this church. And the attitudes of this type are reflected in the church program. Ample consideration has been given the ends and actions of the three types of churches, and therefore to enlarge further upon these would be useless repetition. Nevertheless, attention is being

1 Even with increased integration in the system of action, a degree of variation is expected, however. The individual factor cannot be disregarded.

2 This classification is made for convenience; it signifies a religion which *emphasizes* empirical ends in spite of the existence of some non-experimental values for most of the persons in the system.

redirected to the ends in order to re-enforce the relationship between type of religion and educational and occupational status.

Religious division is an index of internal division in a community. Thus the presence of various types of churches in a community is indicative of differences in education and occupation. A certain type of church attracts a certain type of follower. Men seek churches in which their ends can be achieved or nearly so. That church which offers a fulfillment of their ends and is most nearly approximate to their religious goals is the church which they join.[1] Thus there is prevalence of a certain type of person in a church. Although a "restrained church" tends to be consistently unified in belief and practice, greater variety is found in a "semi-restrained church," which is in a phase of adjustment to diverse elements. This is generally true. Nevertheless, the latter type of church is undergoing change, and as ends are formulated in harmony with the normative principle, unity of belief and practice increases.

In the third type of church, the emotional, the members are strikingly similar in belief and action. This unanimity is understandable in view of the "place" of this group in the community; that is, the attitudes of those guided by the norm toward them, and the origin of the church in the community. The cult performs a residual role of an established church. This position is seen in the departure of groups not greatly guided by "the unemotional norm" from the established church because of unfulfillment of goals. In urban areas, especially in metropolitan centers, the general tendency is the displacement and dismissal of the emotional members by an attitude of literally "freezing them out of the church." This attitude of disdain results from incompatibility of interests of types of men. However, the conservative type of church, which is immediately above the emotional type in the action system, is beginning to reconsider its action because of loss of financial and numerical strength; therefore, a more considerate view is *about* to be taken toward the ends of the emotional type of person by those clerical leaders who are conscious of the effects of their attitudes upon the established Protestant church. Those leaders on the verge of a reversal of position are not many, because few have perceived the actual course of events, and because some leaders are so strongly imbued with the normative principle that they continue to relegate "the emotional" to a subordinate status.

At the same time that this trend of development (that is, expulsion from the established Protestant church) occurs, an opposite related reaction develops during the process of change. Those in popular

[1] This is particularly true of urban churches inasmuch as a city affords variety, and the force of traditionalism is not so strong as in the country.

Protestant churches who find action restricted by the continued presence of some transcendental types and the continuation of some forms of non-empirical actions, withdraw from the established church and seek some other type of religion.[1] In a rural area, however, where transfer of membership may not be feasible, those guided by the norm remain as communicants and suppress the demonstrative.

Church Two (an example of the second type of church) in Boston, which retains some spiritual warmth and yet gradually participates in community life, occupies an intermediate—as well as intermediary—position in the community. There are a *few* professional people; there are some semi-professional, and business persons; and there are some persons engaged in servile work or unskilled labor. In spite of the representation of various occupational groups, the vast majority of the members are of the working class. There is variety of occupation and of education. Educational attainment ranks from the elementary to the university level of instruction. However, there is prevalence of those with some elementary and some high school training.

In addition, the membership consists mainly of southern rural migrants and their descendants who are not greatly removed from "the old religion." That is, at the time they migrated, Negro religion was in a moderate rate of change. Since their residence in Boston, emotional behavior has further declined. Although some rural practices are carried to urban churches, migrants tend to respond to urbanization.[2] Thus Church Two may be considered a decaying rural institution.[3] Another factor to consider in interpreting the program of Church Two is the presence of many elderly people in the congregation. Because of the diversity in education, occupation, age, and

[1] In departing from the established church there are, of course, some other motives. However, consideration of vacillating members who seek the new and constantly shift from church to church is unessential. Likewise, those who seek other faiths for personal advantage are unimportant in an analysis of the system.

[2] And in fact there has been a more rapid and noticeable departure from emotionalism in some urban churches, which contain rural and semi-rural migrants, than in Church Two. In this respect, class is an important factor. Those churches which have the largest number of uneducated, unskilled laborers are most emotional. It is necessary to point out that not all emotional people are in Apostolic or similar churches. New Baptist churches, for example, "spring up" in the community to take care of emotional members not welcome in Baptist churches conforming to the system of normative rules. Some of the traditional religionists who do not feel comfortable or welcome in those churches emphasizing rationality of action do not desire to leave their denomination and do not wish to identify themselves with the cults, which are on the periphery of religion; therefore, under the leadership of a preacher, who sometimes finds this a good opportunity for livelihood, special churches are established for the traditional type.

[3] Significant changes have occurred in this church within the past six years. Some transcendental forms of religious expression have greatly fallen into desuetude; the type of service has changed. Beliefs of this group are becoming crystallized.

origin (both rural and urban) of the membership, the church has a program which seeks to provide some degree of satisfaction for the various elements. Consequently, transcendental values are stronger in this church than in church type one. This simply reiterates the proposition that the rate of change proceeds more slowly in a church which has in its midst conditions similar, in some respects, to those which characterized "the old system." Experimental and non-experimental ends are important to the conservative church, which comprises all types of worshippers. And the kinds of ends pursued by men are greatly conditioned by education and occupation. For the Negro collectivity, the more significant factor in change is education inasmuch as there is not great occupational diversity for the group.

Transcendental ends and emotional action are more common among those of "unfavorable" socio-economic status than among those of high educational achievement. Traditionalism is strongest among those of meager education; they tend to retain non-empirical values and practices, although they also tend slowly and eventually to regulate their ends in harmony with the guiding principle of action. The type of clerical leadership, as has been shown, is important in retarding or facilitating change.

Consideration of class division according to ends pursued in the religious community brings us to further consideration of the third type of church, which consists primarily of the very emotional. In rural and urban areas, there is insecurity of the traditional religionist in the Protestant church as a result of changing religious attitudes and practices. Generally, the rural traditionalist remains in the Baptist or Methodist church because of the existence of only a few Holiness churches in the community and because of censorship of withdrawal.

However, the group which finds its integrity damaged in the system of action seeks a religion which will repair integrity by offering recognition and by providing outlets for ends. Hence the group which leaves the established Protestant church either by "will" or by force, finds opportunity for expression of transcendental ends and emotion in a Holiness church or some related type of institution. An example of this kind of association is that of Church Three in Boston, especially as it was before the Director assumed control of it. Since sufficient consideration has been given this church with reference to ends, etc., only condensed information is now presented on the status of the members of this group. There are a few clerical and semi-professional members, who have a high school education or the equivalent of two years of college training. Most of the members are unskilled laborers, with an elementary education or less. Most of the members are migrants. The traditional type of churchman predominates. This is an emotional church; and at some services, extreme emotional behavior is manifested by some of the communicants.

However, under the influence of the Director, emotion is being guided into practical channels.

In connection with the variation of experimental ends according to socio-economic status, church goers show a consciousness of recreational needs in relation to the type of church to which they belong. Those of retarded education and economic inadequacy less readily perceive recreational ends in religion than those of advanced education and income. That is, a consciousness of needs increases proportionately on a graduated scale. (This is especially true in the types of rural churches. Successive stages in the series can be seen as there is advancement from the emotional, the semi-emotional, and the restrained types of churches.)

Saintliness, Mysticism, and Magical Ritual, According to Education and Economic Circumstance.—As religious actions fall within the logical framework, beliefs regarding saintliness, mysticism, and magical ritual are longest retained by persons of low income and meager formal education. There tends to be correlation of these traditional non-experimental beliefs and actions, whenever found, with subordinate education.[1]

Saintliness and asceticism (an aspect of saintliness) are found mainly among groups of poverty or subsistence level, and of inferior or mediocre educational development. This is in keeping with the continued manifestation of emotional behavior accompanying religious sentiments by these groups. Examples of self-denial, sacrifice, piety, equanimity, calmness in adversity, control over the carnal impulses, abandonment of worldly things, and devotion to religious pursuits are seen in the religious experiences of various types of worshippers; but these manifestations are more common among persons in rural churches and in Church Three in Boston than among those in the other churches.[2] Saintliness and asceticism are conspicuous

1 Care is used in stating this generalization in order to avoid overstatement. Some educated persons attempt to achieve harmony of living (sometimes through philosophy rather than religion) through the principle of saintliness. Also, some educated persons—think of other religions strongly emphasizing faith—adhere to the principle of mysticism either by physical or mental relationship with the Deity. In addition, educated persons are followers of religions which make strong recourse to some form of ritual, often involving magic. And magical ritual is sometimes practised secularly, though not religiously, by the formally educated. As far as magical ritual is concerned, today in the Negro Protestant collectivity, it is essentially without the domain of religion. Only fragments of it are vaguely connected with actually religious ceremonies.

2 Many Protestants are indeed skeptical of the saintly. They maintain that positive principles as promulgated and practised in the Holiness churches are counteracted by negative principles outside of the church.

features of the religion of the worshippers in Church Three. Although asceticism is common, it is not exclusive. These persons are not far removed from the old system; hence there is continuation of the traditional religion. The saints tend serenely to resign and abandon themselves to the will of God in their religious experiences.[1] Among this group, asceticism takes the form of the principle of veracity, sincerity, humility, and purity of life.

As non-experimental actions diminish, mysticism survives longest among uncultivated groups of low income. Although mysticism is not prevalent today, some evidence of it is seen in the most retarded, isolated groups or sections. Those individuals in other areas for whom mystical experiences are a reality are usually the most educationally retarded persons in the community. Some worshippers in church type three undergo absorption with the Deity. To the individual who feels the presence of the Holy Ghost and communes with the Deity, through visitation, the awareness of the presence of God is incontrovertible. The experience is authoritative to the individual who concentrates upon the image of Christ during the mystical state. He feels and knows mystical truths, although they are not actually perceived by the senses and are therefore nonexperimental.

As religion proceeds within the empirical realm and rationalism becomes apparent, saintliness, asceticism, and magical ritual diminish. Magical ritual, which has almost disappeared, exists longest among the illiterate, whose religion is simple and unsophisticated. Groups in whom traditionalism is strong react more slowly to the system of normative rules than educationally advanced groups. Magical elements are discarded with increased rationalism in the system of action. Magical ritual is a form of non-experimental action based upon non-experimental beliefs; that is, the sentiments motivating the action are not compatible with sensory experiences; the validity of the act is not in terms of empirical fact. Those manifesting ritual actions use inappropriate means to attain an end because of illogical connections between means and end. Since the theories regarding the actions are not scientifically valid, effective means are not applied to the attainment of the end.[2] The person for whom the magical beliefs are valid goes through certain rites or ceremonies in order to obtain an empirical end; it is believed that the act will serve as a means of preventing calamity, or ensuring success. However, there is a faulty relation of means and end. Since subjective and objective ends do not correspond, the act is unscientific.

[1] The contemplative attitude has been modified, to some extent, because of the influence of the Director, who emphasizes transforming the social midst.

[2] Homans and Curtis, *op. cit.*, pp. 70, 72.

With educational advancement of the group, with increasing empirical knowledge, and with the motivation of action according to normative concepts, there is great opposition to the employment of ritual means to the realization of empirical ends.

* * * * *

In conclusion, religion becomes more logical with diminution of non-empirical values. For the traditional religionist, knowledge is perceived beyond human experience. By a spiritual relationship with a Supreme Being, reality is determined. Man seeks to comprehend and to explain the mysterious, and the repulsive aspects of existence by entering a relationship with the Supernatural. The Supernatural is the origin of legality. What is real is in terms of a transcendental ideal. Attitudes of respect and sacredness adhere about the Supreme. Great emotion is manifested in relation to the Divine, partly because of God's powerful role in the destiny of man. Fear is one of the strongest emotions in the stage of a religion which elevates the Supernatural.

As a religion moves from transcendental values to empirical standards, the most negative emotions (those accompanying emphasis upon the evil aspects of existence, from which the concept of Hell and punishment develops) first become weak. The emotion of fear, which expresses itself in overt religious action, loses its efficacy. Being released from the emotion of fear, man's actions advance toward logical standards in spite of the continued presence of non-empirical elements.

The more positive emotions, as love, which do not restrict reflective action nearly so strongly as fear, remain longer as experimental values become important. The brighter aspects of existence become more visible, and man progressively directs his action toward attainment of the abundant in this world.

With further diminution of non-empirical ends and emotion, and an increasing emphasis upon empirical values, action tends to increase in logicality. The diminution of non-empirical and illogical action (as reflected in a changing attitude toward salvation) means a religion which is instrumental in shaping social institutions and promoting change. Religious action proceeds toward the community and religion becomes a vital social force.

There is a direct relationship between type of religion and level of education. An "empirical religion" develops with educational advancement, and there is submergence of non-experimental and emotional elements of action. There is a direct correspondence between the type of education (whether empirical or religious) a society emphasizes and the nature of its religious beliefs and actions. It follows that a church which has a membership consisting of those who have absorbed the education of the society will emphasize those features of the situation of action which are characteristic of the society. Since the emphasis is today upon science, those churches having a dominance of the educated tend to minimize the non-empirical while seeking to transform and ameliorate social life. The following summary of church types brings out the relationship between education and religion.

Churches One and Three are similar in many respects in spite of some dissimilarities. Church One is consolidated in belief and action, abhors emotionalism, moves into the community and is a literary, social, and recreational center. Traditional religion is unimportant.[1] However, some strictly religious functions remain in spite of the fact that the sermons are mainly expository-persuasive lectures, which appeal greatly to thought. This church consists mainly of middle and upper classes. In other words, the class status of the members is nearly the same or similar in spite of the presence of a few members of a subordinate economic and occupational status.[2] In Church Three, there is solidarity. Attitudes toward emotionalism and saintliness are identical. This church too is a center of community life and moves into the community in religious and business aspects. Whereas Church One has established a community center (recreational and literary), Church Three has established a home for the aged and provides other social services under the influence of the Director. Church Three has a preponderance of unskilled laborers, with little formal education.[3]

Church Two occupies an intermediate position with respect to ministerial leadership, class status, emotionalism, and church program. Diversity characterizes this church. It comprises all levels of education and occupation, with a majority of its membership being of the clerical and unskilled labor level. However, the educational and economic level of the congregation as a unit excels that of Church Three. Church Two has recently established a community center (re-

[1] So much so that some of the Boston preachers in whom the religious tradition is strong, consider this institution a cultural and recreational center instead of a church.

[2] So much is this group regarded a "class church" that some members of Church Three state that presentation of a social card is necessary in order to be admitted in the church. Though exaggerated, this statement is certainly indicative of the type of membership of Church One. Educated professional, business, and clerical classes mainly comprise the church membership.

[3] It has been pointed out that the practical program of this church has resulted from the leadership of the Director. The type of church with this level of membership usually does little to improve community life.

ligious, and social in the sense of teas, banquets, etc.). It sponsors recitals, concerts, and dramas. Though experimental and non-experimental ends operate, this is a conservative church responding to the principle of "the unemotional norm."

The generalizations regarding educational and economic status as far as urban churches are concerned are valid for rural churches. Those rural churches having educated, land-owning classes more readily conform their actions to the normative system of rules. This is especially true as pertains to emotionalism. Reasons for retardation in regard to practical programs have been enumerated. However, the semi-rural communities are beginning to establish playgrounds.

Though there is a relationship between class and emotionalism, it is emphasized that sentiments manifested in emotional action are diminishing in all levels of the collectivity. Nevertheless, transcendental ends and emotionalism are longer retained by the "uncultivated" and by rural audiences, as empirical ends become noteworthy in urban churches, and as action is guided by the system of norms.

As the Negro advances educationally and socially, his ends will progressively proceed in the direction of experimental rather than non-experimental values, and there will be further diminution of the manifestation of sentiment in emotional behavior. Also, transcendental ends of action will further deteriorate with increased city contacts and experiences.

PART II

Negroes in the South and the Northeast

CHAPTER VI

Statistics on Population and Church Membership

Preponderance of Negroes in the South.—Since this is a study of the religion of the American Negro, it is appropriate briefly to indicate the proportion of Negroes in the population of the United States, with particular reference to the South inasmuch as most Negro rural churches are located in this section of the country. In 1940, there were 12,865,518 Negroes in the United States, or 9.8 per cent of the total population of 131,669,275.[1] The Negro population, though less than 10 per cent of the total in the United States in 1940, comprised one-fourth of the population of the South. Negroes comprised 9.7 per cent of the total population of the United States in 1930. Sixty and six-tenths per cent of these resided in the District of Columbia and nine southern states, including South Carolina.[2]

Negro Population in South Carolina and Massachusetts.—The figures which follow indicate the population statistics for the areas in which this particular study was made. The total population of South Carolina in 1940 was 1,899,804.[3] Negroes comprised 814,164 of this number.[4] The population of Orangeburg County, South Carolina, in 1940 was 63,707.[5] The Negro population of Orangeburg, South Carolina, the vicinity in which the rural churches herein considered are located, was 4,748, or 45.1 per cent of the total population of this city in 1940.[6] The actual population of Oragneburg exceeds this number by thousands in view of the fact that there are heavily

[1] Murray, Florence, *The Negro Handbook,* 1946–1947, Current Books, Inc., New York, 1947, p. 3. These figures were taken from the Bureau of the Census.

[2] Bureau of the Census, *Negroes in the United States,* 1920–1932, United States Government Printing Office, Washington, 1935, p. 13.

[3] *The World Almanac,* edited by Eastman E. Irvine, New York World-Telegram, New York, 1947, pp. 208–209.

[4] *Ibid.,* p. 217.

[5] *Ibid.,* pp. 208–209.

[6] Murray, *op. cit.,* p. 9.

populated residential suburban areas not designated as within the limits of the city. This is especially true of Negro sections.

In 1940, the population of the state of Massachusetts was 4,316,-721.[1] In 1940, the population of Boston, Massachusetts, was 770,816.[2] There were 23,679 Negroes, or 3.1 per cent of the total population of this city.[3]

Negro Church Membership in Rural and Urban Areas.—In 1926, the total Negro church membership in the United States was 5,203,-487; of this number, 2,964,616 were in rural churches and 2,238,871 were in urban churches. Various Methodist denominations and the Baptist church showed a higher distribution of rural than urban members, whereas the Roman Catholic and the Protestant Episcopal churches had a greater concentration of their church membership in cities.[4]

In the South, the total Negro membership in 1926 was 4,288,621; rural membership comprised 2,903,473 while urban membership was 2,385,148. In the North, of the total Negro membership of 875,748, most of this membership comprised city churches, 816,608 being urban. There were only 39,118 Negro church members in the West.[5]

In New England, only 653 Negro members out of a total of 28,048 were rural. In Massachusetts, only 76 Negro members out of a total of 13,822 were rural. In the South Atlantic Section, of a total Negro membership of 2,159,295, rural churches had 1,484,675 members. In South Carolina, of a total Negro membership of 405,614, rural churches had 327,011 members.[6] These figures indicate that in the South rural church membership is large, whereas in the North most Negro church members are concentrated in urban areas. They also show that southern Negro church membership is appreciably higher than northern. Since these figures were compiled, however, many rural churchmen have migrated to northern urban areas. This does not, nevertheless, make void the conclusion that the percentage of Negro church membership in the South remains higher than in the North.

There was a decline in rural Negro membership in the decade 1926–1936. In 1936, there was a total Negro church membership of 5,660,618, or 2.3 per cent greater than in 1926. Of this total, 2,701,-988 members were in rural churches, while 2,958,630 members were

1 *The World Almanac, loc. cit.*

2 *Ibid.*, p. 205.

3 Murray, *op. cit.*, p. 8.

4 Bureau of the Census, *Negroes in the United States, op. cit.*, p. 532. This information was taken from Tables 1 and 4.

5 *Ibid.*, p. 536, Table 8.

6 *Loc. cit*

in urban churches.[1] This decrease in rural membership is accounted for through migration to surrounding towns and cities in the South, as well as migration to the North. The 1930 census shows that 43.7 per cent of the Negro population resides in cities.[2]

There has been a constant increase in Negro church membership over the years in proportion to the rate of growth of the population as seen in the following figures:

Year	*Membership*
1906	3,691,844
1916	4,602,805
1926	5,203,487
1936	5,660,618[3]

These figures do not actually portray membership growth in various decades because of denominational changes in definitions of members and because of the failure of some churches to reply to inquiries regarding membership.[4]

Increase of Negro Urban and Northern Population.—Negro and white church membership in America has increased proportionately with population growth.[5] Urban Negro church membership has increased while rural membership has decreased because of cityward migration. Mobility of population has been characteristic of America. The following table shows this trend.

Year	*1910*	*1920*	*1930*	*1940*
U.S. population	91,972,266	105,710,620	122,775,046	131,669,275
Urban	41,998,932	54,157,973	68,954,823	74,423,702
Rural	49,973,334	51,552,647	53,820,223	57,245,573[6]

Thus there is a positive correlation between movement of the population to urban areas and an increase in the membership of city churches, with a corresponding loss in the rural group. Many rural churches have closed or consolidated because of dearth of membership. At the same time, many southerners organized churches in the North during the twenties and thirties, and they are continuing to establish churches.

Although Negroes in the South greatly exceed Negroes in the North numerically, the percentage of Negroes in the South sub-

1 Bureau of the Census, *Religious Bodies:* 1936, Vol. I, United States Government Printing Office, Washington, 1941, pp. 850–851, Table 33.

2 *Ibid.*, p. 74.

3 Bureau of the Census, *Negroes in the United States, op. cit.*, p. 530. Also see Bureau of the Census, *Religious Bodies:* 1936, p. 84.

4 *Loc. cit.*

5 See pp. 102–103.

6 *World Almanac, op. cit.*, p. 200.

stantially declined within the last fifty years. In 1880, Negroes comprised 36 percent of the total population of the South, about the same as in 1790. This percentage decreased to 33.8 in 1890; 32.3 in 1900; 29.8 in 1910; 26.9 in 1920; and 24.7 in 1930.[1]

The increase in percentage of the Negro population in the North since 1860 has been remarkable. Beginning with 1915, the influx of southerners to the North was appreciable. Not less than 500,000 Negroes changed their residence during the years 1915–1918.[2] There has been a striking change in the territorial distribution of the Negro as a result of phenomenal migration. Notwithstanding, Negroes comprised only 3.3 per cent of the total population of the North in 1930.[3]

With population changes, characteristics of religion change. There was alteration of religious action with the influx of migrants to urban areas. It is important to note the type of religion which survived in the North after Negro southerners went to metropolitan areas in tremendous numbers, beginning with World War I and continuing through World War II. Traditional religion diminishes with urbanization.

[1] Bureau of the Census, *Negroes in the United States*, 1920–1932, *op. cit.*, p. 13.

[2] Brawley, Benjamin, *A Short History of the American Negro*, The Macmillan Company, New York, 1919, p. 171.

[3] *Negroes in the United States, loc. cit.*

PART III

Churchmen's Religious Attitudes and Experiences in the Rural South and the Metropolitan Northeast

CHAPTER VII

Conceptions of the Divine

The Decline in Supernaturalism

In the theoretical system, the essence of the propositions established is as follows: Religion contains empirical and non-empirical elements of action. With a decline in emphasis upon the supernatural, there is diminution of non-experimental and emotional action. Accompanying this process, religious ends are increasingly directed toward the community rather than toward Heaven. With this trend of development, the influence of a normative system of rules regulating the choice of means and ends cannot be minimized. In spite of some diversity of attitudes toward the norm, the principle enjoys institutional authority; and there is an approach to integration of ends of the Protestant church.

In order to relate further the theoretical analysis of this study to the empirical phenomena, it is necessary to supply the values of the categories embodying the system of theory.[1] This can be done by presenting data concerning the beliefs and actions of the members of the Protestant church. The empirical data show the significance of non-scientific beliefs to action.

Men assign motives to their actions. And since many of their beliefs are philosophical, it is important to understand the relation between men's non-scientific ideas and their actions.[2] Religious ideas consist of the active attitudes of men toward the non-empirical. These ideas and attitudes are reflected in action. Social action is understandable "in terms of men's ideas of and active attitudes toward the non-empirical."[3]

Believing that the nonempirical aspects of existence have significance for life, men seek to attain salvation. Correspondingly, their actions are motivated by ascertainment of the ideal in a variety of ways. Hence it is necessary to consider the manifold attitudes and

[1] Parsons, *op. cit.*, p. 71.
[2] *Ibid.*, pp. 8, 26.
[3] *Ibid.*, p. 427.

actions which result from motivation by the nonscientific aspects of existence.

The Principle of Divine Control, and Retribution.—The presence of transcendental ends in religion is seen in men's attitudes toward the Deity. The ideologies of the theories associated with non-experimental actions indicate the extent and nature of ultimate value attitudes and their influence upon the ends of action. The end, a subjective category, has reference to something in the state of mind of man.[1] Being motivated by sentiment, he formulates propositions which evolve into nonscientific theories of action. From the sentiments expressed in nonempirical beliefs regarding a Supreme Being, men regulate their actions, to some extent, according to religious principles and conceive practical programs the church should inaugurate in order to promote "community betterment" and harmonious social relations. Though the ultimate-end system of the majority of churchmen is nonexperimental, values are greatly regarded from a social point of view, and the non-empirical phase of religion is subordinated.

Churchmen variously express theistic views. Although most informants do not question the existence of God, some do not maintain the anthropomorphic view of a Supreme Being characterized by human attributes and affections. Some do not fear provoking the wrath of God and believe that God does not control the destiny of man. Some, who do accept theism, ascribe to God a limited function. Some do not repudiate the existence of a Deity; yet, in their agnosticism, they regard any advantages accruing from the doctrine of Christianity as having social value only. Jesus is a great social teacher whose precepts are beneficial to man; hence there should be application of his prescriptions to life.

In spite of the departure from orthodox religion, some fervent religionists believe in a Creator, who directs and controls the destiny of man. They attribute their successes to the providence of Christ, and they believe that God's influence affects the realization of empirical ends. Some pious Christians fervently beseech God's blessings, unchallengingly anticipate the Second Coming and make preparation for it. The knowledge of God is a reality and the Omnipotent is a great comfort and help in personal difficulties, such as death, economic, moral, and social adversities. They have staunch faith in God's power and mercy and are inspired to surmount obstacles because of past personal experiences in which the Almighty did not fail them. They pray for divine protection and guidance and believe that a receptive attitude and confidence are indispensable. They are positive that God is a solace and a fortress in the time of trouble and

[1] *Ibid.*

cite examples of his unfailing love. "I know the Lord will make a way for me" is the spiritual which portrays their attitude.

Since belief in nonscientific theories motivates action in a variety of ways, examination of the beliefs of informants in the following table is appropriate.

TABLE ONE

Beliefs in God and Prayer

	God	Prayer
South Carolina		
Church A	12 out of 12	12 out of 12
Church B	13 out of 13	13 out of 13
Church C	13 out of 13	13 out of 13
City Church	4 out of 5	4 out of 5
College Students	40 out of 40	40 out of 40
Massachusetts		
Church One	11 out of 12	12 out of 12
Church Two	12 out of 12	12 out of 12
Church Three	15 out of 15	15 out of 15

The above table shows the beliefs of informants in Methodist churches in South Carolina, of Protestant seniors at State A. & M. College, Orangeburg, South Carolina, and of Boston Congregational, Baptist, and Apostolic churches.

Most of the informants do not doubt the reality of God, although their conceptions of the role of the Supreme in the natural order of events vary. Most of the persons interviewed expressed the idea that God is active in directing and controlling mundane occurrences, and they have faith in the efficacy of prayer. Nevertheless, a few do not ascribe an omnipotent, omnipresent, omniscient status to the Deity.

The two informants who manifested agnostic attitudes are university students. Although one of them prays whenever she encounters perplexing problems, she attributes the act of prayer to the traditional influence of religion upon her in spite of uncertainty as to its beneficial results. Any value accruing from the act might result from its psychological effect upon her. Although most informants affirm the existence of a Supreme Being, not all of them manifest the same attitude toward the Deity. There is variation in the strength of the belief regarding a Supreme Ruler who manifests interest in the lives of his followers. The traditional type of Christian has inveterate faith in the Divine, and the active intervention of the Almighty in human affairs. Reference to the Deity has an invigorating effect upon him; confidence is seen in glowing facial expressions and in the prolongation of words. There is an electrifying effect of the Holy Ghost upon the physical and the spiritual being. The individual possesses a serenity and calmness which stimulates and inspires him in the pursuit of his ends. Other types of Christians are more restrained and subdued in their expressions.

The table showing the degrees of belief is indicative of the trend from transcendental values inasmuch as Christians in the past were firm in their knowledge of the existence and mercy of God. Observe variations in attitudes according to church.

With the emphasis upon sensory knowledge, and the increase in urbanization, there has been a decline in supernaturalism and in the vitality of traditional religion. Man believes less fervently in a Supreme Being, in prayer, and in after-life. Changing beliefs regarding the transcendental are reflected in the attitudes which the subjects manifest toward the Deity. One of the propositions set forth in the theoretical system is that non-empirical ends diminish in the religious system with changing attitudes toward the Supernatural. Religious ideas (men's active attitudes toward the Deity) influence the type of ends pursued. Furthermore, transcendental ends are longest retained by those in the system of action whose conditions are most nearly approximate to those in the state of static equilibrium. A glance at Table Two reveals this; observe, for example, that Church Three (characterized in the religious system as the traditional type, whose membership consists of those of subsistence level and of meager education) manifests a more intense belief in the existence of a Supreme Being and a more confident attitude regarding the belief that God answers the prayers of the sincere than the other two Boston churches (the unemotional, and the semi-restrained types, Churches One and Two respectively).

It was also established that emotionalism diminishes with a wane of emphasis upon the nonempirical. There is a close relation between non-experimental and emotional actions. Substantiation of this generalization is seen in the attitudes of Church Three, the traditional or emotional type, toward the Deity.

Attention has been called to the fact that there is not a great degree of variation among the rural churches in some respects. However, there are differences; consequently the type concept is applicable to these churches. Note that Church A is comparable in attitude with Church Three. The former church consists mainly of landless, uneducated members. Churches B and C, which manifest a weaker degree of belief in the divine order than Church A, have a membership consisting of various socio-economic groups. Although there is

TABLE TWO

Classification of Beliefs in God and Prayer

	Beliefs in God Type of Response			*Beliefs in Prayer Type of Response*		
South Carolina	*Moderate*[1]	*Warm*[2]	*Enthusiastic*[3]	*Moderate*	*Warm*	*Enthusiastic*
Church A	4	2	6	4	2	6
Church B	6	5	2	5	4	4
Church C	8	3	2	9	2	2
City Church	1	2	1	1		3
Massachusetts						
Church One	10		1	11		1
Church Two	11		1	11		1
Church Three	5	5	5	5	5	5

not a great difference between Churches B and C, the former is comparable with Church Two, while the latter is comparable with Church One, in some respects.

In connection with the idea that those living near the submarginal or marginal level of existence tend to manifest a closer relationship with the Deity, people having perplexing problems sometimes tend to lean upon a Supreme Being to alleviate uncertainty and calamity. For example, ten veterans of Church B assert a strengthening of faith in the Almighty as a result of their war experiences. These men, who saw their comrades die in battle, believe that God's protection enabled them to survive and return home. On the other hand, some persons become more doubtful of God's active interference in human events because of difficulties they encounter; this attitude is assumed gradually as frustrations multiply.

In regard to the effect of mobility upon religious beliefs, fifteen veterans of Church B report a disintegration of religious beliefs as a result of their experiences in the armed forces. Traditional ideas of God underwent a decided change so that there is doubt of the omnipotent character of the Deity. Contact with all types of people in many places, harassing experiences, and uncertainty of the future prompted

1 This indicates those believers giving a mere affirmation—"Yes."

2 This response signifies affirmation with a nod of the head, or the statement, "I do," "I surely do."

3 This response signifies those who answer emphatically, "I KNOW there is a God," etc., upon being asked, "Do you believe there is a God seeing, directing, and controlling the affairs of men?"

a change in the customary manner of doing things to the extent that irreverent, profane, and epicurean attitudes were assumed. This illustration amplifies the former assertion of the decline of orthodox religious views with migration and heterogeneity.

Further diminution of beliefs regarding the Supernatural is seen in the weakening of ideas of compulsion. This reiterates the position of a trend from the grosser forms of supernaturalism as transcendental ends diminish in a religious system. The idea that the more negative emotions first decline with a decrease in non-experimental elements was developed in the theoretical system. Various replies were given to this question: "Do ideas of God, Heaven, and Hell influence your everyday relations and life as constraining forces (causing you to do or not to do some things)?" Table Three shows a decline of fear as a motivator of men's actions.

Beliefs regarding the principle of retribution convey the transition in attitudes toward the nonempirical. Informants' conceptions of the Supreme are revealed in their attitudes toward Heaven and Hell. Churchmen more sharply adhere to beliefs in God and the efficacy of prayer than to the concepts of a nonempirical Heaven or Hell influencing their conduct. Attitudes toward the application of sanctions in regard to conformity or nonconformity with sacred commandments are changing. In addition, concentration upon Heaven as a recompense for social dissatisfaction noticeably diminishes with a declension of Heaven as a constrainer of action.

According to informants, God influences their conduct by causing them to refrain from, or to pursue, certain ends of action. However, many informants are not influenced from the standpoint of incurring the disfavor of God and provoking punishment. Although they concede that principles of God influence their actions, the negative aspect of action is minimized. Since God's teachings have social value, church members strive to mould their conduct in harmony with the Christian ideal. In fact, some informants who doubt the existence of God are influenced by Christian precepts because of advantages which result from inculcation of these norms in the social group. Although this view is more widely held by those of elevated educational, economic, and social attainment than by the less favorably situated, it is also expressed by those whose formal education does not exceed the elementary level. Among traditional religionists, however, this view is somewhat subordinate to that of approbation and distribution of rewards. They desire and seek to attain a nonempirical Heaven, "where the wicked cease from troubling and the weary are at rest," as is sometimes stated in testimonials.

According to informants, conduct is more greatly influenced by positive ideas of God than by ideas of Heaven and Hell. The God-concept is a basic, primary one, the Supreme, being the shaping force behind the universe. Consequently, of "the constrainers of action," God, the Creator, is foremost in the minds of men. Heaven and Hell are subsidiary; and though they complement the idea of the transcendental, they are declining in importance. Table Three reveals that "tapering off" proceeds with the principle of retribution. Some informants who retain remnants of the conception of a non-empirical Heaven, also affirm that the ideal is realizable in this world. There is a further refinement of this idea among those who affirm that the traditional idea of Heaven is purely imaginary; any heaven which might exist has a possibility of realization on earth. Their actions are not motivated by traditional conceptions of Heaven.

The idea of constraint in the three respects is stronger among South Carolina churchmen than among the Boston group. The decline in the Hell-concept as a motivator of action is indeed striking, especially among South Carolina informants.

TABLE THREE

God, Heaven, and Hell as Constraining Forces

	God		*Heaven*		*Hell*	
South Carolina	*Yes*	*No*	*Yes*	*No*	*Yes*	*No*
Church A	11	1	10	2	7	5
Church B	13	0	12	1	8	5
Church C	13	0	11	2	9	4
City Church	5	0	1	4	0	5
College Students	40	0	31	9	14	26
Massachusetts						
Church One	8	4	7	5	7	5
Church Two	9	3	9	3	9	3
Church Three	13	2	12	3	12	3

Clergymen, who are cognizant of this trend from the nonempirical, have correspondingly minimized emphasis upon the nonexperimental in their sermons. The audience today is less responsive to the other-worldly appeal than it was in the past. Christians express and manifest less ardent belief and interest in the transcendental aspects of life.

In connection with this, it is interesting to observe the attitude of an urban South Carolina informant who expressed belief in the existence of Heaven. She stated that she likes to think of the passage,

" 'In my Father's house are many mansions. . . .' A spacious, commodious Heaven is attractive to me. . . ." Then she added, "But if there is no Heaven—then that's too bad." This attitude reflects an uncertainty of nonempirical aspects of existence for some informants. Another urban lady, who gave an affirmative reply regarding the existence of a Supreme Being, added that she hardly knows what she believes. These examples are given to show that doubt penetrates the mind of some informants who answered positively. And they indicate a variety of attitudes toward the Supernatural.

Attitudes Toward the Supernatural in Relation to Education and Occupation.—Attitudes toward the negative aspect of the principle of retribution change more rapidly among persons of advanced education than among others. Generally, the highly educated tend to be less orthodox in their religious attitudes than those of little or ordinary education.

The more rapid decline in the sentiment of fear than in the more positive aspects of existence is revealed in the attitudes of college students toward the Supernatural. Value attitudes toward the transcendental are seen in students' beliefs in God and the efficacy of prayer. The decline in these attitudes is observable in regard to the concepts Heaven and Hell. Although thirty-two out of forty students pursue the supremacy of the higher principle over the lower, thirty of them believe that there is a possibility of heaven on earth. This shows the decline in nonempirical ends; and it reveals that attitudes toward the Deity are changing. Five of the students interviewed regard Heaven as an imaginary traditional concept. Furthermore, they deny the possibility of a predominance of the ideal in a nonempirical or an empirical realm. These findings in this respect are of the same nature as those made by Allport. Doctor Allport's study of Harvard students reveals declining beliefs in immortality. Although only one-half of the students studied believe in personal immortality, a rigid theistic view in regard to an infinite Creator who is solicited by prayer and worship is accepted by one-fifth of the men and two-fifths of the women.[1]

The actions of thirty-one out of forty South Carolina State College students are influenced by traditional conceptions of Heaven. Although thirty out of forty students believe that there is a Hell, the conduct of only fourteen is influenced by traditional ideas of Hell. This substantiates the trend from fear as a motivator of action.

Although men tend to be released from the sentiment of fear with education and urbanization, the trend from compulsion is observable

[1] Allport, Gordon, *Lowell Lectures,* Lecture II, pp. II, 20.

among groups of varied educational and occupational levels. The principle of retribution (in regard to punishment for offense) does not influence action today to the extent that it did formerly. Table Four shows the changing religious attitudes among all groups.

TABLE FOUR

South Carolina Churchmen's Attitudes Toward the Transcendental, According to Occupation and Education

	Beliefs in a Deity and Prayer				*Constrainers of Action*					
	God		*Prayer*		*God*		*Heaven*		*Hell*	
Occupation	*Yes*	*No*	*Yes*	*No*	*Yes*	*No*	*Yes*	*No*	*Yes*	*No*
Unskilled Laborers	3	0	3	0	3	0	3	0	3	0
Skilled Laborers	1	0	1	0	1	0	1	0	1	0
Business Men	1	0	1	0	1	0	1	0	1	0
Farmers	26	0	26	0	25	1	22	4	14	12
Professionals	9	1	9	1	9	1	5	5	3	7
Education										
College	5	1	5	1	6*	0	4	2	2	4
1–3 years College	8	0	8	0	8	0	4	4	4	4
High School	2	0	2	0	2	0	2	0	0	2
1–3 years High School	4	0	4	0	4	0	4	0	1	3
Elementary	23	0	23	0	22	1	20	3	14	9

* This "apparent disparity" signifies the type of person who does not adhere to traditional ideas of God but seeks to apply Christian teachings to life.

Table Four corroborates the proposition that negative, repulsive features of religion first decline with a cessation of emphasis upon the nonexperimental elements of action.

In spite of some differences in ultimate ends (that is, the manner in which the ideal is pursued), there is a degree of integration of the ends of the members of the action system. Although there is some variation in attitudes toward the ideal, the essence of "the principle of group welfare" is obvious. There are common ends for the members of the religious system. Some aspects of the individual and group systems of action are shared by all of the members of the religious body. Being motivated by some "imaginary ends," individuals in the Negro Protestant church believe that religion should be integrated with life. Thus emphasis is at present being placed upon the immediate end sector of the intrinsic means-end schema rather than upon the ultimate-end sector.

Men's Conceptions of and Attitudes Toward Religion.—Although there is a decline in supernaturalism, religion continues to have significance for its followers. Religious conceptions are being modified, however. With diminution of the transcendental, the social character of religious beliefs is more apparent. Twenty-five out of 43 South Carolina churchmen report a change in religious attitudes over a period of years. Nineteen of this group variously attribute an increase of religious sentiments to prayer, reading the Bible, regular church attendance, deeper appreciation of the principles of Christianity, perplexing problems, experience, and observation. Six of the 25 informants who report a change state that there has been a decrease in religious sentiments in that their views are less orthodox. They attribute the transition to professed Christians' lack of application of Christian precepts to life, an increased knowledge of philosophy and religion, reasoning, association and discussion. Eighteen informants report no changes in religious attitudes.

Religious Sentiments over the Years

South Carolina	
Total number of informants	43
Increase	19
Decrease	6
No change	18
Massachusetts	
Total number of informants	39
Increase	12
Decrease	5
No change	22

According to informants, the religious attitudes of 17 out of 39 Boston churchmen have changed over a period of years. Of the 12 who report an increase in religious sentiments, 9 are members of Church Three; they impute the transition to spiritual absorption with the Deity, deeper communion with Christ, a knowledge of the reality of God, deeper faith in Christ and the Bible resulting from a closer relationship with the Divine, appreciation for the practical aspects of religion, and failure to participate in worldly activities. Recall the position of this church in the system of action. The 3 members of Church Two ascribe the change to a deeper appreciation of the church as a valuable institution to society, and integration of religion with life.

Five members of Churches One and Two attribute the decrement of their religious sentiments to physical and mental maturity. They have become more skeptical of the Bible and theism as a result of studying religion and philosophy.

The informants who state that there has or has not been a change in their attitudes toward religion had reference mainly to traditional religion. The failure of 18 South Carolina informants and 22 Boston informants to report a change in subjective attitudes shows that they regard themselves as being religious persons. Objectively, however, churchmen themselves are not conscious of the marked change in religious attitudes. Their attitude toward programs churches should institute indicates change. There is a decided shift from the nonempirical to the empirical.

A comparison of religious motivation of South Carolina and Boston informants shows the similarity between rural church members and those in Church Three. Rural informants and urban informants in Church Three give related reasons for an increase in religious sentiments.

The motivation of those who indicate changing attitudes toward religion signifies the importance of empirical and nonempirical elements to Protestants.

The active attitudes of churchmen toward the Deity are reflected in the meaning of religion. To informants, religion means living according to Christian principles with the end in view of eternal salvation, the satisfaction of spiritual aspirations, a norm for living, and relating Christianity to life. The number of replies given to each religious value signifies its importance. The emphasis is not upon attainment of the ideal in terms of a nonexperimental entity; it is upon integration of religion with life. Present attitudes indicate the changing process of religion.

TABLE FIVE

The Meaning of Religion to Informants

	S.C.	*Mass.*
Everything	9	9
A guide for living	8	8
Abundant living	3	2
Applying Christian precepts in all social relationships	9	17
Serving humanity	5	–
Obeying Christ and receiving his protection	8	1
The satisfaction of spiritual aspirations	5	1
Inner peace and comfort	–	3
Salvation	2	2

Emphasis upon the social aspect of religion confirms the proposition relating to a changing type of religion accompanying a decline of interest in the nonempirical. Informants' replies regarding the principle determining their relationships with others indicate the importance of the Christian religion as a norm. Efforts to conform action with the Golden Rule show the importance of religion as a guide for living. Churchmen strive to pursue ends according to this prescription, which promotes harmonious group relations. Religious attitudes are changing; men now regard religion as a means of teaching them how to live. (Although there was inculcation of the principle of charity in the past, Christians tended to withdraw from the world and contemplate the Blessed Eternal.) Religion is thus a means of fulfilling empirical aspirations. It has potentialities for abundant living.

TABLE SIX

The Principle Governing Churchmen's Social Relationships

	S.C.	*Mass.*
The Christian religion	10	19
The Golden Rule	33	20
Source of the principle:		
The Christian religion	14	19
Personal philosophy	3	4
Institutional influences	2	4
Combination of the three	24	12

It is usually traditional or conservative types of church members who give the answer that action is regulated according to "the Christian religion." Various replies (such as "the Fatherhood of God and the brotherhood of man," "Love thy neighbor as thyself," "the principles of God," "the Spirit of God," and "the Ten Commandments") are included under the classification, "the Christian religion." All of the rural informants who regard religion as the sole factor motivating their social relationships gave the reply, "Christianity." The majority of the informants consider "the Golden Rule" as the principle guiding action.

Some impute the source of the guiding principle to the Christian religion, while others ascribe the adoption of the rule to institutions other than religion. Some ascribe adoption of the norm to ideas absorbed from institutional life; others accept the principle as a result of reflection. The fact that religion is not alone regarded by men as the source of the norm regulating their actions indicates the subjective importance of values other than religion. And it also indicates the social nature of religion as a collective expression of the ideals of society, with some consideration given to individual attitudes.

College students believe that the ends of action should be pursued according to the Christian religion. Forty informants consider Christianity a helpful social philosophy and believe that its precepts should be applied in daily living. All of them seek to govern their lives according to the principle and to manifest the embodiment of religion in social action. Although forty informants state that the Christian religion greatly determines their attitudes and actions, the conduct of twenty-eight out of forty students is also motivated by a personal philosophy. The influence of a personal philosophy is indicative of the individualistic trend.

The Waning Authority of the Deity in Regard to Pastime Activities.—With a decrease of the authority of the Divinity, men are, to some extent, released from the sanctity of custom, and fear. With a diminishing strength of belief in the transcendental, various attitudes toward the Supreme being are reflected. Correlative with the decline in the common value attitude toward the nonempirical (as existed in the past) is the diminution of a common system of values in society. This observation does not invalidate previous statements of empirical fact regarding some degree of integration in the collectivity. It simply reiterates the position of imperfect integration and the dereligious trend (that is, from a traditional point of view). It has been established that religion is in a process of change and that an empirical type of religion is developing. Churchmen are less inclined to think in terms of transcendental values; and, as a result, personal standards tend to overbalance religious codes.

Man formulates his own philosophy, which may manifest surviving religious influences. The church is not the regulator of moral standards that it was formerly. Instead of looking to the church to formulate moral principles, the individual looks within or without to some agency or institution other than the church. So long as ends of action do not seriously conflict with legal codes, the individual seeks pleasures mainly as they are important to him, with perhaps some subsidiary religious influence. Allport's study of religious attitudes reveals a trend from the theocentric to the ethical.[1]

The following lists of activities in which Christians should not participate show changing attitudes toward the sacred norm.

[1] Allport, *op. cit.*, pp. 18–19.

TABLE SEVEN

Activities in Which Christians Should Not Engage, According to South Carolina Informants

Restrictions	*No. of Times Listed*
Treachery	1
Promoting strife	2
Gossip and slander	4
Lying and falsification	8
Profanity	4
Stealing	5
Committing adultery	3
Attending ball games and theaters	6
Attending dances	26
Attending parties, roadhouses and cafés	11
Playing cards	17
Gambling in any form	34
Drinking	28
Drinking excessively	2
Selling intoxicants	4
Desecration of the Sabbath	3

This list indicates that Christians should not violate the Ten Commandments. Also, the aspect of saintliness is apparent in that Christians should withdraw from worldly activities or "things of the flesh." Nevertheless, rigid observance of the Ten Commandments is not regarded necessary by many informants. Under certain conditions, the activity which the commandments and other religious norms restrict is exonerative. For example, four semi-urban (originally of the country, now residing in the city and holding their membership in rural churches) informants believe that dancing and moderate drinking are permissible for Christians provided they engage in these activities with "social equals," and Christians rather than "sinners." Another indication of changing attitudes toward the sacred norm is that some of the informants listed only two or three commandments which should not be violated. A few stated that dancing, card playing, and athletics are permissible, but not gambling. Five of the informants believe that there is a time for everything. Others regard secular activities adequate on certain occasions. Decadence of religious beliefs is seen in the separation of "the sacred" from "the profane" in some respects. Some refrain from attending card parties on prayer meeting nights, although they may not actually attend the prayer service. Some informants do not attend the theater on prayer meeting nights nor Saturday nights. Saturday night is set aside for meditation and preparation for the Sunday services. "Christians should not desecrate the Sabbath by attending theaters, games, and entertainments," some of the informants stated.

A comparison of the enumerations given by South Carolina informants and those in Church Three in Boston is revealing.

TABLE EIGHT

Activities Banned by Boston Informants in Church Three

Restrictions	*No. of Times Listed*
Smoking	1
Drinking	4
Drinking excessively	1
Dancing	6
Playing cards	7
Gambling in any form	8
Attending theaters, night clubs, etc.	4
Being entertainers	2
Violating any of the commandments	2

There is a greater similarity between the South Carolina list and the Church Three list than between the South Carolina enumerations and those of the other two Boston churches. It has been shown that rural groups are more conservative than urban; furthermore, Church Three was given as an example of a traditional type of church as far as transcendental values are concerned. Rural audiences and type three audiences tend to preserve the old religion longer than types one and two. Thus a degree of distance between the spiritual and the temporal is expected among traditional religionists, inasmuch as the authority of the Deity has not declined nearly so rapidly as among other types of religious men. It has been shown that persons in church type three almost exclusively pursue religious pursuits.

In the theoretical system, there was development of the idea that there is variation in attitudes toward the sacred norm according to type of religious man and type of church. Differences in belief regarding religion as a motivator of moral action reflect differences in ultimate value attitudes according to type of Christian and the numerical strength of the various types in a particular church. Recall that church type two preserves fewer traditional religious values than church type three, and it retains more conservative elements than church type one.

TABLE NINE

Activities in Which Christians Should Not Engage According to Informants in Church Two

Restrictions	*No. of Times Listed*
Group One	
Profanity	1
Attending public dances	4
Drinking	3
Playing cards	2
Gambling in any form	8
Professional gambling	4
Group Two	
Attending Sunday entertainments	1
Applauding in church	1
Church teas	1
Church fashion shows	1
Church auctions and raffles	1

The above list indicates that even conservative types of churches are departing from maintenance of strict standards of conduct according to moral prescriptions of the Bible. Observe lenient attitudes toward Christians' participation in sensuous activities. Only three informants in Church Two specified that consumption of alcoholic beverages by Christians is prohibitive. Christians may dance; but it is not permissible for them to attend public dances, according to four informants. This attitude signifies that recreational pursuits, which formerly were condemned, are allowable provided Christians associate with persons of their social status. Four churchmen condone social gambling inasmuch as it is prevalent; yet professional gambling is tabooed.

The enumerations of restrictions under Group Two relate to respect for the Sacred Day, and to extra-religious activities which churches should not sponsor. Although the question asked informants pertained to activities from which Christians as individuals should refrain, three informants disapprove of the extension of the church into "things of the world." In other words, some conservative Christians believe that the church should not acquire characteristics of the secular world. The fact that there is a greater frequency of condemnation of gambling in any form on both rural and urban lists shows that many informants are intolerant of churches sponsoring games of chance, as well as critical of "the moral laxity" regarding gambling.

In Church One, designated in the theoretical system as the unemotional type with a prevalence of "empirical-minded" men, observe the further deterioration of transcendental value attitudes.

TABLE TEN

Activities From Which Christians Should Refrain, According to Informants in Church One

Restrictions	*No. of Times Listed*
Gossip and slander	3
Excessive drinking	1
Commercialized vice (adultery)	1
Gambling	1

The fact that the informants in church type one hardly place any restrictions upon the pleasurable or sensuous ends of Christians is significant. This scant list shows a striking decline in attitudes toward the sacred norm according to the occupational and educational status of members of churches.

Church Three is a traditional type of church, with a prevalence of "the transcendental type" of man. Church Two is a conservative type of church, with a prevalence of "the moderate religionist." Church One is an unemotional type of church in which "the empirical type" of churchman is predominant. The following figures give a condensed picture of the attitudes of informants toward the Supernatural as a source of legality for personal conduct.

Church Three

Number of informants	15
Number of informants listing restrictions upon Christians	12
Number not listing restrictions	3
Number of times restrictions upon Christians listed	35

Church Two

Number of informants	12
Number of informants listing restrictions	10
Number of informants not listing restrictions	2
Number of times restrictions listed	27

Church One

Number of informants	12
Number of informants listing restrictions	6*
Number of informants not listing restrictions	6
Number of times restrictions listed	6

The above classification of churches reveals the differences in religious attitudes, and it also shows the similarity of belief between church types two and three.

Those persons who place no limitation upon the recreational activities of Christians regard pursuit of pleasurable ends according to religious standards a matter of individual conscience and reflection.

The lists of both rural and urban churches denote a decay of traditional religious values. The enumerations reveal that Christians are given almost as much freedom in regard to pleasurable ends as non-Christians. However, some limitation is placed upon the pursuit of leisure activities. Restrictions, nevertheless, are generally placed upon Christians in church type three (the type conserving established standards). Activities most greatly banned for Christians are as follows: dancing, card playing, gambling in any form, and partaking of intoxicating beverages. Of the forms of temporal activity or amusement most rigidly condemned for Christians, there are some differences in attitude toward the activity. For example, some informants accept dancing as a legitimate pastime for Christians, while others restrict dancing in public places. Some accept gambling "for small stakes" among friends, while others prohibit all games of chance involving gifts, prizes, or money. Some informants condone drinking, while a few taboo constant drinking or intoxication.

	Drinking	*Dancing*	*Card playing*	*Gambling*
South Carolina	30	26	17	34
Boston				
Church Three	5	6	7	8
Church Two	3	4	2	12
Church One	1	0	0	1

Attitudes toward temporal pleasures are changing. At one time, it was considered inappropriate for Christians to consume alcohol, to dance, to play cards, to gamble, and to participate in other secular activities. Attitudes toward pastime activities gradually changed. Change proceeds more slowly in rural areas than in urban. Observe

* Although one informant believes that there are activities in which Christians should not engage, she did not list any. However, in a comparison of attitudes of rural and urban churchmen, she is computed in the total restrictive activities.

that the total number of South Carolina restrictions regarding dancing, cards, etc., exceeds that of Boston.

Rural churchmen more rigidly adhere to traditional religious ideas than urban. The charismatic norm has more significance for action in a homogeneous area than in a heterogeneous one. A comparison of the activities listed, the number of times listed, and the number of persons who restrict or fail to limit the activities of Christians shows a difference in rural and urban attitudes. The following figures reflect the difference in attitudes toward the Supernatural as a source of moral rules regulating conduct.

South Carolina	
Number of informants	43
Number of informants listing restrictions	42
Number of informants not listing restrictions	1
Number of times restrictions upon Christians listed	158
Massachusetts	
Number of informants	39
Number of informants listing restrictions	29
Number of informants not listing restrictions	10
Number of times restrictions listed	68

Although five informants in the South Carolina group are members of an urban church, all of them place restrictions upon the conduct of Christians. Furthermore, some of the rural informants reside in the city and retain their membership in rural churches; thus they are subject to urban influences.[1] The rate of change in religious ideas tends to proceed more slowly in the South than in the industrialized urban North.

Some rural and urban informants rationalize their attitudes. The tendency to justify a course of action, the tendency of some churchmen to consider observance of religious codes a personal matter for the individual to decide, and the variety of attitudes toward the sacred confirm the subordination of traditional religion.

[1] In the rural churches studied, informants were selected according to residence, age, sex, education and occupation in order to reflect the attitudes of various types of worshippers in the church. In the urban churches, a representation of the religious beliefs of different groups of men in a church was secured.

CHAPTER VIII

The Alteration of Institutional Religion With Cultural Change

Modification of Religious Ends and Actions with Social Change.—Diminution of interest in transcendental ends indicates changing religious conceptions. Churchmen continue to regard religion as a norm; however, religion is conceived as a means of attaining empirical ends, with some regard to eternal values. With changing attitudes toward the Supernatural, the social value of religion is emphasized. Many conceive the potential value of Christianity as a means of promoting harmonious group living. In spite of changing attitudes toward the nonempirical, religion continues to maintain some influence over its followers. Church membership in America has not decreased.

Although there is a transition from the transcendental to the empirical, the American population is not less greatly churched than it was in the past.[1] The rate of growth of church membership has been constant with population changes. Church membership between 1906 and 1926 grew at about the same rate as the population. Even though membership in 1936 was only 2.3 per cent greater than in 1926, this small increase is primarily a result of some churches not reporting the number of members they had in 1936.[2] In 1916, there were 41,926,854 church members in the United States; in 1926, there were 54,576,346; and in 1936, there were 55,807,366.[3] The rate of growth of urban church membership has exceeded that of rural as a result of population mobility.[4] Consequently, religious attitudes change in an urban environment. A diminishing strength of traditional religion is expected in the city.

In spite of some degree of attraction to the church, traditional religious values are continually being modified. With scientific discovery, industrialization, and urbanization, emphasis is placed upon

[1] See page 79.
[2] Bureau of the Census, *Religious Bodies:* 1936, *op. cit.*, p. 85.
[3] *Ibid.*, p. 17.
[4] See page 78.

sensory rather than supersensory values. Thus men's religious attitudes and interests reflect cultural standards. With supremacy of the physical, traditional religion has diminished as a value system.

With a predominance of sensory knowledge, there is diminution of religion as a moral force. Concomitant with the emphasis upon sensory experience, there is diminishing influence of the ethical norm to regulate personal conduct as seen in Christians' attitudes toward temporal pleasures. Emphasis upon the secular rather than the spiritual is seen in the attention given the pursuit of pleasurable ends. The American consumer spends more money for liquor, tobacco, and cosmetics than for all charitable and religious purposes combined.[1] In 1944, the American public spent these sums for the following personal luxuries:

Alcoholic beverages	about	$7,100,000,000
Tobacco	almost	2,800,000,000
Recreation		2,800,000,000
Personal care		3,300,000,000
Toilet articles & preparations		1,100,000,000*

These figures not only indicate an interest in things of the world rather than the spirit, but they also reveal that the church is not the medium for personality expression that it has been in the past. Diversion is sought mainly through extra-religious channels. The church is no longer the center of activity and life; its position of prominence has been usurped by other enterprises and agencies. Thirty South Carolina clergymen have observed changes in the function of the church as a social center over a period of years. Two ministers consider the change insignificant; four regard it moderate, while twenty-four observe a decided change in the position of the church as a center of community life. Eighteen ministers state that there is less intercourse and fellowship among communicants today than in past years. In the past the church was a great meeting place for members to fraternize, converse, and picnic. The informants attribute the change to many factors, the principal factor being the interest of churchmen and others in secular pastimes. People in the community are attracted to amusement centers, cafés, theaters, and ball parks. Twelve of the rural clergymen state that the people are frequenting "piccolo joints," and so forth, instead of attending church services. Four informants observe that organized community agencies are providing recreation, and consequently the informal church gathering is being supplanted

[1] Burkhardt, Roy A., *How the Church Grows,* Harper and Brothers, New York, 1947, pp. vii–viii.

* *Methodist Statistical Department Chart.*

by institutional diversion. Six clergymen note that the church is providing recreation and entertainment as a substitute for the old form of association. There are others who have begun programs and plans for church community centers because the church has become a competitor with commercialized recreation and hence must provide an attraction in order to maintain its membership. The church is adjusting itself to the present trend of society by sponsoring various forms of recreation instead of relying upon the traditional method.

Secularization has influenced church members' attitudes toward the Supernatural and their conceptions of religion. The church, too, has not escaped present trends, and its position has been altered. The church is not the cynosure nor the regulator of life that it has been in past eras. As the state and social agencies assume and execute some of the former functions of religion (in regard to sex, marriage, drinking, etc.), legality rather than religion is in some respects followed as a guide for personal conduct. Observe, for example, the weakening influence of the church as an agency of social control with respect to drinking. At one time the Board of Temperance of the Methodist church exerted considerable influence regarding alcoholic consumption. With the repeal of the eighteenth amendment to the Constitution of the United States, the church was left relatively impotent in regard to temperance. With legalization of whiskey, drinking became widespread even among Christians. Although there is still a little temperance endeavor, the Methodist church, realizing the shift in its position and its corresponding diminution, has not manifested as much interest and activity in promulgating temperance programs. With the division of function, the church is relegated to the position of attempting to influence legislative enactments, regarding liquor permits, licenses, etc.

The institutional church has perceived changing religious attitudes and has attempted to modify its perspective in keeping with its changed position. Religion is imbedded in social organization, and it is an expression of the characteristic value-system of a particular society and of a particular age. Its outlook is colored by that of the culture which it reflects. Its functions, too, tend to manifest themselves in terms of the *modus operandi* of the society. Although the church may exert some influence in helping to formulate ends of social action, its role is greatly conditioned by society and men's active attitudes toward the non-empirical.

Considering its subordinate position, the church has attempted to adjust itself to a sensate society in order not to be incongruous with the culture of the age. In the process of accommodation, the church has retained some former values and functions and has acquired new characteristics. Institutional religion has changed in the framework of the church. Leaders have observed the changing attitudes and practices of church members with respect to drinking, dancing, etc. There has been violation of church ordinances as a result of men's attitudes toward the sacred norm. The church observed these tendencies, and therefore some denominations changed their rules to harmonize with beliefs and actions of churchmen. Some conservative denominations, which have not departed from established procedures, are beginning to visualize the trend and to anticipate changes in church doctrines.

Some church leaders are becoming tolerant of the deviations of Christians and hence fail to censure or to apply rules against nonconformers. Some churches have been more striking in their assumption of secular characteristics and thus promote dances, raffles, lotteries, fashion shows, etc., in order to raise funds and in order to placate members whose interests are not transcendental.

The Methodist denomination is cited as an illustration of the changing policy of the institutional church with respect to churchmen's attitudes toward the sacred. Failure of the Methodist discipline specifically to condemn some amusements which were previously restricted for church members is an indication of the shifting position of religious bodies. Over a period of twelve years, regulations of the Methodist church have changed. The 1932 discipline expressed deep concern about the increase of "demoralizing" amusements and warned members of the church against "attendance upon immoral, questionable, and misleading theatrical or motion picture performances; against dancing; and against such games of chance as are frequently associated with gambling; all of which have been found to be antagonistic to vital piety, promotive of worldliness, and especially pernicious to youth."[1] The 1940 and 1944 disciplines did not specifically designate any of the above activities as formerly. By 1944, the church had set up milder prescriptions, as seen in the advice given Christians to refrain from "such diversions as cannot be used in the name of the Lord Jesus."[2] The church retained some of its regulations, however. Class leaders were expected to advise, reprove, and exhort members and to inform the minister of disorderly members who failed to correct their conduct. Furthermore, members were advised against use of the name of the Lord in vain; working, buying,

[1] *Discipline of the Methodist Episcopal Church, 1932,* John W. Langdale, Book Editor, p. 72.

[2] *Doctrines and Discipline of the Methodist Church, 1944.* The Methodist Publishing House, Nolan B. Harmon, Jr., Book Editor, p. 35.

and selling on the Sacred day; buying, selling, or drinking liquor; intoxication; speaking evil against others; violating the Golden Rule; wearing gold or costly apparel; fighting, quarreling; laying up earthly treasures; engaging in usurious practices, borrowing or taking credit "without a probability of paying"; singing songs or reading books which do not pertain to "the knowledge or love of God," etc.[1]

Although the church urged against profanity, irreverence, drinking, personal adornment, gossip, etc., and threatened the application of sanctions against members who did not respond to persuasion and admonition, many churchmen ignored and violated the precepts of the church. Seldom were there any cases of excommunication because of immorality or disobedience to the discipline of the church.

By 1948, the Methodist church further modified its position by acknowledging the prevalence of dancing and other secular pastimes among members, and by refusing to admonish them in this respect.

The shifting policy of the church is not only characteristic of the Methodist denomination. The church alters its doctrine to correspond with changing individual attitudes and societal trends. Whenever there is no explicit alteration of doctrine, church rules are ignored to some extent. Hence this method of failure to attempt to restrain action indicates adjustment of the church to its relegated status. Although the church has not kept pace with social transition, efforts are being made to adjust church programs to the changing beliefs and actions of constituents. While accepting its subordinance with respect to moral action, the church seeks to cooperate with other institutions which have acquired functions once regarded as religious.

[1] *Ibid.*, pp. 34–35.

CHAPTER IX

The Status of Emotionalism in Rural and Urban Areas

Attitudes Toward the Manifestation of Sentiment in Emotional Action

Efforts of the Negro Protestant collectivity to conform its action to normative principles are reflected in attitudes and practices with respect to emotionalism and church programs. There is an attitude of moral obligation to the norm, which prescribes patterns of behavior under given circumstances.[1] There is general adherence to the system of normative rules, in spite of some dilatoriness in its observance by certain groups in the action system.

Increasingly the individuals in the religious unit are motivated by the belief that emotionalism is a barrier to a religion which promotes the intellectual and social growth of its adherents. Although there has not been eradication of emotional action in the collectivity, the selective principle has an outstanding result in the action of the group. Feeling is generally more subdued than in the past. And from this restraint, religious action of a practical nature is precipitated. Consideration of "the unemotional norm" in the collectivity is indispensable inasmuch as the selective factor is pertinent to an analysis of concrete action. Its causative, dynamic nature is apparent in the outcomes of action. With an increase in adherence to the norm, its weight in determining action will be more conspicuous. With further diminution of non-empirical religious expressions, there will be an increase of church and community coalescence.

Attitudes Toward Emotionalism.—There has been theoretical development of the proposition that emotional action diminishes with a declining importance of supersensory values. It has been demonstrated that there is diminution of the transcendental with the progression of action in the Negro religious collectivity. Since emotional action deteriorates with an impairment of non-experimental action,

[1] Parsons, *op. cit.*, pp. 414–415.

it is essential to consider subjective attitudes regarding the expression of religious sentiments in emotional behavior.

There is a variety of attitudes toward "the unemotional norm." There are reasons which account for emotional action among rural and uneducated churchmen. Heredity and environment influence the type of religious expression. To understand the course of religious action, it is necessary to consider the non-normative aspects of action. Non-normative factors condition the individual's choice of ends and means employed to attain a particular goal. The type of action manifested by the agent results from normative, as well as non-normative, aspects.[1] Effort is necessary to coordinate the non-normative and normative factors.[2] The influence of hereditary and environmental factors is seen in the action of the individuals and groups in the various churches and sections.

In regard to the relation of the system of normative rules to the course of action, attention was directed to the attitudes of the traditional type of person and church toward "the unemotional norm." Those for whom the sanctity of authority and custom is strong manifest some resistance to the normative principle because it has not been totally accepted and because other elements in action are significant.

At the same time, there are individuals in the action system who do not reject the normative principle; they abhor emotional action for themselves and believe that there should be subordination of emotion in religion. Nevertheless, they take cognizance of non-normative elements; thus they are somewhat tolerant of those whose actions do not conform to the norm. This attitude is reflected in the following statements:[3]

I do not subscribe to emotionalism and regard emotional action as unnecessary for myself. However, emotionalism depends upon temperament and intellectual level. Worship is an individual matter. People should worship according to their desires and circumstances.

In considering the question of emotionalism, it is important to consider the section of the city or country where the church is located. There is no fixed law which can be universally accepted and applied as a standard for all worshippers.

Informants who manifest these attitudes (that is, expression of religious sentiments in emotional action is undesirable for themselves; but, on the other hand, the type of worshipper and type of church,

[1] *Ibid.*, pp. 252–253. [2] *Ibid.*, p. 253.
[3] Each paragraph represents the attitude of a different person.

and the factors impinging upon the person must be considered, while the collectivity seeks to conform to the normative principle) are classified in tables as being tolerant of emotionalism. Because of this attitude, there is a larger number of replies indicating a favorable attitude toward religious emotion than there is of persons who themselves give overt expression to religious sentiments during the church service. Informants' ostensible liberality in regard to emotional action of others cannot be accepted literally, because even in this group various attitudes are apparent. That is, some informants are actually sincere in their utterance. However, there are others whose actions tend to belie their statements to the extent that they are inclined politely to ignore or restrain the emotional worshipper so that he refrains from emotional action after a few attempts to give vent to his feelings. Moreover, those who tend to endure overt manifestations are held in check by ardent advocates of unemotionalism. Some "tolerant" informants believe that worshippers should identify themselves with churches which satisfy their emotional needs. Not all members seek to eliminate emotional churchmen from the established Protestant church; some persons in this group, as well as the hostile group, wish to divert the emotional from extreme action.

One group of men is hostile toward and intolerant of any form of emotional behavior in church. Although this group is not strong numerically, it exerts considerable influence in the action system. Influence is disproportionate with numbers. Therefore, this group is effective in restraining demonstrative persons. Some persons request or insist upon the silence of the traditionally emotional type during church services. The attitudes of men who are extremely critical of emotional persons are visible in the following utterances: (Each paragraph represents the attitude of a different person.)

I totally object to emotionalism in the church. People who respond to emotional appeals, respond to almost any kind of idea that is suggested to them. Furthermore, many of the emotional border on insanity.

Emotionalism is unnecessary. It is mainly a result of ignorance. Those who are mentally deficient or mentally undeveloped display themselves and manifest irrational action in church in order to attract attention. Being unable to command attention or respect because of their feeblemindedness or uncultivation, they satisfy their egos by making themselves ridiculous in church. Thus they detract from the effectiveness of the service and are a source of annoyance.

There is another group of churchmen who regard the overt expression of emotion desirable. The following statement reveals the attitude of this group:

Emotionalism is not inappropriate. Some groups are subject to economic and social pressures. They are suppressed and frustrated. The church is the one place where they can release pent-up emotions. The manifestation of emotion is valid, psychologically understandable, and psychologically desirable. The church should inspire and encourage these groups and provide satisfaction for their emotional needs.

The quoted statements show differences in attitude toward the expression of religious sentiments in emotional action, and they indicate a variety of beliefs with respect to the selective principle and its application. Consideration of these beliefs in the system of action shows that there is some degree of integration of ends as the collectivity moves toward the regulation of action by the guiding principle. It is important to remember that this analysis presents the presence of normative and non-normative elements in the religious system; action is precipitated by experimental and nonexperimental ends. There are some normative elements which are not subjectively stated, inasmuch as some men do not clearly perceive ends even though their actions tend to conform to the system of norms. This subconscious motivation has been amplified in many respects. The trained observer is able to discern various shades of belief and their impingement upon action. There is an analysis of material in diverse respects in order to focalize the trend from nonempirical and emotional action elements.

Extreme emotional action is generally regarded with disdain. Nevertheless, a subdued or semi-subdued manner of emotional expression is still permissible. Table Eleven reveals the general unpopularity of traditional emotional action; it shows that shedding tears and sanctioning the speaker's ideas are more common than shouting. Informants were asked whether they give overt expression to religious emotions. Simply classifying replies as affirmative or negative without a division of positive replies would be misleading, inasmuch as classification of emotional actions shows a departure from extreme manifestations.

In response to the question pertaining to informants' attitudes toward overt emotional expression of others, there are various attitudes recorded under the term "desirable." A few persons specified that moderate emotional expression is not objectionable; some limited acceptability to "amen"; and several added that emotionalism is not objectionable if the worshipper is sincere. The spuriously spectacular is condemned. Nevertheless, a genuine expression of religious sentiments in a restrained or semi-restrained manner is generally condoned by the group designated as considering emotionalism "desirable."

TABLE ELEVEN

Laymen's Attitudes Toward Overt Expression of Religious Sentiments

	Number Emotional and Type of Response				*Emotionalism of Other Worshippers*		
	Shed Tears	*Say "Amen"*	*Shout*	*Number Unemotional*	*Desirable*	*Tolerable*	*Objectionable*
South Carolina							
Rural Churchmen	2	16	6	14 out of 38	29	6	3 out of 38
City Churchmen	0	0	0	5 out of 5	0	3	2 out of 5
College Students	2	4	0	34 out of 40	15	5	20 out of 40
Massachusetts							
Church One	0	0	0	12 out of 12	1	4	7 out of 12
Church Two	2	0	2	8 out of 12	3	6	3 out of 12
Church Three	4	2	6	3 out of 15	15	0	0 out of 15

The table shows that the normative principle is significant inasmuch as emotional action is rapidly declining, according to the attitudes of churchmen. There continues to be emotional expression in the church, but extreme manifestation of religious sentiments in overt action is held in contempt. Only 6 out of 38 rural persons interviewed manifest extreme action while emotionally stimulated.

Rural informants express their emotions in some form during the church service more frequently than urban, and they are also more tolerant of emotional action than urban worshippers. Twenty-four out of 38 rural persons are emotional, while 16 out of 39 Boston informants are emotional. Three out of 38 rural informants object to any form of overt emotional expression, while 10 out of 39 Boston informants do so. In spite of the disproportionate weight of Church Three informants, who have a Holiness background, the table shows that Boston informants as a unit are more restrained than rural.

The effect of urbanization upon traditional religion is also seen in the similarity between the attitudes of South Carolina urban informants and Boston worshippers. At the same time, the factor of education is seen in the close correspondence between attitudes and practices of the South Carolina city churchmen and college students, and Churches One and Two. Recall that the transcendental is more significant in action for rural and uneducated churchmen than for urban, educated groups. The connection between nonexperimental and emotional action has been established.

Nevertheless, the collectivity as a unit minimizes emotional expression of religious sentiments. In spite of the fact that professional groups are more unemotional and hostile to emotional action than other worshippers, churchmen of all occupational and educational levels are not favorably disposed toward the manifestation of religious sentiments in extreme action. The following table shows that persons of various levels do not manifest emotional behavior during the church service. Also, some informants in various educational and occupational groups are hostile to any form of emotionalism. Bear in mind that not all positive replies indicate predisposition to extreme emotional action. Table Eleven gives a more precise classification of attitudes and actions than does the following table, inasmuch as the latter is designed simply to portray attitudes of persons of various statuses.

TABLE TWELVE

South Carolina Churchmen's Attitudes Toward Emotionalism, According to Occupation and Education

	Overtly Emotional in Some Form		*Emotionalism of Others Desirable or Tolerable*	
Occupation	*Yes*	*No*	*Yes*	*No*
Unskilled Laborers	3	2	4	1
Skilled Laborers	1	0	1	0
Business Men	1	0	1	0
Farmers	17	9	24	2
Professionals	2	8	8	2
Education				
College and above	0	6	3	3
1–3 years College	2	6	8	0
High School	1	1	2	0
1–3 years High School	3	1	3	1
Elementary	18	5	22	1

The declining influence of the supernatural is seen in the type of service conducted in churches. The services today do not as strongly appeal to nonexperimental and emotional action as those of the past. In spite of this, communicants are emotionally satisfied. Satisfaction with a serene type of worship substantiates the changing religion of the collectivity. Thirty-three out of 38 rural informants consider their emotional needs as being effectively met. Five out of 5 South Carolina urban worshippers are emotionally satisfied. And 35 out of 39 Boston informants regard the church service satisfactory. Only 9 out of 82 informants in South Carolina and Boston churches are not emotionally satisfied. The significance of transcendental values for the unsatisfied informants is seen in their replies. The service does not stimulate traditionalists to "grow in grace." Some lament the passage of the era of intense emotional stimulation. They cannot give overt expression to their religious sentiments because of fear of censure.

In stating the manner in which the church service is satisfactory, informants designated answers which amplify the trend from the nonempirical to the empirical. Half of the comments indicate a relationship with the Supreme, while the other half reveal an appreciation for instructive sermons which facilitate social adjustment. That is, replies show that informants give some consideration to spiritual as well as temporal values. Ten replies indicate mystical, emotional and nonexperimental values, such as absorption with the Deity. Twenty-six designations make reference to values, such as the church service satisfies the need for religious expression, Christian fellowship, reverence, and communication with the Divine. Fifteen replies indicate an appreciation for logical sermons which stimulate the intellect, while 21 replies signify satisfaction with a message which encourages the integration of religion with the community.

Most informants regard their churches as amply meeting their emotional needs. Furthermore, they appreciate the trend from the nonexperimental to the experimental. Communicants still are conscious of transcendental values. The service satisfies a need for the spiritual, a need for something beyond the temporal. Thus a service which retains some warmth through prayer and song is inspiring. However, a service which makes appeal to the emotional only is not appreciated. Increasingly, worshippers seek a service which stimulates thought and which pertains to the solution of personal or social perplexities.

Clergymen's Attitudes Toward the Manifestation of Religious Emotion.—Ministerial leaders elicit diverse actions with respect to the normative principle. However, subordination of the emotions in religion is seen in the frequency of statements regarding the importance of control of emotion under the influence of religious objects. Almost all South Carolina and Boston clergy indicated that religion should stimulate thought and action of a constructive nature. However, attitudes regarding the place of emotion in religion are not identical. The variation in attitudes is seen in regard to the desirability and extent of emotion in religion, and the manner in which the norm should be pursued. Although most clergy believe that annihilation of emotion from the collectivity is not feasible (because of various considerations), the informants generally disfavor extreme manifestations of emotional action. Hence the normative principle is significant in the motivation of action. The following table shows the number of clergy who manifest a variety of attitudes toward religious emotion.

TABLE THIRTEEN

Clergymen's Attitudes Toward Emotionalism

South Carolina	*Encourage*	*Understand or Tolerate*	*Discourage*
Rural	4	7	7
Urban	4	4	4
Massachusetts	1	5	4
Total Number of Attitudes	9	16	15

Most South Carolina clergy oppose an unbounded expression of enthusiasm and are hostile to extreme emotional behavior. However, informants manifest diverse attitudes toward the expression of religious emotion. Some consider the traditional role of emotion in religion and therefore do not advocate the total submergence of emotional action in the system, although they themselves tend to restrain their feeling. Some ministers regard it essential to give adequate consideration to motivation and circumstance. Some consider a subdued manner of emotional expression adequate and legitimate. Most informants believe that there should be a combination of emotion, thought, and volition in religion. A few leaders are hostile to the overt expression of emotion, however; and they seek to stifle spontaneity. Even a few of the rural ministers manifest an intolerant attitude and interrupt the expression of extreme emotional action, which sometimes takes the form of exhibition, whenever the members proceed to display or dramatize themselves.

Various replies indicate a predilection to the control and direction of religious emotion. The informants who discourage the manifestation of religious sentiments in emotional action seek to direct emotion to practical action. And, in fact, most of the South Carolina clergy (even those who regard emotionalism desirable) are making some efforts to lead worshippers from a transcendental type of religion.

The following excerpts (each paragraph reflects the attitude of a different person) concretely present attitudes of South Carolina clergymen.

Personally, I don't care for emotionalism, but the people should not be suppressed, considering traditional religious fervor.

The church service is more effective without emotionalism.

There should be some expression of religious emotion. However, I try to sublimate emotion by directing it into wholesome, practical channels of thought and action. I promote the educational and cultural advancement of the people by breaking down traditional attitudes and practices. I promote a program of activity through instruction and church organization.

Although I used to like emotionalism, I don't care for it now. And most of our preachers are getting away from the emotional type of discourse. They are trying to teach the people, and the people are demanding a thoughtful sermon. Nevertheless, some feeling of a subdued nature should be retained in the church.

We are trying to teach our people that religion is not all emotion, but it is a sincerity of the heart and mind inclined to a full understanding of God's purpose.

I neither like nor approve of emotionalism. I use the intellectual approach in my sermons.

The old religion is not suitable today; it is inappropriate and useless. A modern religion with emphasis upon social and recreational activities is needed to attract youths.

Do not teach a burdensome religion that requires refraining from secular activities. Show youths that they can participate in sports as a part of their religious experience and can manifest sportsmanlike attitudes and the spirit of fair play while engaging in athletic contests. The sermon emphasizing the Supernatural and stimulating emotion is outmoded.

Emotionalism is very desirable. It engenders spiritual warmth and cooperation.

Emotionalism should be nurtured. It is a traditional religious expression. Take it away, and the race will die.

Enthusiastic expression of feeling has a helpful influence upon men religiously and secularly.

Emotionalism provides an outlet for restricted feelings; it gives a sense of release from restraint, and it gives tone to the church service.

Emotionalism is appropriate according to place and circumstance. It is beneficial when it is directed by reason. It should not be annihilated completely nor taken to the extreme.

People should be permitted to worship as they desire. I like emotionalism, and the average preacher likes it if he can produce it. When he can't, he doesn't like it.

I do not condemn emotionalism so long as it expresses the desires of the individual and satisfies him in worship. People usually worship according to their understanding and knowledge. If emotional expression were discouraged in my parish, the service would be a complete failure.

I am tolerant of emotionalism. The cultural level of the worshipper and the geographical location of the church must be considered. Man is basically emotional; therefore there should not be suppression of the natural. Sudden joy or sorrow in sport or religion may upset the individual to an uncontrollable extent and produce an extreme reaction. However, exaggerated pretensions of emotion are not acceptable. Nor is the stoical attitude manifested to be labelled "intelligent" appropriate.

With respect to Boston clergy, there are manifold attitudes toward emotion. Those who discourage emotion conceive it differently in some respects. Attitudes toward the manner of pursuit of the norm vary. Two of the Boston clergy are opposed to any form of emotional action accompanying religious sentiments. They totally favor a serene form of worship and they are harsh in their judgment of emotional audiences. Two other informants who discourage emotional action are not condemnatory in their judgment of emotional worshippers, though they seek to lead their congregations to a more subdued manner of worship. They gradually institute a religion which submerges the traditional form of worship. However, they desire the retention of spirituality in the church.

The group which understands or tolerates emotionalism is motivated by the belief that emotion is one phase of religion. Semi-subdued or subdued emotional expression is beneficial. It has its place and should be harnessed into other channels. The church should not be devoid of it; nor should there be an excess of emotion. The individual factor must be considered. Too rigid suppression of the emotional type will produce spiritual stagnation and church disintegration. Nevertheless, emotional persons should not be permitted to disturb the effectiveness of the service and to disrupt its continuity. Overt manifestation of emotion to attract attention should not be allowed. Another attitude related to individual freedom of worship is that of considering the level of the worshipper in the church.

It is difficult to take a man without a background of culture and bring him to the level of an educated man. The leader must promote adjustment through a sympathetic, understanding approach. He should appreciate the position of the masses, deal with them on the realm under which they live, and try to lead them on to something which their background makes possible. . . . So many times we take away from people what they have, without giving them anything in its place.[1]

One clergyman in "the tolerant group" regards emotionalism as "a vanishing cultural expression." He does not oppose nor promote emotionalism but accepts it as a fact.

It is a cultural heritage. It has some enriching results, and it has often led to useless extremes. It affords release (particularly in northern communities) from circumscription, inadequate social expression, and frustration.[2]

The informant who encourages emotionalism considers spontaneous expression of feelings as being understandable, wholesome, beneficial, and desirable. Emotional expression provides release for individuals who experience social pressures. "However, my primary objective is not to arouse emotion, but to teach, to convert, to encourage, to inspire, and to stimulate action."[3]

Education is a factor in the decline of emotionalism. Nevertheless, some youthful educated clergymen who express tolerant attitudes were formerly hostile to the overt manifestation of religious sentiments. Their education and experiences have contributed to a reversed attitude of understanding toward the traditional type of church worshipper. Education in respect to emotion has two effects upon the individual—either intensification of intolerance or moderation of rigid attitudes. The flexible attitude indicates an approach to reintegration of ends of the Protestant collectivity.

There is a relation of ends of the leaders of the action system. Ministers of the various Protestant denominations manifest the three types of attitudes toward emotionalism. The thirty South Carolina informants are of the Methodist denomination. Hence it is observed that differences in attitude toward "the unemotional norm" are reflected in terms of type, and not denomination. (That is, denomination is not the principal influence in a transcendental or an empirical religion in spite of some subsidiary influences.) The Boston informants comprise a motley group with respect to attitudes and denominations. Two are of a nonsectarian faith (formerly Holiness); one is a Congregational minister; one is an Episcopalian; three are Baptists;

1 Interview, The Reverend Dr. Charles B. Copher, June 26, 1947, Boston, Mass.
2 Interview, The Reverend Dr. Stokes, February 20, 1947, Boston, Mass.
3 Interview, The Reverend L. S. Odom, July 3, 1947, Boston, Mass.

one is a Methodist, and two are of the African Methodist Episcopal church. Irrespective of the difference in attitudes toward emotionalism, there is a degree of integration of the various end systems of action.

Types of Sermons Preferred by Churchmen.—The decline in emotional and nonempirical action is exhibited in the kind of sermon which is esteemed by worshippers. Men in the collectivity are demanding a type of discourse which appeals to reason, although nonempirical elements exist in a religious sermon with its basis in nonexperimental beliefs. Instead of desiring a mainly illogical sermon appealing to emotion, church goers seek a sermon which is provocative of thought and which aids man in his quest for an abundant life. The type of sermon expected and sought today gives an index of the importance of transcendental ends to men in the religious system. Evidence of the trend from the nonempirical and the increasing importance of empirical values is reflected in attitudes toward sermons.

An indication of the nature of the ends sought by rural and urban laymen is seen in the following table.

TABLE FOURTEEN

Type of Sermon Preferred by Church Members

South Carolina	*Biblical*	*Combination Biblical and Practical*	*Practical*
Church A	8	4	0
Church B	12	1	0
Church C	11	2	0
City Church	0	1	4
Massachusetts			
Church One	1	3	8
Church Two	4	2	6
Church Three	7	8	0

The practical sermon is preferred to the religious or Biblical type in the city. City worshippers tend to appreciate a sermon which bears direct application to life or a type of discourse which relates religious teachings to contemporary events and experiences. Some informants state a desire to hear current events related to the Bible (the religious-practical type). Some indicate a preference for a presentation of local, national, and international problems over a rendition of Biblical stories, which are remote. Eighteen informants desire instructive, pertinent sermons. Twenty-one seek a sermon which provides instruction according to a religious reference. They like a combined spiritual and intellectual sermon. Thus there is a total of 39 out of 82 informants who believe that religion should pertain to or be applicable to life. This type of worshipper regards an empirical or intellectual approach superior to a nonempirical or emotional approach. The moderate and the empirical types of Christians designate a desire to integrate religion with life, not especially from a transcendental perspective. Worshippers with this point of view are found in type one and two churches, whereas the type of worshipper for whom the authority of the Deity is significant is found in the traditional type three church. It has been shown that there is a close similarity of belief in many respects between South Carolina rural informants and urban Church Three informants. Forty-three out of 82 laymen prefer a Biblical or religious type of sermon. Five of these informants state a desire to hear "a clear explanation of God's word"; they regard the Ten Commandments as being authoritative. Five prefer a Biblical sermon which makes no reference to the Commandments. Four of the traditional group like messages descriptive of "the glory and adoration of God." Two wish to hear discourses pertaining to the Coming of Christ. These samples of attitudes indicate the importance of the transcendental for churchgoers who wish to hear an elaboration of traditional religious values. In spite of the presence of nonempirical ends, the other-worldly sermon designed to stimulate the emotions is not popular today. The religious sermon, in terms of the Gospel, continues to enjoy moral authority in rural areas. But there is disapprobation of the emotional sermon. Those clergy in rural churches who do not supply a religious sermon which contains some elements of logic are falling in ridicule and disrepute. A few rural churchmen are indicating consciousness of a need for a sermon which will be of some practical benefit to them. The increasing preference for a sermon which tells men how to live and quickens their intellect shows the importance of experimental rather than nonexperimental ends of action.

The sermon is the most attractive feature of the church service. For laymen in South Carolina and Boston, the sermon is the most satisfying part of the church service. Note the attitudes which follow.

Forty-nine out of 82 informants enjoy the sermon most. A few qualify their appreciation according to the type of sermon delivered. If the type they seek is not presented, the music is the most important part of the service. These discriminating informants desire a logical rather than an emotional approach. Even those who did not add a qualification generally indicated during the interview that a sermon designed to stimulate emotion rather than thought is not acceptable.

Churchmen's attitudes toward the sermon show that nonexperimental elements are diminishing in the action system. Laymen's attitudes and the elevation of rational ends in the changing religion are an important point of consideration for leaders of the Protestant collectivity.

TABLE FIFTEEN

The Most Satisfying Part of the Church Service, According to Laymen

South Carolina	*Prayer*	*Music*	*Sermon*	*All*
Church A	0	0	11	1
Church B	0	3	8	2
Church C	0	2	8	3
City Church	0	0	4	1
Massachusetts				
Church One	0	3	6	3
Church Two	1	6	2	3
Church Three	1	1	10	3

CHAPTER X

The Status of Emotionalism in Rural and Urban Areas (*Continued*)

THE MANIFESTATION OF SENTIMENT IN NONEXPERIMENTAL AND EMOTIONAL ACTION IN SOUTH CAROLINA

Practices in South Carolina Churches

AS RELIGIOUS beliefs are modified, nonempirical elements of action deteriorate less slowly in the country than in the city. Actions of rural worshippers during the church service indicate that transcendental value attitudes continue to be significant. Some men enter a dependent relationship with the Supreme, from whom blessings are sought as a means of sustaining and ameliorating life. The principle of retribution, especially from a positive point of view, has some outstanding effects in action irrespective of its increasing insignificance. With diminution of the nonempirical, there is a rapid decline in emotional action.

I. ALTERATION OF ACTION WITH RESPECT TO THE SERMON

Classification of Rural Sermons.—The "religious" sermon, which is more common than other types of sermons in the rural church, consists of three kinds. First, there is the religious sermon in which nonexperimental elements are significant; however, it is devoid of appeals to emotional action. Second, there is the Biblical expository type as a guide for moral action. The Supernatural is regarded as a source of authority for personal conduct and social relationships. Although a sermon of this nature appeals to sentiment, there is no attempt to induce extreme emotional action; an intellectual approach is combined with a submerged emotional appeal. This kind of religious sermon is usually delivered in the rural churches studied. Finally, there is the emotional religious sermon, which consists of no central unified point of view; its chief aim is to arouse feeling.

The "practico-religious" type of sermon (the second main classification of sermons), which conceives religion as a norm for community life, principally makes use of the intellectual appeal. This type of sermon makes fewer references to the nonempirical aspects of the universe than the religious type.

The "practical" sermon (the third basic classification) is informative in nature and contains only a few references to transcendental values.

Of 13 sermons delivered in rural churches by five clergymen, 8 were of the religious type; 3 were of the religious-practical type, and 2 were practical. Of the religious sermons, four emphasized problems of life and their cessation in a nonempirical world; these sermons were designed to arouse emotion. In the meantime, two of these sermons were informative, whereas the other two consisted essentially of emotional elements. Because of revival season, the emotional appeal was strong; however, audiences were generally unresponsive, although a few persons in some of the audiences reacted positively to the speakers' efforts to stimulate feeling. In the other four religious sermons, the intellectual approach was followed. Two of the sermons were persuasive and the other two were expository. At one time, rural speakers concentrated upon the Supernatural. At present, there is diminution of negative transcendental values and of emotional action, irrespective of the presence of nonexperimental beliefs and actions. The decline of nonempirical ends is observed in the changing status of religious sermons. That is, there is variation in the religious types of sermons delivered to the extent that the principle of retribution is considerably less significant today than yesterday; the more positive aspects of existence are appealing, and emotional audience response is infrequent.

Ideas in Sermons Producing Audience Response and Emotional Action.—Persons reacting positively to the Supreme Being's power to relieve situations of stress and tension are usually the traditional type of churchman. The inclusion of responses does not imply that there is general audience response to nonexperimental appeals; it does show, however, the importance of transcendental values to certain types of men and churches in the action system. Those groups of church goers who feel the pressures of existence strongest tend to identify themselves in some manner with the Deity. Being in an insecure, precarious position, they tend to rely upon a Supreme Being, the Animator and Bestower of Life.

Emotional response is most intense with an elaboration of (1) trouble, tribulation, adversity, and disappointment, (2) agony, crucifixion, victory of Jesus,[1] (3) faith in Christ, (4) protection of the Al-

[1] Sometimes the speaker identifies the audience with Jesus by comparing Jesus' suffering with that of the audience; then he proceeds to point out the eventual success of

mighty in difficulty, (5) personal knowledge of the power of Christ, and (6) the inevitability of death, and the attainment of Heaven, where there will be termination of present struggles in communion with Jesus and deceased relatives. References to these ideas in the past produced extreme emotional responses, often in the form of screaming and shouting. Today, manifestation of feeling is somewhat restrained; response to the preacher generally takes the form of a semi-subdued or subdued verbal expression, such as "amen," although stronger expletives are sometimes employed. In addition, nonexperimental ideas and emotional appeals usually create no favorable audience response in the observed churches. Speakers experience extreme difficulty in inducing emotional reactions. After repeated efforts, the speaker sometimes secures positive response from a few persons in the audience.

The following excerpts from sermons delivered in rural churches indicate the diminution of emotion: the increasing unresponsiveness of audiences to nonexperimental or other-worldly sermons, and the sanction of various types of ideas by audiences. As speakers expressed some ideas, there was "warm" audience response. "Warm response" designates audience reaction of two to seven persons in verbal expressions, such as a vociferous "Amen," "Yes, Lord," "Have Mercy," and in bodily action in the form of handclapping and footpatting.

There was warm response to these transcendental value attitudes:

The Necessity of Faith in God—In this atomic age, faith in God is necessary. No atomic power is equal to Christ's. In this age of destruction, God Almighty will save men. All nations must bow and confess that Jesus is Christ Almighty![1]

God's Fatherly Protection in Difficulty and Despair[2]—God can do things nobody else can do. Many times I've been shipwrecked, threatened, almost killed; but God took care of me. Yes, God will take care of you. In a few more days all of my trouble will be over. I'll go home. God has been a father to us, a mother to us. I like to pray. I like to talk about prayer and God. He is a rock in the weary land, a fortress in the time of trouble. . . . I want to be in that number. I've been talked about, called everything but a child of God. We are they who have come up through trials and tribulations.

Christians in spite of obstacles. Occasionally the pastor of Churches A and D takes this text: And Jesus saith unto him, The foxes have holes, and the birds of the air *have* nests; but the Son of man hath not where to lay *his* head.—Matthew 8:20.

[1] Sermon, The Reverend M. J. Porter, Quarterly Conference, Church A, August 10, 1947, Orangeburg County, South Carolina.

[2] The first part of this revival sermon consisted of an historical account of government, philosophy, and religion. Later, the speaker discarded the intellectual approach and made use of the emotional appeal. This device indicates an effort to satisfy various elements in the audience.

O for a closer walk with God,
A calm and heavenly frame,
A light to shine upon the road
That leads me to the lamb!

Church, this may be the last time you ever hear me preach. Church, this may be the last time you ever hear me sing, but when the roll is called up yonder I'll be there.

Sometimes I'm beset with trouble; water is up around my head. I pray on. In a few more days, I'll go to Jesus. God is going to say, "Jones, come up on high." I've got my ticket in my hand. Hold on and be in that number.

Unresponsiveness to Emotional Appeals.—Warm response to sermons, whenever found, usually occurs on certain occasions, notably revival season. Most of the excerpts in this section of audience reaction to sermons are taken from revival sermons. This warrants the conclusion that emotionalism is conspicuously decreasing since ideas other than the transcendental type create response, since references to the most popular feeling-generator (termination of the struggles of life in everlasting peace) sometimes create no response other than a mere "amen," and since this reiteration of the speaker's thought is by far the most common form of overt expression. This point of view is forcibly demonstrated in the failure of some audiences to respond during revival season.

Rural audiences of all levels increasingly depreciate the emotional type of sermon. The revival audience at Church C were amused, uninterested, and bored with the repeated attempts of the evangelist to arouse feeling as he grimaced and pranced while delivering his sermon. During some revival sermons, there was no verbal response. During others, positive response took the form of an infrequent unadorned "amen," uttered mainly to prevent embarrassment of the speaker. (It must be remembered that rural audiences tend to be much more sympathetic, cooperative, and natural than city audiences.) At the same time, nonexperimental ideas retain some value for a few rural communicants. But most worshippers are unresponsive to other-worldly appeals since their interests run counter to traditional religious conceptions and since some rural churchgoers are adopting the sophisticated manners of some urban groups.

The fact that emotionalism is restricted to from one to seven persons in a revival audience of fifty to one hundred persons indicates the paucity of overt expression of emotion.

There was only an unemphatic "amen" response to these ideas related to nonempirical values.

The Necessity of Faith in Difficulty.—You must have patience to lead others and to wait upon God. . . . I need faith and trust in God. . . . When beset with problems and difficulties, you must have patience to wait upon God. You've got to have faith to face and overcome the storm of life. When the road is rugged, you must get on your knees and pray. Prayer is powerful and has been in the past. . . . Prayer ensures success.[1]

God Relieves the Troubled.—Speak to God about your trouble and disappointment. He will hear you. David said, "Not only will He hear you, but He will answer." When your heart is heavy, speak to God and your trouble will pass away.[2]

The Assuaging Power of Christ.—When you're in despair, God will answer your prayer. In this dreary life of disappointment, we sometimes shed tears. We can tell the world, "I have light, though the way is cloudy." During the past war, mothers shed tears while their sons were away. . . . Through their tears, they talked with the Father, and their hearts were uplifted because of God's presence and inspiration.[3]

Protection of the Righteous and Purification of the Sinful.—God will take care of the righteous. . . .

The cleansing power of God removes idolatry and sin and makes a new creature in God.[4]

It has been shown that the sermon appealing to nonexperimental values is not so widely accepted today as formerly, with the advancement of experimental ends in the religious collectivity. Nevertheless, traditional value attitudes continue to be reflected at times; some preachers continue to strive partially to allay the fears and despairs of men by making reference to the Divine Order of the universe. This potential method of remuneration (concentration upon the Supernatural to offset unsatisfied empirical hopes and aspirations) is not very acceptable today; hence there is a diminishing frequency of reference to Christ as a comfort to the distressed. However, changing religious functions are, in some respects, more retarded in rural than in urban areas. Probably the general poverty level of worshippers in the country church, the unattractiveness of the rural environment (not from a natural point of view), and the extent of dependence upon the church (that is, for traditional Christians) as a source of diversion contribute to the continued, though modified, inculcation of the Spirit of God as a source of help and inspiration.

1 Sermon, Church A, August 17, 1947, Orangeburg County, South Carolina.

2 Revival Sermon, Church C, August, 1947, Orangeburg County, South Carolina.

3 Sermon, The Reverend Joseph Mitchell, Orangeburg District Conference, Bethlehem Church, July 24, 1947.

4 Revival Sermon, Church B, July 23, 1947, Orangeburg County, South Carolina.

Other Ideas Producing an "Amen" Response.—There are frequent sanctions to ideas of a this-worldly nature. Of course, there are non-empirical elements in most religious sermons; however, there is moderation of these values from an emotional standpoint in sermons. The intellectual appeal is mainly relied upon in some discourses. A religious sermon which contains some transcendental elements undesigned to produce emotional action is common. This type of sermon and its response bears out the changing religious attitudes and actions. Listeners expressed agreement with these ideas: willingness to proclaim the Gospel, personal knowledge of Christ, adoration of the Deity, the necessity of applying religion to life, and confidence in the eventual triumph of Christianity.

Ideas of an expository nature stimulating mild response are as follows:

> The Eventual Victory of Jesus.—
> Peace will begin in men's hearts.
> There will be no peace in this world
> until men decide to do right and
> treat each other right. . . . You
> can't live in this world without
> Christ. . . .
> Regardless of where you go, you'll find someone
> serving God. . . .
> Regardless of how wicked you find
> this world, someone will pray. . . .
>   Jesus shall reign where'er
> the sun
>   Does his successive journeys
> run;
>   His kingdom spread from
> shore to shore,
>   Till moons shall wax and
> wane no more.[1]

Knowledge of the Presence of the Lord.—The spirit of the Lord is with me in this world. . . . Four elements necessary to a Christian are wisdom, patience, courage, and faith. . . . Through knowledge, you must avoid evil and realize God's expectation of making this world a paradise.[2]

The Meaning of Religion.—There are three important aspects in this sermon. (1) Knowledge. We cannot have the religion of Jesus Christ unless we know it. . . . (2) Feeling. Unless you have feeling, you are not a Christian. . . . (3) Conduct. Changing your conduct is necessary if you

[1] Revival Sermon, The Reverend W. W. Toomer, Church B, July 24, 1947. The speaker quotes Isaac Watts' hymn.

[2] Quarterly Conference Sermon, The Reverend M. J. Porter, Church A, August, 1947.

are going to be a Christian. . . . Religion affects the whole circle of your activity. . . . Religion takes possession of the entire being. Religion as knowledge illuminates the intellect. . . . Knowledge guides the individual's thinking in the right channels. . . . It awakens the right actions and provides a rule for conduct.[1]

The Necessity of an Active Religion.—The Lord wants active Christians, those who spread sunshine among others. No man liveth to himself nor for himself. . . . Christians must live a useful life. Their activity will demonstrate their Christianity. . . . The wheels of the machine must move; if they do not move, there is no progress. . . . If you are a child of God, if you've been washed in his blood, the wheel will move. . . . You must work for humanity. . . .

Feeling religion is all right, but emotion must be transferred to action. Feeling should put you to work for humanity. . . . God wants active Christians.[2]

The above attitudes toward the Supernatural show changing conceptions of religion, and they reveal that attitudes and actions are tending to correspond.

The Transfer of Feeling from the Sermon to the Spiritual.—Speakers are gradually refraining from attempts to elicit emotional action. Some clergymen have remarkably altered their approach, while others are moderately adjusting themselves to changing religious attitudes by using both emotional and intellectual appeals. Yet others still deliver the old type of discourse, which audiences increasingly disparage. The expository sermon is taking the place of the emotional sermon in rural churches.

Although the dramatic after-life appeal is more prevalent during revivals than at other times, some revival audiences are unresponsive to the traditional type of sermon. A few persons in Church B sometimes respond, while at other times no one elicits emotional action. There is general unresponsiveness of Church C during revival regardless of the type of sermon. Absence of emotionalism is conspicuous in this church, only occasional exceptions being noted.

As emotionalism diminishes in rural churches, spirituals supply the warmth formerly generated by sermons. Spontaneity is expressed in the spiritual. Manifestation of emotion in singing of the spiritual is greater than overt audience reaction to the speaker's ideas. This is true partly because of disapproval of traditional forms of emotional action by various aged groups, especially young people, in the audience. Also, elderly emotional Christians are "dying out of the church," and some of the remaining elders are themselves intolerant of emo-

[1] Revival Sermon, The Reverend S. A. Funchess, Church C, August, 1947.
[2] Sermon, The Reverend S. A. Funchess, Church B, September, 1947.

tional action. Expressing emotion in song is less noticeable and objectionable than expressing it in extreme action. Emotional needs are conceived differently today.

A Comparison of Types of Responses According to Church.—Differences in spontaneous expressions of worshippers in various rural churches are noted. In classifying types of response, the following distinctions are made: (1) "Cold" response refers to general audience unresponsiveness, sometimes with an occasional mild "amen" to sanction the speaker's ideas. (2) "Warm" signifies exclamations, such as "Amen, yes, Lord" and "O, Lord, have mercy!" It also denotes movement of the hands and feet. Sometimes there is only one form of response. The manifestation of warm response in action is usually limited to singing of the spiritual. (3) "Hearty" denotes action in the form of shouting and rhythmic dancing. Sometimes "cold" is used synonymously with unemotional, or restrained. "Warm" may describe a semi-restrained audience. And "hearty" may be used to characterize emotional audiences.

The following table shows variations among rural churches. In noticing the table, take cognizance of special occasions, such as revival or Young Men's Christian Association Day, as influencing the type of response. Churches B and C are usually subdued in their religious expression.

Observe the similarity between the type of service at Churches B

TABLE SIXTEEN

Type of Audience Response

Name of Church	*Number of Services*	*Response*
Church A	4	warm
	1	hearty[1]
Church B	2	cold
	2	warm[2]
	1	hearty[1]
Church C	5	cold
Church D	5	warm
Miscellaneous	1	cold
Churches	2	warm

[1] On Y.M.C.A. day, persons of various denominations and churches conduct joint service. Some in the audience usually give overt expression to their religious sentiments. Therefore, some leaders in Church B oppose Y.M.C.A. meetings.

[2] Revival services.

and C; however, extreme manifestation of emotion is not general at any of the rural churches. Churches A and D are more expressive than Churches B and C. The two former churches sometimes manifest emotion in action as they sing the spiritual, which is more popular than at the latter two churches. Anthems and hymns are popular at Churches B and C, although spirituals are sung occasionally. There is general decadence of emotional action. Verbal and vocal expression of religious sentiments is the most common form of emotional manifestation in all of the rural churches studied. On special days, nevertheless, a few persons in the audience do manifest somewhat extreme actions; hence emotionalism does vary according to occasion and circumstance. The reservation of emotional action for special occasions or services verifies the trend from the overt manifestation of sentiments with respect to the Supernatural.

There is similarity of action in services at Churches A and D; also, the conditions under which the people live are comparable. In order to substantiate the relationship between type of religious expression and socio-economic conditions, concrete material on living standards will be presented at the conclusion of this section.

II. THE STATUS OF THE SPIRITUAL IN THE RURAL CHURCH

Disparagement of the Spiritual.—Some churchmen enjoy spirituals and express emotion by singing them in a submerged or restrained manner since extreme emotionalism is held in contempt, with the application of the normative system of rules. Expression of emotion in the spiritual (which is a native traditional expression of the religious aspirations of the Negro) is permitted, whereas manifestation of emotion with respect to the sermon has declined more rapidly. Toleration of emotionalism on certain occasions and in certain forms indicates a degree of accommodation in the action system, inasmuch as there is some resistance to the normative principle.

Traditional religious men who have not fully accepted the normative system of rules seek to manifest emotional action in a modified form at least. Being maladjusted to the progressive equilibrium, some traditional Christians seek to give overt expression to their emotions and nonempirical aspirations. Thus they form combinations consisting of those of similar interests in order to protect their individual and group integrities. Gospel choruses or choirs are permitted to sing during special programs at rural and urban churches. But since some of these spiritual singers dramatically manifest emotional action at times, they tend to be unfavorably received and are regarded with disgust by some persons in the system who seek a quiet form of worship. For example, at Church B some of the spiritual singers are submerged and restrained by some of the leaders of the church. An officer and some of his followers walked out of church during the gospel program; therefore these singers refrain from presenting performances at Church B, although they will appear at Churches A and D, where they are more cordially received. Some spiritual leaders, who find folk melodies spiritually stimulating, hesitate to sing and shout because some rural and urban members regard emotional persons with contempt. As a result of present tendencies, some class leaders who led spirituals ten years ago lead only hymns today. Because of the application of pressures against spiritual singers, some persons have refrained from singing this emotional type of song.

Nevertheless, some of the rural preachers seek to offset intolerance by giving recognition and encouragement to spiritual singers provided they are not extremely demonstrative. Being motivated by the system of norms, the tolerant type of leader believes that the choruses should be trained to sing in an appropriate manner and instructed in church decorum. This type of leader regards it improper to parade while singing and to pervert the natural beauty of spiritual songs by adding jazz elements.

Attitudes toward the spiritual vary according to type of person and church. Some churches sing the spiritual with appreciative gusto; for instance, the spiritual is popular at Churches A and D. The former church has a group of jubilee singers who are regarded with esteem. A rigid attitude of disparagement of the spiritual in the rural church is not general; this type of song represents the chief form of music in country churches. It is unnecessary to enumerate reasons for the prevalence of the spiritual in the country church. With respect to Negro churchmen, there are different attitudes toward the spiritual. Some persons are proud of this folk music; however, some in the favorably disposed group prefer a restrained, refined manner of singing spirituals. Some persons are not interested in this form of music and see no need for it today. Some informants believe that other ethnic groups are not interested in this type of music and do not understand or appreciate it; hence they refuse to sing the spiritual. Some impute attitudes of disdain of emotionalism to others. There are some who consider the integrity of the Negro damaged as a result of being regarded emotional; therefore they seek to repair group integrity by declining to manifest emotional action in any form. At any rate, it is obvious that the group is striving to conform its action to the normative system of rules; and there is diminution of all forms of emotionalism with changing religious attitudes and practices. The spiritual remains, but its declining status is reflected in disdain toward it, in the increasing frequency of hymns and anthems in the rural service, and in the trend to relegate the spiritual to the revival service, which has become unimportant. With the diminution of nonexperimental and emotional action in the religious system, there has been a decline in the popularity of the spiritual in the rural and the urban church.

Attitudes Toward the Folk Song with Respect to Education and Urbanization.—Ideas expressed in spirituals indicate a close relationship with the Supreme. Since there is subordination of nonexperimental and emotional action with the ascension of empirical ends, emphasis upon the sombre aspects of life and contemplation of a transcendental ideal where happiness is supreme with a cessation of earthly toil are not generally condoned in the action system. Thus there is disparagement of the spiritual as religious attitudes change. Those groups most critical of the spiritual tend to possess common attributes.

Educated Negroes generally have little or no interest in the spiritual. (However, some trained Negroes sing the spiritual for various reasons, such as publicity, financial remuneration, and emotional satisfaction.) The spiritual is mainly sung by those of modest status. In the rural and the urban church the spiritual is usually led by the same few persons, who have a fourth-grade education or less. Some persons in the audience join the leaders in a subdued manner, while others refrain from singing. College-trained churchmen and persons they influence tend to restrain spiritual leaders, since this traditional emotional song is not regarded as being appropriate to present interests of the collectivity. In those churches possessing a trained membership, in those churches where living conditions of members are not dire, in those churches in which there has been rapid transit to and communication with the city, the spiritual does not possess the vitality, force, and popularity that it does in churches with a lesser degree of these tendencies. The influence of education, economic and social circumstances upon the manifestation of sentiment in nonexperimental action is seen with respect to attitudes of Churches A and D toward the spiritual as compared with Churches B and C.

III. REVIVALS, CONVERSION, AND TESTIMONIALS

Lack of Interest in Revivals Today.—The changing status of ends is revealed in attitudes toward the service which seeks to transform the worldly man into a religious being conscious of the spiritual aspects of life. With modification of nonempirical attitudes, practices with respect to nonexperimental entities change. Thus there is a decline in nonexperimental and illogical action in the religious collectivity with the variation of attitudes toward the Supreme Being. Although there is some toleration of emotional action accompanying religious sentiments during revivals and prayer meetings, some audiences are intolerant of emotionalism under any circumstances and suppress demonstrative members on all occasions.

With the changing religion, there is a lack of interest and response in revivals. Church members fail to attend the services which introduce the convert to the sacred world. Some South Carolina clergy state that only twenty-five or thirty church members attend revivals, and some of these do so simply as a matter of custom. Furthermore, clergymen regard the revival successful if they are able to persuade four persons to pursue a Christian life. In the rural churches studied, only a few persons finally responded to conversion invitations after continuous entreaty by the evangelist over a period of a week at each church. There was general absence of spiritual warmth during revival services.

Changing Forms of Conversion.—The changing religion is reflected in men's attitudes toward the transcendental. With the subordination of nonexperimental aspects of religion, men's actions with regard to the Supernatural change. Sentiments of remorse and joy accompanying the process of supremacy of the higher self over the lower self are insignificant. The victory of the positive principle over the negative was at one time an occasion for the manifestation of gratitude to the Divine whose help and inspiration made possible or probable the pursuit of a Christian life and the final attainment of Heaven. Religious sentiments accompanying the introduction of the convert into the Christian society are not as voluble as in the past.

During the past, conversion signified restimulation of collective sentiments. The importance of spiritual transformation was indicated by a detailed process extending over a period of days. The aspirant walked through a dark wilderness and finally saw the light of day. He underwent a series of tests and interrogations before he was admitted to the body of spiritual élite. This form of conversion was gradually succeeded by a less exacting process which involved a prayerful attitude at the "mourner's bench." These ceremonies were designed to impress upon the aspirant the necessity of repentance and denial of sin in order to ascertain the state of grace. Conversion meant a supremacy of the good aspects of the individual over the evil. It denoted a departure from the secular world and absorption with the spiritual world. Conversion signified strengthening of the sentiments of group life through religion.

The crisis form of conversion was supplanted by a decision form, lysis.

Weakened solidarity is reflected in the variation and variety of conversion practices today. In some churches, candidates for conversion simply go to the altar to shake the minister's hand as evidence of their spiritual rebirth. In some churches, aspirants kneel at the altar during a prayer or a song. In other churches, converts are questioned regarding loyalty to the church as they are accepted as members; in this way, there is a combination of conversion and church membership. Some churches have no formal conversion. The religious community exemplifies little or no common interest in assumption of the sacred life by the unconverted, or the spiritual transformation of the converted.

Present attitudes toward the Supreme reflect the changing conceptions of religion. At one time, reliance upon the Creator was ardently, emotionally, and gratefully expressed in relation to the spiritual metamorphosis. But with the decline in a nonempirical religion, emotion accompanying religious sentiments or actions diminishes. As evidence of their conversion, rural converts did not undergo an emotional upheaval nor verbally declare their regeneration; they calmly shook the minister's hand as they stood at the altar. The decline in traditional religion is seen in the failure of church members to address the converts after the pastor of Church C had asked them to do so. Formerly, spiritual regeneration was an occasion for rejoicing as transmuters were gladly received into the fold.

In spite of the trend toward a decision form of conversion, a few churches in culturally retarded isolated sections retain the ritual form of conversion. Some clergymen in remote island sections of Beaufort, Colleton, and Charleston counties, South Carolina, seek to modify customary procedures by instruction and activity as they gradually ignore traditional conversion practices. Although some elders resist changes which tend to disrupt the equilibrium to which they are accustomed, youths more readily accept the new elements introduced in the action system.

Rural and urban leaders of the collectivity are instituting changes in conversion ceremonies. They seek to promote understanding rather than to appeal to emotion as aspirants or candidates for conversion are indoctrinated with respect to the values that accrue from Christian living. Clergymen explain the meaning of religion in terms of a changed attitude involving a personal decision of acceptance and acknowledgment of Christ through a change of living. At the same time, there is some alteration of attitudes regarding the trend from nonexperimental actions. Some ministers believe that there should be reinjection of spiritual elements. There should be confirmation of the role of the Deity in redemption from sin. Hence they seek to combine the practical approach with a conservative approach. One leader's attitude toward the unemotional trend and conversion is as follows:

> We need more feeling in religion today. . . . Although it is not desirable to submerge jubilance over acceptance by Christ, religion does not end with conversion. It is the responsibility of Christians to manifest catholic attitudes rather than selfish attitudes in terms of family, race, local and national groups alone. . . . An indomitable spirit of sacrifice is necessary. It is the responsibility of Christians to engage in foreign and local missionary work. . . . Churchmen must christianize, educate, and elevate mankind morally, economically, and socially. Religion must be active and practical.[1]

Although the Supernatural retains some significance for action, the importance of the empirical is seen in present conceptions of religion.

The Declining Testimonial.—Another action manifested with reference to the transcendental is the declaration by redeemed persons of the active influence of the Deity upon their conduct, the acknowledgment of the role of the Supreme in material, physical, and spiritual accomplishments, and the expression of an avowed purpose to continue to pursue a Christian life, which will lead to final supremacy of the higher principle in an eternal home. This statement of the power of God in the physical world was intermittently expected of Christians. It served to strengthen religious ties and solidarity by keeping religious values foremost in the minds of men. It inspired and aided the individual by vitalizing action in the pursuit of temporal ends.

With the decline of nonexperimental action in the Protestant collectivity, there is deterioration of this form of religious expression. Testimonials, which are seldom heard except during revival prayer meetings and New Year's Eve services, are further evidence of the diminishing strength of traditional religion. It has become increasingly difficult to attract communicants to this religious expression.

The unpopularity of the testimonial in the church is seen in these respects: It is a vanishing expression, relegated to a subordinate position. Most persons in the audience do not testify. In the past, Christians were so eager to attest the divine principle that three or four persons testified simultaneously. Today, only a few rural churchmen testify after being urged to do so. For the most part, only traditional Christians proclaim the influence of the Deity upon their lives. Young

[1] Sermon, Bishop Willis J. King, missionary, Trinity Methodist Church, Orangeburg, South Carolina, June 27, 1948.

people usually are not interested in this religious manifestation. Testimonials are of short duration; two-thirds of the testifiers in rural revivals limited their expression to one sentence. There has been a decrease in the frequency of spirituals between testimonials. Piano or organ music has been substituted for singing in some urban churches. The content of the testimonial has changed to the extent that fewer, less ardent references are made to the Supreme. Emotional action accompanying the statement of sentiments is infrequent.

Although some testifiers express themselves with feeling, the average testifier goes through a mechanical rendition, sometimes in response to the insistence of the leader of the prayer service. In past days, churchmen eagerly and fervently expressed their Christian living and a determination to attain Heaven, where there would be a solution to the problems of life. As a result of changing religious conceptions, there has been alteration of this customary procedure. Examination of present testimonials shows that many testifiers simply request the prayers of the audience; others state either a desire or an intention to attain the final triumph of good. Although religious men speak less frequently and less forcibly of their Christian living since many assume secular attitudes, some devout Christians affirm a close communion with the Divine, whose active presence ensures peace and harmony of action.

Ideas Expressed in Testimonials.—Even though nonexperimental ends of action are expressed by rural churchmen, there is a decline in the importance men attach to supersensory values. With the diminution of the grosser forms of supernaturalism, positive religious values are more significant than the negative, which emphasize the evil or dreary aspects of existence. A classification of ideas expressed in rural revival testimonials indicates that the largest number of testifiers, 39, simply asked the audience to pray that they would become stronger spiritually or morally. (Christians today are not as positive that they are living according to the Ten Commandments as Christians of the past.) Five persons serenely spoke of their adoration of and love for the Deity because of his daily presence, assistance, and inspiration. They were grateful for the peace and equanimity resulting from living according to the teachings of Jesus. For them, the charismatic norm is significant in action. Tremendous benefits result from a close relationship with the Supernatural. Five individuals expressed gratitude for God's love. Four persons said they were trying to apply Christianity in family and social relationships. Four persons remarked of God's salvation of their souls. Eleven Christians expressed a desire to attain Heaven. Seventeen churchmen indicated a *determi-*

nation to attain a celestial home, where there would be communion with the Almighty and reunion with deceased relatives. For the traditional Christians who testified, the nonexperimental aspects of existence influence nonempirical and empirical action in various respects. Some attitudes indicate a close relationship and absorption with the Divine, who is foremost in the thoughts and actions of the testifiers. Some attitudes reveal a dependence upon the Supreme, whose active presence produces striking results. Others reveal respect for the charismatic norm and an effort to regulate action according to it, in spite of deviation.

IV. MODIFICATION OF PRAYER

Present Attitudes Toward Prayer.—The decreasing significance of nonempirical aspects of existence is seen in attitudes toward prayer and practices with respect to the Divine. Although churchmen generally have some degree of faith in God and his intervention in human affairs, weakening confidence is indicated by the assumption of active instead of passive roles by the persons themselves. They tend not to delay action for God to accomplish the miraculous or to hasten the realization of empirical ends. This is expected inasmuch as value attitudes with respect to the Supernatural are in a process of modification.

The decline of prayer is seen in these respects: Prayer is less ceremonious than it was formerly. Prayer during the church service is brief and infrequent. Less reverent attitudes toward the Deity are manifested in frequent failure to kneel during the inner communion with God. Because of the apathy of Christians, many churches have either eliminated or contemplate eliminating prayer meetings and Sunday evening services. Although some persons assume neutral, indifferent, or mild attitudes toward prayer, some Christians speak assuredly of their knowledge that God answers prayer and cite experiences to affirm their belief in an anthropomorphic Deity.

Irrespective of diminishing fervency and reverence, traditional Christians reveal the inner self to the Maker, who has the power of redemption. Some souls in distress devoutly and pleadingly seek the salvation of the Almighty. And they are encouraged to pursue their daily activities because of a firm belief that God relieves them and provides some means of fulfilling experimental or nonexperimental ends. For the traditional religionist, spiritual benefits accrue from the Divine. The rural churchman addresses adorational, petitional, and anticipatory prayer to the Deity, who inspires him and adds meaning to life, which is sometimes amazing and baffling. Underprivileged or economically insecure communicants also tend to manifest a close relationship with the Director of the universe, upon whom they depend to bestow blessings of animation. The vitalizing principle is effective in action for the traditional religious man.

The Content of Prayers.—Concrete statement of the religious sentiments of traditional Christians is as follows. Aside from expressing gratitude to Christ and beseeching his blessings, the two ideas most commonly expressed in prayer are these: (1) dependence upon the Deity in trial and disappointment frequently related in terms of God as a "father to the fatherless" and a "shelter in storm and deep water," and (2) anticipation of Heaven, where the struggles of existence will subside in joyous eternal life.

Reliance upon Christ as a means of overcoming difficulty is expressed in requests for wisdom, understanding, and strength to endure hardship until "the battle of life has been fought" and Heaven is a reality. Aspirations are often expressed in a natural flowing force of language. In exuberant simplicity, the rural traditional churchman reveals his innermost feelings to God and does not refrain from using the eternal verities—right, soul, and salvation.

The following excerpts from prayers reveal the attitudes of conservative and traditional rural communicants. (Each paragraph represents a quotation from a different prayer.)

Expressions of Gratitude

We are grateful for the message of God and the privilege of hearing it. May it enter our hearts this morning.

We thank thee, O Lord, for thy teaching, for that is truth.

Beseeching Grace, Understanding, Guidance, Protection, and Strength

We pray for guidance, understanding and strength. In our distress, throw thy arms of protection around us. You told us to ask, and you would grant our needs. In the past, your mercy and protection have been ours. Lord, we know your protection is with us in the present.

Reliance upon the Deity

We don't know what to do, where to go. We're trusting in thee. This is a rugged road; help us through our trials. Throw thy strong arms of protection around us in our trouble. We're trusting in thee, Lord . . . My mother and father left me here by myself . . . Build me up. Lord, I'm weak. Where I'm weak, make me strong. . . . When I can't pray no more and am done with this world, take me into Heaven, Dear Lord, for Jesus' sake. Amen.[1]

[1] This fervent plea was made by a member of Church D.

Desires for Life Everlasting

Lord, when I'm done with the trouble of this world and the struggles of life will be no more, take my soul to the Throne of God.

When we come to the end of our journey and Heaven is within our reach, help us to put our trust in thee.

We are graveyard travelers. . . . We soon expect to die. . . . Some have already crossed beyond. . . . Jesus the name that calms our fears and bids our sorrows cease, Jesus the name that sets the prisoner free, Spirit of the Living God, I want to make Heaven my home when I die. . . . When the time comes we'll have no more prayer meetings and you can't hear my voice, raise my soul to Heaven, O Lord. Amen.

Although there is diminution of the supernatural in prayer, some rural churchmen continue to manifest a direct relationship with the Supreme. The nonexperimental phase of religion is especially significant for traditional rural Christians. Nevertheless, the content of prayer is changing and feeling with respect to the Omnipotent is far more restrained than formerly.

V. CHANGING RELIGIOUS PRACTICES, AND FACTORS IN THE DECAY OF TRADITIONAL RELIGION

The Trend from Emotional Action.—With the deterioration of nonexperimental beliefs, emotional action diminishes irrespective of the presence of nonexperimental elements of action. Sermons, spirituals, conversion, testimonials, and prayers show that there is diminution of the supernatural, although the rural churchman continues to express religious sentiments in terms of adoration of and dependence upon the Supreme Being, and anticipation of eternal life. It is true that there is manifestation of feeling with respect to nonempirical values. But with changing attitudes toward the transcendental, emotional action declines significantly.

South Carolina clergymen have observed a striking departure from emotional action in the religious collectivity. Twenty-four out of thirty ministers state that there has been a general decline of emotionalism in the Negro church over a period of years. Of the 24 leaders who attest the change, 5 have directed rural churches only; 18 have served at rural and urban churches, and one leader has ministered to urban churches only. Clergymen's observations cover a period of 10 to 50 years as ministers of the Gospel. (See page 139.)

These clergymen, who have had ample opportunity to observe religious changes in urban and rural communities, attribute the decline of emotionalism to various factors. Three leaders state that the recession of emotion is concomitant with the general religious decline. Seven ministers correlate the modification of action with an increase of education and with changing conceptions of the meaning of religion. Nine clergymen relate the change to a wider functional program of the church; emotions are directed into other activities. Five leaders attribute the decline to facility of travel and communication. Twenty-four ministerial informants relate the decrement of emotionalism with the decline of the church as a center of community life. At any rate, leaders believe that cultural and social change has hastened the decay of emotional action in the collectivity.

Period of Years	*Number of Clergymen*
10–14	3
15–19	6
20–24	3
25–29	3
30–34	4
35–40	5
41–50	6

In regard to the present status of emotionalism in the religious body, audiences are not inclined to manifest religious sentiments in emotional action, according to clerical informants. Communicants tend to express themselves in a restrained or semi-restrained manner.

TABLE SEVENTEEN

Emotional Responses in South Carolina Churches, According to Clergymen's Findings

Pastors	*None*	*Few*	*Many*
Rural	4	12	2
Urban	5	6	1

The above table shows that out of 30 churches, 9 are unemotional, 18 are semi-emotional, and 3 are emotional. It also indicates that rural churches tend to preserve traditional religious action to a greater extent than urban as change rapidly proceeds in all areas. And it reveals the presence of the three types of churches in the rural environment. There is increasing subordination of emotional elements in the religious system.

With respect to the manifestation of religious sentiments in nonexperimental and emotional action, there is diversity in both the rural and the urban church. Religious action tends to correspond with certain features of existence. Even though there is diminution of supersensory values, a degree of relationship exists between type of religion and educational and economic attainment.

There is not a great difference in the religious beliefs and actions of rural worshippers; extreme emotional action is not characteristic of rural churchmen. Although there is general submergence of feeling, the degree of restraint varies with the conditions under which church members live. In spite of warmth in Churches A and D, members tend to express themselves in a semi-restrained manner. However, constraint is not a significant feature of action in these churches. Irrespective of the manifestation of feeling on certain occasions, Church B usually has a serene type of service. This church tends to follow the pattern of service at Church C, while Churches A and D conduct similar services. Churches B and C tend to be intolerant of emotional action.

Communication and Residence as Factors in Change.—In the system of action, contact and communication promote change, whereas physical and cultural isolation retards the progression of action in harmony with the norm. The infiltration of urban ideas in the rural environment has an influence upon religious worship.[1]

The rural churchman's communication with the city influences his attitudes. He absorbs the attitudes of the urban inhabitant; hence his religious actions tend to acquire the character of those of the urban churchman. Through sensory perception, the rural churchman is stimulated to act according to urban norms. Through newspapers, magazines, and radios, he becomes acquainted with urban ideas and occurrences. Visual and auditory perception precipitates change in rural attitudes. Cultural contact is seen in respect to the extent of rural travel and communication. Table Eighteen reveals the acquaintance of the rural inhabitant with city patterns of action.

Rural informants are in contact with the city in various respects. Out of 38 laymen, 30 subscribe to newspapers, 18 read magazines, 24 have access to radios, 11 have resided in metropolitan areas, 25 have relatives living in large cities, and 16 have children who were in the armed forces during World War II. Through communication and mobility, the rural worshipper becomes familiar with city attitudes

[1] The converse of this is true also. The penetration of the rural churchman in the urban milieu signifies the transferral of rural patterns of action to the city. Nevertheless, there tends to be modification of practices of migrants partly as a result of constraint in the action system. Through request, ignorement, or excommunication, the demonstrative newcomer is suppressed. As a result of the application of sanctions, the traditional type (in spite of some resistance) tends gradually to conform to the system of normative rules. The process of change and adjustment to it is a feature of action in southern and northern urban churches.

and hence acquires some of the characteristics of urban men. Although the travel of 13 informants has been restricted to southern cities, 13 have visited cities from Maryland to Massachusetts. Twenty-five informants have relatives who have resided in various cities of the Middle Atlantic States from a period of three to eighteen years. Furthermore, interchange of ideas and adoption of new attitudes were hastened as a result of the travel and experiences of children in and outside of the United States during the recent war. Becoming acquainted (through direct or indirect contact) with various attitudes and practices in a heterogeneous environment influences the religious beliefs and actions of the rural churchman.

TABLE EIGHTEEN

Communication and Travel of Rural Informants

	Audio-visual Communication		
	Newspapers	*Magazines*	*Radio*
Church A	9	4	5
Church B	10	7	9
Church C	11	7	10

	Travel			*Migration*	
	Local[1]	*Neighboring States*	*Distant States*[2]	*Residence in Metropolitan Areas*	*Relatives Residing in Metropolitan Areas*
Church A	0	2	2	3	6
Church B	1	5	5	4	9
Church C	4	1	6	4	10

[1] Visited various cities of South Carolina.
[2] Travelled beyond Washington, D. C.

Communication is a factor in change. The rural churchman who migrates and associates with city inhabitants tends to assimilate and acquire urban attitudes; thus religious action tends to conform with city standards. The relationship is seen in this respect: Churches B and C, whose members visit and reside in the city to a greater extent than those of Church A, are unemotional. The residence of members of the rural churches intensively studied is as follows: Thirty-five per cent of the members of Church C live in Orangeburg, South Carolina; 15 per cent of the members of Church B live there, while only 2 per cent of the members of Churches A and D live there. Sundays on which services are not conducted at the rural churches to which these city residents belong, these rural church members worship in Orangeburg churches, where emotionalism is rapidly diminishing because of the application of sanctions against emotional members.[1]

As communication facilitates transfer of ideas, isolation hampers the inculcation of action according to certain standards. Those churches located in remote areas tend to preserve the static equilibrium to a greater extent than the rural churches to which specific reference was made. Thus actions of members of isolated churches do not rapidly progress in harmony with the normative principle.[2] Culturally retarded groups, which tend to preserve traditional religion, react slowly to change. Therefore, there are some emotional rural churches. Rural island churches in the vicinity of Walterboro and Charleston, South Carolina, tend to maintain the customary form of religious worship. Semi-rural churches in this vicinity, which communicate more extensively with outside areas, depart more rapidly from the old religion than remote churches. Correspondingly, town and city churches of this area manifest a greater variety of attitudes than semi-rural churches, which have fewer means of communication with other sections and which have inadequate educational facilities.

Irrespective of isolation, distance, and educational retardation, churches in remote areas are slowly responding to the normative system of rules.

The Relationship Between Type of Religious Action and Socio-Economic Status.—In the system of action, nonexperimental attitudes and practices are longest retained by those whose situation is in

[1] Some of the formerly rural inhabitants, who might be described as semi-urban men, prefer to retain their rural membership partly because of a desire to continue an association with rural friends and relatives and partly because of desires for recognition. The force of traditionalism is seen in a desire to remain in "the home church." Furthermore, the rural service is in some ways more satisfying than the urban service. The transplanted rural churchman identifies himself with the rural and the urban church as his religious attitudes and actions are in a process of modification. Correspondingly, competition and conflict exist between the urban and the rural clergyman and church since the city preacher seeks to induce the worshippers to join his church, while the rural minister attempts to maintain a grasp upon them. Rivalry exists between churches of the same denomination and it also occurs among various denominations. Some of the rural members who join the urban church seek a denomination in the established church other than their own because of the superior attitudes of the professional and business groups who comprise the membership of the Methodist church and because of pressures against emotional persons.

Regardless of a desire to captivate migrants, established urban churches are not especially interested in extremely emotional persons, who are discouraged or omitted; hence those who manifest religious sentiments in an exaggerated manner are more favorably received in Holiness churches, which provide satisfactory emotional expression.

[2] This is the reason some South Carolina clergymen stated the impracticability of total suppression of emotional action.

some respects analogous to that during the stable form of equilibrium. Uneducated, economically insecure groups respond somewhat slowly to change as the collectivity is motivated by the system of norms. Thus nonempirical ends are important as the collectivity seeks empirical values. There is a decline in the manifestation of religious emotion in extreme action with progression from one economic status to another.

A comparison of living standards of rural churchmen indicates the significance of nonexperimental beliefs in action according to socio-economic status. A census of rural churches shows differences in occupation, earning capacity, and educational attainment of members of Churches A-D. The position of members of Churches A and D is less favorable than that of members of Churches B and C. Recall that transcendental value attitudes are more outstanding in action in the former two churches than in the latter. Although none of these churches are inclined to manifest extreme emotional action, Churches B and C are assiduous in their disparagement of emotionalism. In Churches B and C, the presence of some members who attach considerable importance to the pursuit of ends according to the normative standard limits and retards the action of a few traditional religionists, who wish to give overt expression to their religious emotions. Note the following table.

TABLE NINETEEN

Occupation of Rural Laymen, According to Church

	Type of Farming				*Other Occupations*	
	Day Laborers	*Share-croppers*	*Farm Renters*	*Farm Owners*	*Teachers*	*Business Men*
Church A	6	11	5	0	0	0
Church D	3	7	0	0	0	0
Church B	4	3	1	8	5	0
Church C	5	7	2	4	4	3

The occupational status of members of rural churches varies. The position of insecure dependence of members of Church A is reflected in the fact that none of the members own land. Out of 22 adult heads of families in this church, 11 are sharecroppers. All of the farmers in Church D are sharecroppers. Out of 14 adults in this church, 4 are unemployed. Farmers in Churches A and D are tenants. There are more sharecroppers, day laborers, and unemployed persons in the communities of Churches A and D than in the communities of Churches B and C. Although there are no farm owners nor professional and business men in the former churches, there are some in the latter. Out of 21 heads of families in Church B, 8 are farm owners, while only 4 farmers are landless. The membership of Church C is somewhat diversified. Out of 25 adult heads of families in this church, 4 own farms, 3 operate businesses, and 4 teach school.[1]

In Churches A and D, members' incomes are substantially lower than incomes of members in the other two churches as the following table shows.

Table Twenty shows that more than half of the heads of families in Churches A and D earned less than $150 in 1944. Three sharecroppers in Church A earned nothing but were said to be in debt when the year ended. Only two members of this church earned not less than $600. In Church B, two-thirds of the heads of families earned not less than $400, which more than doubled the income of more than half of the members in Churches A and D. More than half of the members in Church C earned not less than $400; one farm owner earned $5,000.

In 1945, ten out of 22 members of Church A were earning not more than $100; only three were earning more than $500. Six out of 10 in Church D had incomes not exceeding $300, while 12 out of 21 in Church B received not less than $600, which was the highest income of any member in Church D. Two members in Church B were earning not less than $2,000. Twelve out of 25 heads of families in Church C were earning not less than $600, while only one member in Church A had an equivalent income. One farm owner in Church C was earning $2,100 and another was earning $5,700.

In 1946, fifteen out of 22 heads of families in Church A earned not more than $300; seven of this number earned not more than $100. Only four of this group earned not less than $500. In Church D, five out of 10 members earned not more than $300, while there were only 2 out of 21 in Church B who earned not more than this. Thirteen out of 21 in Church B earned not less than $800; only two out of 22 members in Church A earned the equivalent. In Church B, two farm owners earned $2,200; one earned $3,000. In Church C, fifteen out of 25 earned not less than $500, while only 4 out of 22 in Church A had this income. Six members of Church C earned not less than $1,000; no member of Church A reached this income. One farm owner in Church C earned $2,400; another had an income of $6,100, which exceeded the total income of members of Church D.

[1] Rural clergymen indicate a tremendous influence of school teachers upon religious action; educated persons, who manifest little interest in traditional religion, quench the spirit or warmth of the service by ridiculing demonstrative persons.

TABLE TWENTY

Annual Income of Members of Churches A–D for the Years 1944–1946

1944	Less than $50	$50 to $100	$100 to $150	$150 to $200	$200 to $300	$300 to $400	$400 to $500	$500 to $600	$600 to $800	$800 to $1000	$1000 to $1500	$1500 to $2000	$2000 to $2500	$2500 to $3000	More than $3000
Church A	3	6	7	1	2		1	2							
Church D	1	2	3				4								
Church B	1	4			1	1	4	4	2	1	1	2			
Church C		2	4	2	1	3	3	3	4	1		1			1
1945															
Church A	3	7	2	4	2	1		2	1						
Church D		2	1	2	1			2	2						
Church B		1		4			2	2	4	5		1	2		
Church C		1	2	1	3	1	3	2	5	3	2		1		1
1946															
Church A		7	2	2	4	3		1	1	2					
Church D				3	2	1			1	1	2				
Church B				1	1		3	2	1	6	4		2	1	
Church C		1	2	1	3		3	2	6	1	3	1	1		1

The above figures reveal wide differences in the economic levels of the members of the four churches on a comparative basis. There is no general diversity in the economic status of members of Churches A and D. The table on income reveals that almost all of the members are of the same economic level. There is wider variation in Churches B and C.

Differences in income are reflected in living standards. Although most rural homes have no screens, running water, and electric lights, the members of Churches B and C have more of these facilities and live in more substantial, attractive houses than the members of Churches A and D. The number of rural members who have facilities in their homes is as follows:

	Running Water	*Indoor Toilet*	*Electric Lights*	*Screens*
Church A	0	0	2	2
Church D	0	0	0	0
Church B	3	3	7	6
Church C	5	4	8	7

Differences in occupation and income correspond with differences in educational attainment. In Church A, there are no college graduates. There is one college student, and there are two high school students. Most churchmen in this community do not have an elementary education. The members of Church D have had little formal education. Few members have attended high school, and none have had advantages of higher education. In Church B, there are several high school students and eighteen college graduates. Many members have had high school training. In Church C, there are twenty-five college graduates and several college students. Table Twenty-One, which includes only persons who were in church the Sunday the census was taken, reveals educational differences among adult members of the rural churches.

The factors of education and income are significant in religious action. There tends to be repression of nonexperimental and emotional action in churches which have trained members whose economic circumstances are fair or adequate. South Carolina clergymen indicate the importance of these factors in religious action. Those churches which longest manifest emotional action have uneducated members who live under adverse circumstances.

Survivals of Magical Ritual.—Magical ritual is subsidiary today; fragmentary magical practices survive in connection with obsequies. By a process of faulty reasoning, illogical connections between means and ends are established. Thus some persons employ magical means to realize empirical ends. Believing that they can obtain certain objectives by appealing to nonempirical forces, some illiterate people seek to appease or dispel evil spirits by performing certain acts at funeral ceremonies. Being motivated by fear, these persons pass a baby over the grave of the departed in order to prevent the spirit of the deceased from returning to claim the living. A few persons, whose empirical knowledge is scant, have not visualized the effects of science in combating disease; hence the utensils (spoon, plate, medicine bottle, etc.) of the dead are buried with the body to prevent the spread of disease in the community.

TABLE TWENTY-ONE

Education of Rural Churchmen

	Elementary and High School					*College*			
	Less than 3 grades	*3–5*	*6–7*	*8–9*	*10–12*	*1 yr.*	*2 yrs.*	*3 yrs.*	*4 yrs.*
Church A	1	13	4	4	0	0	0	0	0
Church D	5	8	1	0	0	0	0	0	0
Church B	0	3	4	5	2	0	0	3	4
Church C	0	6	8	3	1	0	2	3	2

The persons who occasionally manifest this form of behavior (and less objectionable forms, such as display at funerals) are severely reprimanded by ministers for whom the normative principle is significant. Even though persons who manifest archaic actions resist change, they tend gradually to modify their action in concurrence with the logical principle in spite of previous refractoriness.

Magical ritual, as well as other manifestations associated with "the old religion," survives longest in areas of educational retardation and poverty. In spite of the presence of illogical elements in the religious system, there is rapid diminution of traditional religious practices among various socio-economic groups.

CHAPTER XI

The Status of Emotionalism in Rural and Urban Areas (*Continued*)

The Manifestation of Sentiment in Nonexperimental and Emotional Action in Boston

Practices in Boston Churches

I. THE INFUSION OF RURAL RELIGION

Interaction of Rural and Urban Attitudes.—There is modification of religion with migration. Infiltration affects religious action. Migration involves a reciprocal process of action. The stationary resident is influenced by the beliefs of the transient or the migrant who establishes permanent residence in a new locality. Differences in attitudes diminish. As the southerner migrated to the North, rural attitudes were taken to the urban environment, and hence there was interaction of rural and urban religious attitudes. In spite of interaction of relatively contrasting beliefs, one type of resident exerts tremendous power over the other, so that the influence of the established resident tends to counteract and overbalance that of the new resident.

At first, the process of change is slow. In a young area, which depends to a great extent upon the rural area for population, the incoming resident establishes his practices in the new environment; therefore traditional patterns of action are fortified. Customary religious beliefs and practices continue over the years. After a long span of years, conservative religion gradually changes. With age of the city and continued urban expansion, the established religion progressively diminishes.

Eventually rural religious beliefs become ineffectual in the established urban system. With the inefficiency of rural attitudes in the urban church, persons who retain former religious attitudes find their action restricted by the prevalence of empirical-minded Christians in the religious system. With the conflict of attitudes and the retardation of nonexperimental action, the position of the traditional Christian in the religious system is challenged.

This is followed by a process of withdrawal resulting from disharmony of attitudes. Distance between types may be manifested in isolation of traditional men in two ways. First, the person responding slowly to urbanization and change remains in the system in a weak position. Second, those retaining decaying rural beliefs are ejected. Later, there tends to be affinity of opposing views as reintegration proceeds in the religious system.

The preponderance of former southerners in the northern church indicates the extent of the infusion of attitudes of migrants. Churches were erected for Negroes after they had gone north in large numbers. And today most Negroes worship in Negro churches, although a small proportion of Negroes has remained in urban churches which are conducted by white men. Most Boston Negro churches consist of southerners and their descendants.[1] Although there are some persons who were born in the North in these churches, northern attitudes have been influenced by those of southern ancestors. (Nevertheless, the process of mutuality does not nullify all differences between southern and northern churches. At the same time, the extent of change in all areas must not be disregarded; and differences between rural and urban religion in the South should be considered.)

Negro churches in Boston are of southern origin. Many southern clergymen have organized churches in the North. Of the ten Boston pastors with whom interviews were conducted, 6 are of the South; 2 are of the South via the Midwest, and 2 are from the West Indies. The membership of 8 out of 10 churches consists mainly of southern migrants.

Even though traditional religion was significant to migrants who entered the North, there has been a striking change from transcendental religion. The decline of emotionalism among Negro Protestants is observable in types of urban churches. Restrained churches have become ascendant. Out of 15 Boston churches, 8 are restrained; 2 are semi-restrained; and 5 are emotional.

Table Twenty-Two, according to denomination, is included to show that the various Methodist denominations and the Baptist church have within their jurisdiction the three types of church. For

[1] This statement applies to American Negroes. There are many West Indians in the Episcopal church. Although they usually have their churches, some of them worship in mixed racial audiences. Even though most persons of the West Indies and their descendants are Episcopalians, a few are scattered in various Protestant denominations; a small number of the popular Protestant churches in Boston have a large proportion of West Indians.

instance, of the churches observed, Baptists have 2 emotional, 2 semi-serene, and 2 serene churches.

In the city, churches are established for heterogeneous groups in order that there will be some fulfillment of the manifold ends of religious men. There are various types of churches to satisfy diverse Christians in the religious system. The influence of the urban environment upon religious action is seen in the increasing strength of empirical religious action as nonexperimental action diminishes. The role of leaders is remarkable in directing the nature of religious action as change proceeds in the Protestant system. Further empirical substantiation of the conspicuous function of types of leaders in the collectivity is presented in the following pages.

TABLE TWENTY-TWO

Type of Worship in Boston Churches

Denomination	*Emotional*	*Semi-Restrained*	*Restrained*
Methodist	0	0	1
A.M.E.	2	0	1
A.M.E.Z.	0	0	1
Baptist	2	2	2
Congregational	0	0	1
Episcopal	0	0	2
Holiness	1	0	0

II. THE NATURE OF URBAN SERMONS

Clergymen's Attitudes Toward Sermons and Nonexperimental Action.—Urban clergy believe that sermons should carry a message which will aid members to grow spiritually, morally, and socially. They believe that members should be led to pursue a religion which has significance in the realization of empirical objectives. Members should seek to adopt and practice Christian virtues which promote character development. They should be acquainted with and made conscious of opportunities for Christian service. They should be told that obligation accompanies opportunity. "Privilege carries with it obligation and responsibility, responsibility for soul-saving, responsibility for the spiritual enlightenment of the world, and responsibility for the coming of the Kingdom of God on earth."[1]

Religion is a dynamic, progressive process. Religion is action; the belief without its manifestation in action is futile. Church members

[1] Interview, The Reverend William H. Hester, Boston, Massachusetts, July 9, 1947.

should be directed to accept and pursue the Christian ideal, which forms the basis of successful group living.

Although the teachings of God in relation to empirical action should be reiterated in sermons, there should be no emphasis upon a future nonempirical world. "A theoretical hope and a mystical God without any action is futile. . . . Faith with action is essential."[1] Thus urban clergy seek to appeal to intelligence rather than emotion as they direct churchmen to a supremacy of the ideal in the experimental realm.

The Decline of the Transcendental in Urban Sermons.—Although some phases of the Supernatural remain important in urban sermons, religion is regarded as a norm for harmonious group life. Practical aspects of religion are emphasized; the churchman is urged to pursue action according to divine ordinance. Some references are made to sin and the departure of the world from the sacred norm. However, positive features of action are significant. Most speakers make no reference to attainment of a nonempirical ideal; the other-worldly aspects of religion are ignored. Religion is regarded as a means of supremacy of the superior principle over the inferior in this life. Religion is conceived as life.

Clerical leaders are not especially anticipatory of a future life; they consider empirical ends important. While delivering thirty-five sermons, nine out of ten speakers made no reference (except in a disparaging manner) to motivation of action in terms of a nonempirical Heaven or Hell. Pastor Two referred to attainment of Heaven, but not avoidance of Hell. Clergymen believe that redemption of the world depends upon the manifestation of charity in living; consequently they do not seek to motivate audiences with respect to nonexperimental elements of reward and punishment.

Types of Sermons Delivered.—Considering the significance of empirical religious action for urban clergymen, it is not surprising that sermons are of a practical nature. Out of 35 urban sermons, 4 are religious; 20 are of the practico-religious type, and 11 are practical.[2] Urban clergymen rely almost exclusively upon the intellectual appeal in their sermons. Sermons are of an expository-persuasive type, which appeals to logic and sentiment but not emotional action. Speakers used the following approaches in their sermons. Ministers made chief use of the emotional appeal in 2 sermons, the intellectual in 20, and there was a combined emotional and intellectual appeal in 13 sermons.

Compare the types of sermons and audience reaction to sermons

[1] Interview, The Reverend Oddous R. Barber, Boston, Massachusetts, January 11, 1947.

[2] For an explanation of types of sermons, see pages 121–122.

and songs in churches type one, two, and three—restrained, semi-restrained, and emotional churches respectively.

Table Twenty-Three indicates the insignificance of nonexperimental and emotional action in the urban church. Sermons have empirical value for churchmen as there is subordination of nonexperimental action.

TABLE TWENTY-THREE

Types of Sermons and Responses in Boston Churches

	Types of Sermons Delivered			*Audience Response to Sermons and Songs**		
Name of Church or Denomination	*Religious*	*Practico-Religious*	*Practical*	*Cold*	*Warm*	*Hearty*
Church of Christ	1	0	0	0	1	0
African Methodist Episcopal	0	2	0	2	0	0
Methodist	0	5	0	5	0	0
Baptist	1	1	0	2	0	0
Baptist	0	2	2	4	0	0
Episcopal	0	0	1	1	0	0
Episcopal	0	0	1	1	0	0
Church One	1	1	3	5	0	0
Church Two	1	6	0	0	6	1**
Church Three	0	3	4	0	3	4

* In churches in which there was overt manifestation of religious sentiments, emotion was expressed mainly during songs; feeling was generally restrained during sermons.

** Revival service.

With urbanization, there is decrement of transcendental religious action. In spite of the regression of the Supernatural in rural sermons, rural clergy retain nonempirical values in their sermons to a greater extent than urban. Recall that the expository religious sermon remains important in the rural church, and references to the Deity as a means of offsetting and overcoming calamities of life are made intermittently as speakers abandon the emotional appeal for the intellectual.

The intellectual appeal is more frequently used in urban sermons than rural. The comparative importance of empirical religion in the rural and the urban church is seen in the frequency of sermons which carry an instructive message with direct application to life. Out of 48 Boston and South Carolina sermons, 12 are religious; 23 are of the practico-religious type, and 13 are practical.

TYPES OF SERMONS

	Religious	*Practico-Religious*	*Practical*
Rural	8	3	2
Urban	4	20	11

Eight of the 13 rural sermons are religious, while only 4 out of 35 urban sermons are of this type. Recall that rural audiences prefer religious sermons, while urban audiences are interested in a message which pertains immediately to life. Increasingly in the rural and the urban church religious men are considering it essential that religion relate to present situations. Diminution of the transcendental in the religious body is apparent in the type of sermon which is attractive.

The Content of Urban Sermons.—Ideas expressed in urban sermons show the significance of religious action of an experimental nature. The social aspect of religion is essentially considered. Observe the basic ideas expressed in urban sermons.

Urban sermons make some reference to the Divine, and they include accounts of historical and current developments from a Biblical point of view. These sermons refer to the importance of religion as a solution to present social problems and they emphasize the necessity of the application of the doctrine of Christianity as a means of combating individual and social catastrophe. They show the necessity of the assumption of attitudes of faith, patience, perseverance, and courage in withstanding various life situations. Christ is idealized as a norm for action; thus persistence, optimism, and unselfishness are essential to the individual. Action should be regulated according to the Golden Rule in order to realize the Kingdom of God on earth.

With the decline of religion, men have turned from God and have relied upon education, social agencies, and government to promote community welfare. Family disintegration, crime, and war are indicative of the maladjustment in society. Because of the failure of education to solve social problems, men must return to the principles of God as an ideal. Peace will be maintained only through Christ, who is the salvation of the world. It is necessary to apply Christianity in local, national, and international relationships. Social institutions will be effective only with the inculcation of the Christian doctrine, which will triumph eventually.

Religion means service of an individual and a social nature. It means aiding the underprivileged and the laborer through recreation and legislation. It means promoting the welfare of the masses by alleviating the situations under which they live. The Christian must be active. At the same time, he must be conscious of religious values.

Attitudes of Pastor One Toward Sermons and Nonexperimental

Action.—According to Pastor One, ministers should try to convey to their congregations the consciousness of a loving God instead of a vindictive, tyrannical one. Members should be taught to render personal and collective service to fellowmen; the spirit of unselfishness should be exemplified in living.

Ministers must preach a social doctrine which emphasizes realization of the Kingdom of God in *this* world. Preaching should not motivate escape and eternal salvation; sermons should encourage and foster cleanliness, creativeness, peaceful primary and secondary relationships; churchmen should be encouraged to act to promote harmonious family, racial, and social relations. A social order which ensures recognition and respect for the rights of others, development of the individual, and participation in democratic group life is of essential importance. Intelligent people are not interested in non-experimental salvation and damnation; they rebel against a type of religion which is not related to life. An intelligent man wants satisfaction in this world; he wants heaven here. . . . Because I do not preach a transcendental sermon, some clergymen question my religion. Just preaching does not amount to anything; the preacher should help the people. I seek and help people who need clothes, medical care, and legal aid. Our church helps to correct incorrigible boys; it provides trained social workers, and it employs nine full-time workers and six part-time workers. Religion must be of active benefit to the community. . . . The otherworldly sermon is of no practical benefit; it does not lead to a fuller understanding and appreciation of life. . . ."[1]

In sermons, this leader advises his congregation to "live in the world and participate in its activities." He urges against emotional action in the Protestant collectivity. The basic ideas expressed in the sermons of Clergyman One are as follows:

Although education and the pursuit of knowledge are commendable, educated persons should not withdraw from the masses and the church. Most educated persons take no interest in religious work. . . . This church offers facilities for all persons to function. . . . Higher educated groups should actively identify themselves with the church and seek the direction of religion to life.

There should be realization of the brotherhood of man on earth. Understanding and cooperation are promoted through contact with various classes and races.

Religion will alleviate individual and social ills.

The Origin of Members of Church One.—Some laymen withdraw from churches the rules or services of which have become distasteful to them as religious conceptions are altered. Orthodox Protestants

[1] Interview, The Reverend Samuel L. Laviscount, Boston, Massachusetts, February, 1947.

sometimes seek a liberal church, which does not emphasize doctrine and conformity. (For example, some lay informants joined the denomination of Church One because of its liberal attitude toward pastimes.) Church One does not emphasize traditional religion. Individual freedom is permitted, and members' diversions are not restricted. Dancing, cards, and recreational games are permitted in the community center, which serves as a meeting place for educational groups and clubs, and which houses a nursery school sponsored by the church. Certain fundamentals of the Bible are ignored. This church does not emphasize conversion and church membership; members of the Trustee Board are not required to hold their membership in Church One. This church serves the community, its communicants, and constituents of other churches.

Because of the subordination of nonexperimental action, the absence of emotional action, and the prevalence of empirical action, this type of church attracts communicants who are greatly motivated by the normative principle. Hence its membership mainly comprises persons who were formerly of orthodox Protestant denominations. About 50 out of 450 persons are descendants of Congregationalists. Furthermore, almost all of the members are migrants. Although a few members were born in the North, the vast majority were born in the southern section of the United States. About a dozen members are of Canada; a few are of Africa, and a few originally came from the West Indies. Southern migrants who were formerly members of Methodist and Baptist churches mainly constitute the membership of Church One. As rationality increases with the decrement of traditional religion in the Protestant collectivity, certain types of religious men seek churches which disparage emotionalism. With religious changes, churches emerge according to type; thus arises the empirical church, of which Church One is an illustration.

Pastor Two's Attitudes Toward Sermons and Nonexperimental Action.—Pastor Two believes that religion should be related to life.

Clergymen should impart the tenets of Jesus to their congregations so that churchmen will live Christianity as Christ taught it. The principles of religion as Jesus gave them are capable of promoting peaceful personal and social relationships. Life will be adequate in every way if people understand and practice the teachings of Jesus. . . . If religion is interpreted correctly, it will include every phase of life. Although people have misconceived religion so that it does not adequately meet present needs, religion should be practical and social. A religious man is a practical person. Education, business, and industry are related to religion; but people have divorced religion from life. . . . Jesus' teachings suggest that anything which makes one more qualified to serve is acceptable; however, the really religious must be the dominating influence. Participation in the secular world must not retard religious enthusiasm. Inculcation of the spirit of religion would revitalize the world.[1]

Although the attitude of Clergyman Two indicates the decrement of traditional religious conceptions as seen in the belief that there should be fulfillment of the religious principle in all spheres of action, nonexperimental manifestations are not disregarded. Though leaning toward a liberal conception of religion, this leader believes that the authority of the Deity should be accepted. His interpretation of religion is more literal and conservative than that of pastors type one and three.

The mediating influence of pastor type two in the action system has been designated. This type tends to reconcile conflicting attitudes of laymen. And the conservative type of leader tends to harmonize the diametrical positions of empirical and traditional leaders. Though motivated by the normative standard, Pastor Two believes that abrupt departure from traditional religion is not consistent with the real interest of the collectivity. Neither is it expedient to inaugurate drastic changes which ignore the religious ends of traditional Christians. Pastor Two partially conforms to the normative standard in conducting his church service. He is not opposed to spontaneous expression of religious sentiments if it results from communion of worship as the individual is aware of the presence of God. "Emotion which comes from within as a result of religious meditation is acceptable; but emotion created or generated for the sake of demonstration is totally unacceptable."

The undesirability of permitting some groups to stifle completely the religious expression of traditional Christians is expressed by several clergymen who realize that "old religionists" are active in church clubs; and they give more moral and financial support to the full program of the church than moderate and empirical laymen. That is the reason Pastor Two permits the gospel choir, which is opposed by the majority of the members who prefer a serene type of music from the regular choir, to sing during some of the Sunday services.[2] Although

1 Interview, The Reverend Richard M. Owens, Boston, Massachusetts, January 14, 1947.

2 Those clergymen who seek to change traditional religious worship and to organize their churches to operate efficiently do not offer leading positions, such as pastoral assistants and officers, to emotional persons who are considered unqualified. Pastor Two, who seeks to conduct his church efficiently, does not offer positions to "uncapable persons, who are more eager to serve than reluctant capable persons." In order to secure recognition, some members seek a church which satisfies their aspirations.

Persons of subordinate position or of substandard ability are given opportunities to lead in churches which emphasize sanctification.

some of the other Baptist clergymen, who tend to adhere more precisely to the selective standard, permit gospel choruses to sing one or two selections before or after the sermon, Pastor Two accords them more recognition than other conservative, or empirical, churches. Furthermore, unsatisfied members of established Protestant churches were so rapidly entering the Christian fellowship of Church Three that some of the pastors had to alter their course of action by retaining spiritual warmth in their services. Thus it was regarded advisable to make a few minor concessions to traditionalists because of the competition with clerical leaders of expelled Protestants. Realizing that the established Protestant church was being weakened as a result of the application of the unemotional norm in the religious body, some clergymen sought not only to alter their actions in spite of objection from the membership of the church, but they sought to forbid their members to participate in Holiness churches. It was decreed incompatible with the rules of the church to commute and to hold positions in the home church and another church at the same time. Furthermore, restraint was applied in this manner: Remaining members of established popular Protestant churches interrupted some performances (speaking the unknown language and giving testimonials) of those who were transferring religious patterns from one church to another. Considering themselves misunderstood and being embarrassed, some persons who were worshipping in the contrasting types of churches finally discontinued their relationship with the established church after being ridiculed by Baptists and Methodists who disapproved of eccentric religious manifestations. Those who returned were restrained.[1] The general result of the edict and restriction was either submission or withdrawal. However, some remaining unsatisfied traditionalists defy attitudes by worshipping in two different types of denominations at the same time. Furthermore, denominations whose position has been weakened cannot authoritatively control the action of churchmen. If rules are rigidly applied without concession, the remaining position of quantitative membership predominance may be threatened. (In other words, a course of rigid conformity may be impractical for Baptist and Methodist churches, which still possess the largest Negro membership in the United States.) In addition, attitudes of moderation or acceptance indicate

[1] Considerable animosity and antagonism arose over the following which emotional churches were attracting. So strong was the influence of the Director in the action system that a pastor of one of the large Boston churches became attracted to the new religion, responded to evangelistic appeals, and worshipped with the adherents of the new faith. Protestant leaders strongly reprimanded the "commuting" minister, since they considered his manifestations an undesirable influence upon members who were leaving the Protestant church; therefore, the minister ceased communing in the new church.

the tendency of conflicting interests to harmonize in later stages of progressive rationality in the system of action.[1]

Pastors make use of various techniques in order to provide a degree of satisfaction to remaining traditional Christians who are retained as the established Protestant church seeks further to subordinate emotion. Traditional forms of religious expression are permitted on some occasions. Pastor Two, as well as many other leaders, has instituted the following changes while seeking to conform to the normative principle. There has been alteration of the conversion technique in these ways: The word "unsaved" has been substituted for "sinner." There is employment of the invitational method instead of the coercive. "We do not employ the method of ridicule and eternal damnation upon those we seek to christianize. . . . Acceptance rather than embarrassment is sought." An explanatory process of preparation is utilized instead of the emotional form of persuasion. Motivation by fear has been supplanted by voluntary acceptance. "The decision to pursue the Christian ideal follows instruction on the meaning of religion, which should motivate one to act for the general good." As evidence of conversion, the individual goes to the altar to shake the minister's hand instead of kneeling at the altar to pray. In regard to verbal statement of spiritual regeneration and its effect upon action, testifiers in conservative churches can express themselves during weekday prayer meeting, revivals, and New Year's Eve services. Seven years ago, the communion testimonial was discontinued by the pastor who prefers a serene ceremony in commemoration of Jesus. The pastor substituted organ music for singing and testimonials as he explained to traditional Christians that the import and the spirit of the service were disrupted by verbal interruptions which hampered reflection and rededication. Another change was the discontinuation of church dinners which, in addition to being convenient for those who remained for the afternoon and the evening services, satisfied inclinations to fraternize with friends; this made possible the transfer of the afternoon communion to the Sunday morning service three years ago, and it eliminated one Sunday service.

Elimination of Sunday church dinners and reduction of the number of services were in some respects less satisfactory to Christians who prefer extensive Christian fellowship which is possible in some traditional (especially from the point of view of emotional worship)

[1] Clergymen of orthodox popular churches are more amicable than formerly to leaders of emotional groups irrespective of continued animosity, as normative standards are applied. Approach is also seen in the attitudes of some leaders of "nonconforming groups" who are tending to regulate action according to the normative standard.

churches, for example, Church Three. Church One, which has made a more abrupt departure from conservative practices than types two and three, has no Sunday evening service.

The sermons of Pastor Two show the significance of nonexperimental and experimental action as the normative principle is pursued. The essence of the sermons of this leader is as follows.

> Religious teachings should be integrated with life. . . . There should be preparation for life, utilization of opportunities through participation, and attainment of life eternal as a result of the supremacy of the spiritual over the temporal in the pursuit of ends.
>
> There should be coordination of community agencies: the church, the school, the family, the court.
>
> There should be inculcation of religion in personal and social relationships. In family, racial, and international relations, the principle of love should be manifested. The church must be effective and progressive in moral, economic, and social phases of life. Acceptance of God by the world will result in social prosperity. . . . Man must keep in mind the active role of God in accomplishments of the past. . . . Conformity with the sacred norm will result in social adjustment.

Through a combined emotional and intellectual appeal, Pastor Two seeks to satisfy the diverse elements in his church. He does not seek totally to submerge emotion in his church; emotional persons are permitted moderately to express themselves.

In the action system, the type of church which occupies a medium position remains significant in the collectivity because it gives some consideration to empirical and nonempirical action as it seeks to execute a program which provides some degree of satisfaction of ends of various types of men while it recognizes the system of norms. Nevertheless, it loses some members who are departing from the church in two directions because of restriction of ends.

The membership of Church Two mainly consists of southern migrants who are taking account of the norm of rationality as change proceeds in the collectivity. Since this church is responding to the normative system, persons who persistently violate the unemotional norm are banished from or submerged in this type of church, which is less assiduous than church type one in pursuing action according to the norm.

The Position of Emotional Types in the System of Action.—Emotional churchgoers pass through various stages during their religious experience as rationality increases in the Protestant collectivity. First, they are restrained. Second, they are ostracized if they do not respond to religious sentiments of the group as a unit. Third, freedom of action is attained, and there is exuberant expression of attitudes.

There is prolongation of the period of emotional action because of the following reasons: similarity of belief of leader and follower, inability or indifference of the leader, and selfish motivation. (Sometimes the preacher finds the leadership of the emotional type financially remunerative.) This period may be followed by one in which effort is made to reintegrate traditional Christians in the Protestant system.

As action progresses in harmony with the normative principle, emotional churchmen in the collectivity are restrained. If emotional persons do not respond to censure, they are relegated to an inferior position in the church or expelled from the religious body.

Being banished from the established Protestant church, they express their religious sentiments in isolation; however, they do enjoy the fellowship of the community of Christians whose religious interests are similar to theirs. Being aware of the critical attitude of disdain manifested by other types of men and churches, they appreciate the leadership of a director who restores status through recognition, religious education, and rational action.

The Role of the Director of Church Three.—Leaders can reclaim the status of traditional men who were held in esteem because of the regulation of action by the ethical norm during the static equilibrium. The director of Church Three seeks to counteract derogatory attitudes of persons in other types of churches by various methods. He has conceived a philosophy of religion which appears pragmatic for his particular purpose. Being motivated by the principle of brotherhood, he develops a religion which is all-inclusive; he welcomes all socio-economic groups, denominations, and races in his church and seeks to make the Kingdom of God a reality through social action. Believing that religion is of no value unless it is integrated with life, he seeks and partly achieves harmony of attitude and practice.

The Director is motivated by the belief that action should be regulated according to the Christian ideal. Christ's life of unselfish devotion should be a normative pattern for the Christian, whose foremost end should be the exemplification of love and service in order to promote general well-being. In the process of Christian living, the churchman should strive for a higher plane of living. Though the individual may deviate from the Christian standard, there should be a conscious effort to overcome inadequacies through a progressive religious process. Christian virtues the individual should manifest are gentleness, patience, mercy, justice, honesty, and faith. Christianity should give the individual the desire and the *will* to attain aspirations. "The desire without the will is ineffectual." Living Christianity is the real force. Religion is not emotion; it is demonstrating the Christian principle in social relationships.[1] The final judgment of religion is its manifestation in life—its effect upon the character of the individual with respect to others and its weight in determining a productive life. In order for Christianity to work, the individual must exemplify attitudes of love, tolerance, and generosity as a means of promoting social unity. "Christ's gospel is one of reconciliation. It reconciles irrespective of denomination, social position, or race."[2] Living according to the Christian norm will result in establishment of the Kingdom of God on earth.[3]

Respecting the opinions, position, and religion of all, the director and the pastor eagerly accept and welcome everyone and provide freedom of religious expression to all persons who enter the Christian fellowship; hence Church Three comprises communicants of various denominations, creeds, and races.[4] This church does not emphasize formal conversion and church membership; any Christian can enter this fellowship without severing his connection with his home church. "Christianity is above creed; it is a spirit of unity, fellowship, cooperation—a spiritual manifestation." Hence the Director seeks to relate the Christian attitude to all phases of life; his objective is "to make life sacred."[5]

Believing that religion should prompt man to be of active assistance to others, the Director strives to lead others to develop their religious potentialities. He is particularly interested in socio-religious groups whose religious action is restricted. Thus his position with respect to the traditional type of worshipper who feels insecure in the Protestant system is obvious. He does not expect practical religious action among emotional churchmen unless there is active intervention on the part of the leader. Therefore, he believes that the traditional type of Christian should be led to a more comprehensive view of religion. Consequently, he is imparting his conception of religion as comprising all spheres of life to his followers.

When this leader, who was originally a Methodist, went to Boston in 1932, the membership of Church Three consisted of professors of the Holiness faith (formerly members of orthodox Protestant churches) whose nonexperimental religious action prompted them to withdraw from life. They emphasized the Second Advent, miracles,

[1] Sermon, Church Three, Boston, Massachusetts, February 16, 1947.

[2] Sermon, Church Three, Boston, February 9, 1947.

[3] *The Voice of the Temple,* Official Organ of Christ Temple Church of Personal Experience, The Reverend W. Frederic Fisher, Director, February 16, 1947, p. 1.

[4] This religious fellowship is not restricted to Boston; branches of the church are in other sections of the country. This religion is strongest in the North and the Midwest.

[5] Interview, The Reverend W. Frederic Fisher, Boston, Massachusetts, June 2, 1947.

tongues, and testimonials as an evidence of divine contact. In other words, they manifested the types of action characteristic of cults. This Holiness church was based on one doctrine: The Father, the Son, and the Holy Ghost is a title; hence a person must be baptized in the name of Jesus and not the Holy Trinity. Though retaining the name of the church, the Director, who was invited to lead this group while he was conducting an evangelistic program in some of the Boston Protestant churches, reorganized this church and added the name, "the Church of Personal Experience." Though understanding the motivation of emotional groups and respecting their religious attitudes, the Director disparaged nonempirical and emotional manifestations by imparting the idea that those who seek the signs of spirituality designated above miss the significance and proof of religion. A unified conception of religion was presented. Thus gradually the group was directed to different religious conceptions as the Director sought to guide emotion in constructive channels. The Director does not submerge emotion completely; nor does he seek to stifle all nonempirical religious expression. At times he moderately advises his group as follows: "If there is a wounded heart, a troubled soul, speak to God who gives inspiration and strength to the weary." Believing that the motive and the spirit of the individual are important, and considering the level of the communicant in his system, this leader gives some recognition to the religious penchant of his followers as he guides them to practical religious action. "I do not seek to deny religious freedom. . . . I wish to place emotion in its proper place. . . . My objective is to sublimate emotional tendencies to the greatest good for themselves [traditional Christians] and others."[1]

Although one element in Church Three is inclined to retain the old religion, another element has been directed to a different interpretation of religion as a result of the influence of the leader, who seeks to promote the adjustment of traditional churchmen in the Protestant collectivity.

The Director strives to alter religious conceptions by instructing his followers in various ways. Note the attitudes of the Director in the following excerpts from sermons. Detailed features of his sermons are included in order further to grasp his interpretation of religion as he reinstructs and reinspires his followers in order to facilitate empirical action and reinstatement in the religious system.

Religion is inseparable from life. There must be unity of belief and action. Think not in terms of attaining Heaven, as some of you are doing. Religion should be integrated with the community. Service is a prerequisite

[1] *Ibid.*

to salvation. Practice should correspond with testimony. A living testimony is valid; we must offer a testimony in life. Doctrine must be reinforced with action. Reciting the Apostle's Creed means nothing unless there is motivation to improve community living. A practical religion is essential.

Living Christianity is more important than believing it. It is not what you believe; a religion of experience that you can recommend to others is necessary. We have opportunities to manifest the kind of religion we recommend in daily activities outside of the church. There is too much preaching Christ, but not enough application.[1] Only when Christianity is applied is it of any value. . . . There are two kinds of testimony: negative and positive. . . . Testimony is negative if actions do not harmonize with words. A negative testimony is destructive; a positive testimony is constructive and unifying. Professing Christianity is nothing without action. I can accept or proclaim religion, but I must exhibit love and fellowship in my relations with others. Christianity can work and it *will* work if we accept it and act accordingly. We have the opportunity to live the doctrine that the Apostle Paul recommends. . . . I am not concerned about doctrine or creed. I'm talking about a practical religion, a religion of unity and harmony. Doctrine is what you ascribe; what you actually do is a recommendation of what you believe. If you believe in the Gospel of Jesus Christ, you will do good to all men.[2]

We preach Christianity, but we haven't dared to live it. We speak of brotherhood and have not courage to apply it. We must believe in Christianity and act upon this belief. . . . When we talk of the kind of society we want, we must be conscious of the necessity of making our beliefs work. . . . If we think that the Christian way is the way to live for all humanity, we must manifest our belief in action.[3]

Through Christianity, there is unity. Religion allows no division; it fosters coordinated group life. Some people have lost the spirit of Christianity. People today tend to disparage labor. One of the defects of our education is that M.A.'s and Ph.D.'s assume exclusive attitudes and regard laborers with disdain. But Christianity measures greatness by knowledge, not letters. Usefulness is the essential idea. Preparation to serve is important. . . . Every great life has in it some renunciation—the giving up or forsaking of those things which may be pleasant, for a greater good or service. Workers accomplish and turn dreams into reality. . . . Labor is agreeable or irksome according to perspective. If one views labor as onerous, it becomes

[1] The Director invariably expresses the necessity of applying religion in daily experiences. Religion, which must be manifested in action, teaches people to be honest, to pay their debts, to assume their obligations, to be economical, practical, and to place first things first by investing their money wisely and spending it for necessities, such as a home, rather than for frivolities.

[2] Sermon, The Director, Church Three, Boston, January 19, 1947.

[3] Sermon, The Director, Church Three, February 22, 1947.

unpleasant. Labor transforms the ordinary into the elegant. Three men who were working with brick and mortar manifested different attitudes toward their task. One regarded the task laborious and irksome. Another considered the work exacting, but necessary since he was providing maintenance for his family. The third took pride in his work and labored sedulously to realize his dream—a cathedral. Here was a man who had seen the Master's face! When you realize that you are laborers of God, you're not just the janitor, the maid; you're a laborer in the House of the Lord. We are laborers together. Eliminate "together," and there's no Christianity. When we work together, Heaven will be on earth. Christ said, "Get together and I'll be in your midst."

God is a unified personality. . . . Those who do not respect the unity of God are not Christians. Christians must fight everything which divides the church and social groups. Christianity is unity; reconciliation is needed. . . . To promote the Kingdom of God on earth, the spirit of brotherhood must be manifested in all relations. . . . Christianity is not only unity, but service. No one can appreciate that which is not shared. We must do something for people. . . . If you believe in the righteousness of God, you manifest your belief in action. . . . We are laborers together in the Kingdom of God. We are working together in unity. . . . We're seeking the Kingdom of God in righteousness; when it comes to the world, there will be no division, no disunity. The unity of God will be a living principle, producing efficacious results.[1]

In the above sermon, the minister glorifies labor for two reasons. First, he wishes to reinspirit, to ensure self-esteem, and to instill self-confidence in his followers, who perform humble tasks. He identifies the laborer with Jesus, who wrought marvelous accomplishments.[2] And he identifies himself with the audience to show co-unity of living. (Actually, in practice he lives and works with his followers and shares their experiences.) Attitudes of respect for labor will produce more efficient action in the performance of tasks. And they also will help to retrieve lost status and soothe damaged feelings as a result of the attitudes of churchmen whose opportunities and advantages have ex-

[1] Sermon, The Director, Church Three, January 26, 1947.

[2] Pastor One also gives consideration to the humble origin of Jesus and his elevation to a position of prominence. (In effect, this is a general device employed by clerical leaders of submerged groups; religious leaders use the technique of identity either to assuage or elevate subjects or to precipitate union among social groups.) Pastor One disparages some attitudes of educated persons toward the church; however, his perspective is somewhat different from that of the Director. Several rural and urban pastors of the three types of churches state that educated persons destroy the spirit of the church by negative criticism and superiority, and they manifest indifference as far as actually taking an active part in church activities is concerned. Nevertheless, some exceptions are noted.

celled those of his followers.[1] Second, the Director wishes to consolidate diverse groups in the religious system and in society by showing the importance and dignity of labor. Inculcation of attitudes of respect for labor will repair the damaged integrity of the type of follower in his church.

The sermon further develops the idea of religion as integration of belief and action. Religion is a unified principle, which must transform action. The Director advocates an active, creative religion, not a retiring one. (His followers tended to withdraw from the world before his leadership, and they continue to manifest some attitudes of seclusion.) He is not concerned about baptism, the Second Coming, or attainment of transcendental heavenly felicity. (Neither is Pastor One interested in the Virgin Birth or ritual formalities.) The Director discourages some nonempirical manifestations. However, there is emphasis upon the promulgation of peace and harmony in social living. A unified society will result from the manifestation of Christian attitudes in all relationships. "Nothing can redeem men but love" manifested in action.

* * * * *

In conclusion, in sermons urban leaders express attitudes which indicate subordination of a nonexperimental religion. They are essentially interested in coordination of religion with life, although some consideration is given nonempirical values. Orthodox religion has no interest for Leaders One and Three; their interest is in motivation of action according to the essential social principle. They are not particularly concerned about doctrine, creed, or form of religion; their primary interest is in action—manifestation of the Christian principle in group living. Although they do not accept literally all Biblical accounts, they promulgate Christianity as a means of promoting harmonious social relations and effective community organization. They concretely vitalize Biblical references by relating them to present situations of life. Leader Two gives attention to the Supernatural. He more readily accepts the authority of the Scripture than the other types of leaders. Traditional religious values are significant; the ends of action should be pursued according to the sacred norm. Spiritual values are superior to temporal. Nevertheless, some consideration is given the practical aspects of religion as nonexperimental and emotional action is minimized.

[1] Followers of the Director also have acquired status and recognition as a result of becoming saints and Christians in this religious community. Pageantry, color, and ceremony have enhanced the setting: Visible signs of sacredness are seen in a distinguishing attire.

III. URBAN PRAYERS AND TESTIMONIALS

The Nature of Communion with the Divine.—There is less evidence of direct intercourse with the Deity as nonexperimental action recedes. Actions with respect to the role of the Supreme in natural and human occurrences are restrained. Feeling is submerged with the elevation of empirical action in the religious system.

Urban prayers are far more restrained than rural; less direct relation with the Supernatural is manifested in urban communion with the Deity. While communicating with the Divine, the traditional rural churchman is considerably more emotional in his verbal expression than the urban worshipper in Church Three. There is great diminution of supersensory values in urban prayer, although the individual does manifest some degree of dependence upon the Supreme. Some prayers express reliance upon God for security and guidance; others do not. The Director's prayers usually substantiate the central idea of his sermons; they are an explanation of his religious beliefs. There is a general tendency for prayer to be related to the sermon.

Urban prayer is of an elegant quality. Urban prayer tends to be of the adorational type, which expresses reverent appreciation for God's influence in human affairs. There is cognizance of God's power in the natural and the social order. Yet the urban prayer addresses the Supreme with serene beauty of language, whereas the traditional rural churchman tends to express his sentiments to God with eloquent force. Out of 40 prayers in Boston churches, 2 are petitional; 14 are adorational and appreciatory; and 24 are a combination of supplication and adoration. Since the relationship with the Divine is not so intimate as formerly, and since the Christian greatly regards religion as a means to salvation in the empirical realm, the individual tends serenely to express his sentiments instead of pleadingly beseeching God's mercy. Urban prayerful attitudes are restrained. Only a few communicants warmly express their feeling. Eight out of 40 churchmen manifest emotional attitudes during prayer; 32 Christians are restrained in expressing relationship with God.

Special Opportunities for Traditional Religious Expression.—With the decline of emotional action, the traditional Christian is given a limited opportunity to express nonexperimental religious sentiments. The extent of the opportunity depends upon the type of church. For example, church type three gives more consideration to the old religionist than church type two. A conservative church, which gradually submerges nonexperimental religious elements, considers the interests of various levels of the congregation while seeking to regulate action according to the system of norms. Elderly persons in the traditional type three church find opportunity for close communion with the Deity in preservice prayer and Sunday evening services. In Church Three about 10 traditional Christians in an audience of 200 persons moderately manifest nonexperimental sentiments in altar-prayer. Then the refined quality of music is gradually transformed into a bizarre jazz perversion of the spiritual, hymn, or anthem as thirty persons in the congregation manifest emotional action.

These manifestations may be followed by verbal expressions of gratitude, which are comparable with traditional testimonials. Some communicants of Church Three occasionally give testimony of the mercy of Christ and express gratitude for God's solicitous protection in averting misfortune, as the pianist softly plays "Just Think of His Goodness." There is consciousness of God's relief in physical and mental infirmity.

Some express appreciation for the inspiration and assistance of Christ, and the Director, whose close communion with and faith in God imbues him with prophetic powers. The Director can allay the fears and anxieties of the ill by predicting physical restoration through the power of God.

Diminution of the nonempirical is seen in the failure of testifiers to express anticipation of the Blessed Eternal, although there is expression of staunch belief in God's manifestation of the principle of love in everyday experiences.

By appealing to some of the religious sentiments of his audience before the formal Sunday morning service, the Director wishes to win adherents to a more rational type of religion. Thus the introductory prayer service is followed by a restrained, ceremonious type of worship. The audience is emotionally attuned for presentation of the religious conceptions of its leader.

A Comparison of Types of Churches.—There is a relation between traditional religion and type of church. The transcendental is more significant for churches which respond slowly to change than for those which tend to elevate rational action. A comparison of the religious attitudes and actions of Boston laymen shows differences according to church. An enumeration of reasons for joining a particular church or denomination indicates that attitudes toward the nonempirical aspects of religion are not identical. Informants of Church One find their church attractive because of these reasons: A desire to be released from strict institutional control can be realized in Church One, in which there is relaxation of rigid religious codes. This church satisfies the need for religious group experience among persons whose interests are similar. And it satisfies humanitarian desires to improve community life. The social aspect of religion is significant. Institutional influences tend to be important in Church Two. Adherence to church dogma and tradition prompts 10 out of 12 informants to follow the denomination of their family. Some of these informants are conscious of a need to express religious sentiments in group communion. And there is cognizance of the benevolent phase of religion. Informants of neither Church One nor Church Two are motivated by emotional ends in joining the church of their choice. Among communicants of Church Three, traditional religion motivates action strongly. Although 7 informants are conscious of the social role of Church Three, all of them entered this church because of the strength of traditional religious sentiments. Because of a desire "to serve the Lord in beauty" or because of "fullness of spirit," these informants were led to seek a spiritual church in which "the light of Christianity is brilliant."

The type of worship in various types of churches reflects differences in religious attitudes. The church service of Church Two relates to the nonexperimental phases of religion more so than that of Church One. The former type of church expresses greater reliance upon the Supreme than the latter and is more patient "to wait upon God." Although some values other than the truly or conservatively religious are conceived and sought, experimental action is not of tremendous importance. The Supernatural is significant in action, although the church service indicates consideration of the normative system of rules. In prayer, Church Two manifests a closer relation with the Divine than Church One. Both Churches One and Two have well-trained choirs which have completely subordinated the traditional type of music. However, there is more warmth and emotion in Church Two than in Church One. There is a variety of music to satisfy the different levels of the audience in Church Two. In all of the churches, feeling is more greatly expressed in song than in any other form of divine worship. Emotional action accompanying religious sentiments is more prevalent in type three audiences than in the other types of churches.[1]

[1] See table twenty-three for information on types of response during various Boston services in types of churches.

CHAPTER XII

Education, Denomination, and the Cult Movement

THE DECREMENT OF TRADITIONAL RELIGION IN THE PROTESTANT CHURCH

Education a Factor in the Decay of Traditional Religion.—There is a direct relation between religion and education. There is diminution of traditional religion with intellectual and educational advancement. Rationality increases in the religious system with the continuous education of the population. Men's attitudes change as education is acquired. Over a period of years there has been a constant rise in the number of American persons who have had advantages of education. Dissemination of education in society has had a remarkable influence upon religious attitudes. With the trend from the nonexperimental and the increasing importance of empirical knowledge, the religious action of men of all levels of learning has been affected. Contact with persons of advanced or superior training affects the religious attitudes and practices of persons of modest or ordinary education. Cultural isolation is a barrier to change; persons in remote areas or of subordinate position respond slowly to the modification of established procedures inasmuch as communication with advantaged groups is hampered. Nevertheless, there has been general response to the normative system. Irrespective of location or inadequate formal education, there is general adherence to the system of norms as attitudes of respect are manifested toward the normative principle. Education promotes changing religious conceptions.

Statistics show a steady increase in education over the years. A large proportion of the population of the United States has had the advantage of secondary, college, graduate, and professional training. The following tables show the number of graduates of high schools and institutions of higher education in this country over a period of years.

TABLE TWENTY-FOUR

Total Number of High School and College Graduates of American Institutions, According to Year*

Year of Graduation	*High School*	*College*
1870	16,000	9,371
1880	23,634	10,353
1890	43,731	14,306
1900	94,883	25,324
1910	156,429	34,178
1920	311,266	48,622
1930	666,904	122,484
1940	1,221,475	186,500
1942	1,242,375	185,346
1944**	1,019,233	125,875

* *Statistical Abstract of the United States 1946, Sixty-Seventh Number,* compiled under the supervision of Morris H. Hansen, United States Government Printing Office, Washington 25, D.C., 1946. This information was taken from Table Number 149, p. 133.

** Taken from the Sixty-Eighth Edition of the *Statistical Abstract,* Table Number 154, p. 133. This decrease is probably a result of the war.

There were 74,775,836 persons in the population of the United States 25 years old and older in 1940.[1] The median years of school completed for persons of this age grouping in this country was 8.4. The median number of years for the Negro group was 5.7; for the urban population it was 8.7; for the rural non-farm, 8.4; for the rural farm, 7.7.[2] By April, 1940, more than half of the population 25 years or over had completed not less than 8 years of school; 4.6 per cent had graduated from college[3]; 11,181,995 persons 25 years of age or over had 1 to 3 years of high school training; 10,551,680 had four years; 4,075,184 had 1 to 3 years of college training; 3,407,331 had 4 years or more of advanced training.[4] By 1940, the total number of persons 25 years and above who had received high school and college training in the United States is seen in tabular form on page 172.[5]

[1] *Statistical Abstract of the United States 1947, Sixty-Eighth Edition,* U.S. Government Printing Office, Washington 25, D.C., 1947, p. 123.

[2] *Statistical Abstract of the United States 1946, Sixty-Seventh Edition,* p. 127.

[3] Murray, Florence, *The Negro Handbook 1946–1947,* Current Books, Inc., New York, N.Y., 1947, p. 137. The primary source is the Bureau of the Census.

[4] *Statistical Abstract,* 1947, p. 123.

[5] Murray, *op. cit.,* pp. 138–139.

TABLE TWENTY-FIVE

Number of Degrees Conferred by Institutions in Continental United States from 1890 to 1942[1]

Year	1890	1900	1910	1920	1926	1928	1930	1932	1934
Degrees Conferred									
Baccalaureate	6,853	14,018	22,687	38,552	71,529	83,065	91,623	122,538[2]	119,853[2]
Professional[3]	8,686	13,392	14,512	8,774	20,096	19,917	19,788		
Graduate	1,135	1,952	2,541	4,853	11,451	13,834	16,832	21,655	20,442
Ph.D., on examination	126	342	409	532	1,302	1,447	2,024	2,900[4]	2,796[4]

TABLE TWENTY-FIVE
(*Continued*)[5]

Year	1936	1938	1940	1942
Degrees Conferred				
Total Baccalaureate and First Professional	124,614	164,943	186,500	185,346
Masters, including advanced engineering		21,628	26,731	24,648
Doctors	2,768	2,932	3,290	3,497

[1] *Statistical Abstract of the United States 1932, Fifty-Fourth Number,* U.S. Government Printing Office, Washington, 1932, p. 104. This information was taken from Table Number 102, which consists of data of colleges, universities, and professional schools conferring higher degrees. Figures for the years 1932, 1934, and 1936 were taken from the sixtieth number of the Abstract, 1938, p. 109, Table 114.

[2] Including first professional.

[3] Includes recipients of degrees in theology, law, medicine, dentistry, pharmacy, osteopathy, and veterinary medicine.

[4] All doctor's degrees.

[5] *Statistical Abstract of the United States 1946, Sixty-Seventh Number, op. cit.*, p. 134. Figures were taken from Table Number 151 for the years 1938, 1940, and 1942.

	Total (all races)	*Negro*
High school: 1 to 3 years	11,181,995	549,666
4 years	10,551,680	268,481
College: 1 to 3 years	4,075,184	118,280
4 years or more	3,407,331	80,842
Not reported	1,041,970	114,235
Median school years completed	8.4	5.7
Per cent less than 5 years completed	13.5	41.3

There is an increasing number of Negroes graduating from high schools, colleges, universities, professional and business schools. During the period 1820–1909, there were 3,856 American Negroes who held college degrees; by 1925, this number had risen to 10,000. On the basis of estimates of "The Crisis," 9,257 Negroes received college degrees from 1926 to 1931.[1] By 1940, there were 80,842 Negroes 25 years old or above who had received 4 years or more of college training.[2] From 1876 to 1943, three hundred eighty-one persons of Negro descent received the degree of Doctor of Philosophy or its equivalent, according to some estimates.[3] By Greene's computation, there were 368 Doctor of Philosophy degrees or equivalents awarded Negroes from 1875 to 1943. During the 14-year period, 1930–1943, there was rapid higher educational advancement among Negroes. From 1930 to 1943, there were 317 Negroes who earned Doctor of Philosophy degrees. More than four-fifths of the doctorate degrees were earned since 1930. During the period 1935–1939, one hundred nineteen doctorates were conferred to Negroes. From 1940 to 1943, Negroes received 128 doctorates.[4] From 1944 to 1946, ninety-one Negroes received Doctor of Philosophy degrees, and 12 received the degree of Doctor of Education.[5]

By combining Greene's figures with Guzman's there were 471 Negro recipients of doctorates for the period 1875–1946. A condensed pictorial view of doctorates according to period is as follows:[6]

[1] B. E. Mays and J. W. Nicholson, *The Negro's Church,* Institute of Social and Religious Research, New York, N.Y., 1933, p. 49.

[2] Murray, *loc. cit.*

[3] Greene, Harry W., *Holders of Doctorates Among American Negroes,* Meador Publishing Company, Boston, Mass., 1946, pp. 23–25.

[4] *Ibid.*

[5] *Negro Year Book 1941–1946,* edited by Jessie Parkhurst Guzman, Tuskegee Institute, Tuskegee, Alabama, 1947, pp. 20–22.

[6] This table is based upon Greene's chart from 1875 through 1943, and Guzman's figures from 1944 through 1946. Greene, *op. cit.,* p. 26. *Negro Year Book 1941–1946,* Guzman, Editor, pp. 21–22.

TABLE TWENTY-SIX

Negroes Receiving Doctorates, 1875–1946

Period	*No. of Doctorates Conferred*
1875–1914	14
1915–1924	19
1925–1929	18
1930–1943	317
1944–1946	103
1875–1929	51
1875–1943	368
1875–1946	471

There is a constant increase in the number of Negroes pursuing higher education.

There is regression of nonexperimental religious action in the Protestant collectivity with educational change. The manifestation of religious sentiments in emotional action among Negro churchmen has declined commensurately with increasing quantitative and qualitative educational change.

There is a reciprocal relationship between rate of change and educational opportunity. Change proceeds more rapidly in areas of superior education and leadership than in other areas in which there is greater retardation.[1] Hence there is greater acceleration of an empirical type of religion in the urban environment than in the rural. And there has been a greater regression of nonexperimental religious action in the urban North than in the South. Increasing education and industrialization of the South will precipitate further change in religious action.

Some Effects of the Subordination of the Nonexperimental Phase of Religion.—Education is an important element in change. Alteration of religious action progresses with the promotion of education. Transcendental values diminish, and attention is focused upon experimental elements of action. With industrialization, urbanization, and education, the social character of religious beliefs is more apparent. Religious action is partly determined by men's conceptions of the Supernatural. The Supernatural, men's attitudes, and society are in a process of interaction. As education is accessible to the masses in society and as the city becomes attractive as a center of commerce, trade, and habitation, the underlying principle of society as an im-

[1] Those interested in securing statistical comparisons of rural and urban education in relation to religion may refer to the following sources: Monroe Work, *The Negro Yearbook 1937–1938*, pp. 226–227; Mays and Nicholson, *The Negro's Church*, pp. 17–18, 239, 249; Harry V. Richardson, *Dark Glory*, pp. 123–125.

portant basis of religious action becomes conspicuous. Religion promotes solidarity and is an expression of the collective beliefs of men. The basis of religion is the supersensory and the social. In order better to comprehend the inscrutable aspects of life, man enters a relationship with a powerful nonexperimental entity. Cognition proceeds from the authority of the Divine. Concordance results in society as man is motivated by the Divine principle. A degree of collective solidarity results from observance of religious codes, the authority of which proceeds from the nonempirical and the empirical. As rationality and heterogeneity increase in a social system, there is diminution of the authority of the Controlling Power. Men take different attitudes toward the Supernatural, and the individual and the social factors become prominent.

The motivation of religious men is various. Though religious action results partly from the authority of the Deity, supersensory values have diminished considerably.

Nonexperimental and emotional religious action diminishes with the decrescent authority of the Supreme. Though there is retention of some nonexperimental actions, empirical religious ends are significant. The religious body prescribes a standard of action which is in congruence with the progressive form of equilibrium. A norm of rationality limits action. Men should pursue the logical and discard the irrational, according to present standards. Instead of contemplating a supersensory supremacy of the higher principle, men should seek the divine in life. Emotional anticipation of the Day of Retribution is tabooed. The Deity maintains some authority; nevertheless, the negative aspect of religious action is minimized. Faith in the possibility of inculcating the spirit of the Christian religion in society must not be relinquished. Religion is practicable; it will predominate, and it will have bountiful results in social action. As religious practices change, various attitudes are manifested toward the normative system of ends. In spite of some degree of integration in the church, there is disagreement and discord. With an increase of rationality in the religious system of action, the ends of some churchmen are obscured. Discordant sentiments tend to debilitate the Protestant system.

There is curtailment of the action of Christians whose religious values are conceived in terms of the static equilibrium. Traditional Christians who greatly manifest their religious sentiments in nonexperimental action find their action restricted as change proceeds in the Protestant system. Since the transcendental is of essential importance to them, there is not satisfactory realization of their religious ends. As a result of maladjustment in the Protestant system, a mild form of disruption has occurred. In order to realize objectives, there is partial and total disseverance in the religious system.

During the twentieth century there was a tremendous growth of cults. Though some of "the new religions" were founded in America during the eighteenth and nineteenth centuries, it was not until the twentieth century that there was a large exodus of members from the established Protestant church.[1] Although not all of the cults are Christian, most of them are based upon the teachings of Jesus Christ. The significant fact at this point is not the name and nature of the religion but the phenomenal origin and growth of the cult with respect to the particular religion which is being analyzed. The new faiths were founded by Protestants. Though some still bear a semblance of the Protestant church, some have completely severed their connection with the Protestant body. Some dissident groups are autonomously and doctrinally distinct in every respect.

Cults establish a connection between the old order and the new. They combine conflicting dissociated features of action. They merge a variety of religions. They introduce innovations by taking a little of Protestantism, grasping a little of Catholicism, or Judaism, or Mohammedanism and adding religious originality of their own. This is certainly apparent in Church Three with respect to Protestantism, Catholicism, and Cultism. Cults tend to form connections between the past and the present. The cults have taken discarded religious practices, combined these with the spectacular and the novel and partly adapted these to the religious needs of neglected men in the system of action. And some cult leaders have added practical features to religious action. By taking cast-off forms and combining them with new or striking features they have attracted those Christians who are dissatisfied with the progressive change in the system of action. Thus the advanced cult tends to retain values which are significant to some men, and it tends to acquire practices which promote a manner of adjustment to economic and social life. The cult too reflects the changing status of ends by forming combinations which have functions of a nonexperimental, an illogical, and a logical nature. The cult too is an expression of the social order underlying religious sentiments. The advanced cult is adjusting itself to social change.

There is diffusion of Cultism in the periphery action system.

The extraordinary growth and popularity of the new religions is seen in the fact that there were fourteen new religious bodies in 1936.

[1] For information on the history, membership, philosophy, and growth of these groups, see Landis, Benson Y., *The Year Book of American Churches*, 1945, pp. 18–27, 34–35, 58–59, 70, 73, 77, 89; Murray, *op. cit.*, pp. 155–156; *Bureau of the Census, Religious Bodies*: 1936, Vol. I, pp. 51, 84; and Fauset, Arthur Huff, *Black Gods of the Metropolis.*

From 1926 to 1936, the membership of the Church of God and Saints of Christ increased 450 per cent.[1] There has been a 50 per cent increase in the membership of some of the churches which emphasize sanctification. Samples of gains in racially mixed churches are as follows:[2]

	Negro Membership 1936	*Total Membership* 1936	1942
Church of God	1,405	44,818	82,462
Church of God (in Indiana)	4,310	56,911	83,875
International Church of the Foursquare Gospel	28	16,147	250,000

At present there are rapid increases in the membership of Holiness churches or similar institutions. Protestants in urban areas are continually seeking new religions in spite of the decreasing strength of some of the new faiths. Some churches which have experienced a decrease in membership since 1926 are the Church of Christ and the Disciples of Christ.[3] The decline of numerical strength in these particular churches may indicate schisms in the Holiness church, and the consequent loss of members to other churches of this type. It may signify a return of some communicants to the established church. In Boston some worshippers have reidentified themselves with the established Protestant church. This return is a probable result of the modification of policy by some Protestant clerical leaders. During interviews, three Boston clergy stated that they had altered their former positions and were therefore injecting spiritual elements in their sermons. Three others indicated that they are now more tolerant of emotionalism than formerly. Reference has been made to efforts of interfusion. Loss of membership by the new religions is not a general pattern; there is expansion of the cult movement.

There is dissatisfaction in the Protestant system. Since goals of action are not being realized by some, worshippers partially identify themselves with the established church and the innovated church.

Competition of some of the serene popular Protestant churches with the Catholic church in the District of Columbia became so strong that Negro Protestant clergy had to alter actions and provide additional nonexperimental religious ceremonies for members. There was regular migration of Protestants to Catholic churches to attend

[1] *Bureau of the Census, Religious Bodies: 1936,* United States Government Printing Office, Washington, 1941, p. 84.

[2] Murray, *op. cit.*, p. 155.

[3] *Bureau of the Census, Religious Bodies: 1936, loc. cit.*

the novena service, which would ensure successful realization of empirical ends. Some of the Protestant clergy decisively instituted the novena service in their churches in order to re-attract their members. Considerable attention has been given the diminution of prayer and saintliness in the Protestant church. Some Protestants feel a need for a closer relationship with the Deity. Some feel a need for a ceremonious type of worship which is not characterized by emotional action but which does manifest nonexperimental action to a considerable extent. In South Carolina, Massachusetts, and elsewhere there are occurrences similar to that of Washington related above. Members of the popular Protestant churches are participating in Catholic churches.

Though the increase in Catholic membership was only seven per cent between 1926 and 1936, Negroes are becoming attracted to the Catholic faith more so than formerly. Although Catholic, Episcopalian, and Presbyterian churches have a long history among Negroes, these churches have had only a small Negro membership in spite of early establishment.[1] Neither has the Congregational church had a large Negro following. The few Negro Catholics of the past were scattered variously; Negro Catholics were more numerous in Catholic areas, such as Louisiana and Maryland.[2] Although this is to some extent true today, Catholicism is winning Negro converts in various localities. In 1936 there were 137,684 Negro Catholics in the United States, and by 1945 this number had increased to 330,000.[3] Negro Catholic membership is steadily growing in the South and the metropolitan North. In Boston and South Carolina, adherents are being won to the faith. Catholics proselytize among the masses as well as other groups. Protestants and unchurched men are becoming Catholics. And it is expected that there will be an increasing strength of Catholicism among Negroes.

Some Negroes are seeking churches which have ritual and little or no emotional action; others are seeking those which combine ceremony with nonempirical and emotional action, and others are seeking those which emphasize emotional action. Nonexperimental action is a striking characteristic of all of these churches. As change proceeds in the Protestant collectivity, men react variously to the normative system.

Irrespective of loss of membership or potential membership, the

[1] Brawley, Benjamin, *A Short History of the American Negro,* The Macmillan Company, New York, 1919, pp. 201–204.

[2] Washington, Booker T., *The Story of the Negro,* Vol. I, Doubleday Page and Company, New York, 1909, p. 271.

[3] Murray, *op. cit.,* pp. 155–156.

Protestant church remains strong numerically. America is predominantly Protestant although the Roman Catholic church has a larger membership than any one denomination in the United States.[1] In 1936, the next ranking churches were the Jewish Church, the Negro Baptists, the Methodist Episcopal church, the Southern Baptist Convention, and the Methodist Episcopal Church, South, respectively. Observe the following distribution of members in 1936.[2]

Roman Catholic	19,914,937
Jewish	4,641,184
Negro Baptists	3,782,464
Methodist Episcopal	3,509,763
Southern Baptist Convention	2,700,155
Methodist Episcopal, South	2,061,683

As a consolidated group, the established Protestant church is the largest religious body in the United States.

The 1944 membership of some denominations is as follows:[1]

Roman Catholic	
Inclusive membership	23,419,701
Membership 13 years of age & over	17,330,558 Est.
Methodist[4]	8,046,129
Negro Baptists	6,433,700
Northern Baptist Convention[5]	1,555,914
Seventh Day Baptist General Conference	6,581
Protestant Episcopal	2,227,524
Reformed Episcopal	8,939
Presbyterian Church in the U.S.A.	2,040,399
Presbyterian Church in the U.S.	565,853
United Presbyterian Church	193,637
United Lutheran (consultative)	1,690,204
Disciples of Christ	1,672,354
Congregational Christian	1,075,401

Methodist and Baptist churches held large memberships in the past, and the various branches of these denominations continue to excel the numerical strength of other Protestant churches. In 1926,

[1] Church membership is regarded differently among denominations. For example, Roman Catholics consider infants members, whereas Baptists do not.

[2] *Bureau of the Census, Religious Bodies: 1936*, pp. 17–18.

[3] These figures were taken from Landis, *op. cit.*, pp. 60, 70, 73, 77, 89; figures for Negro Baptist denominations were taken from Murray, *op. cit.*, pp. 155–156.

[4] Methodist now outranks Negro Baptists because of consolidation of some of the branches of the Methodist Episcopal church in 1939. The Methodist church resulted from unification of the Methodist Episcopal church, the Methodist Episcopal Church, South, and the Methodist Protestant church.

[5] **Includes Free Baptists.**

Negro church membership was 5,203,487 or 9.5 per cent of all church members in the United States. Baptist churches held 61.4 per cent of the Negro membership. Observe the following percentage distribution of Negro membership in 1926.[1]

Negro Baptists	61.4
African Methodist Episcopal (A.M.E.)	10.5
African Methodist Episcopal Zion (A.M.E.Z.)	8.8
Methodist Episcopal (now Methodist)	6.4
Colored Methodist Episcopal (C.M.E.)	3.9
Roman Catholic	2.4
Protestant Episcopal	1.0
All other	5.6

Negro church membership increased from 5,203,487 in 1926 to 5,660,618 in 1936, an increase of 571,131 members. Some denominations showing a percentage gain in Negro membership during the period 1926–1936 are as follows:[2]

The Church of God and Saints of Christ	450.0
The United American Free Will Baptist	46.4
C.M.E.	33.2
Negro Baptists	18.3
Roman Catholic	10.7
A.M.E.	9.6
A.M.E.Z.	9.3

The Negro Baptist churches had 66.8 per cent of the Negro church membership in 1936. Negro membership in various denominations in 1936 and 1944 is as follows.[3] (Blank spaces do not indicate absence of membership.)

	1936	*1944*
Negro Baptists	3,782,464	6,433,700
A.M.E.	493,357	868,735
A.M.E.Z.	414,244	489,244
C.M.E.	269,915	382,000
M.E.	193,761	
Roman Catholic	137,684	330,000
Northern Baptist Convention	45,821	
Congregational Christian	20,437	
Protestant Episcopal	63,306	
Reformed Episcopal	2,434	

[1] *Bureau of the Census, Negroes in the United States* 1920–1932, prepared under the supervision of Z. R. Pettet, United States Government Printing Office, Washington, 1935, p. 530.

[2] *Bureau of the Census, Religious Bodies: 1936, op. cit.*, p. 84; Landis, *op. cit.*, p. 51.

[3] *Ibid.*, Census, p. 75; Landis, p. 89.

Statistics on denomination are included simply to give the trend of church membership today. The figures cannot be taken literally; there are some discrepancies in reports since not all sources give the same figures. However, presentation of the information from various sources is accurate to the extent that there is not wide disagreement; the same general picture is presented. The statistics on church membership include those churches which replied to inquiry; not all churches reported to the Bureau of the Census.

The figures substantiate observation. It is obvious that some churchmen are being attracted to new faiths in spite of the remaining strength of the established Protestant body.

Summarily, the American population is primarily Protestant. The established Protestant church predominates numerically. The more orthodox Protestant denominations still excel in membership; the various branches of the Methodist and Baptist churches retain dominance of numbers as far as the white and the Negro population is concerned. Increasingly, during the twentieth century there has been a rapid increase in the number of adherents of different faiths or new religions. Some converts to the "new religions" still remain in the Protestant church as such; they simply alter or modify the dogma or ritual of their mother denomination and give a different interpretation to Christianity. Some totally sever their connection with the Protestant church and formulate the basis of an actually new religion. There is one significant common characteristic of the "new religions": Nonexperimental action is prominent. Most of the nonconformists carry decaying traditional practices with them and transfigure these by bizarre sensational additions. This tenacious grip upon old practices indicates cultural or religious retardation as far as the system of action in its entirety is concerned. Though there is variation among the new religions as far as the extent of emotional religious action is concerned, nonexperimental action is a conspicuous general feature.

Retention of old practices by religious men, withdrawal, and expulsion are an index of religious maladjustment in the system of action. Those manifestations indicate religious and social deficiency. As a result of individual, religious, or social dissatisfaction, men are seeking new values. Men are searching for that which they have not found in religious or extra-religious channels. Religious action is a reflection of society.

There is confusion within and without the established religious system. Not being content with the present state of things, churchmen in the Protestant system are striving to modify action in order to attain the ideal, which they regard possible. As values are being conceived differently in some respects, friction results from the different attitudes toward the ideal and the corresponding clash of interests. Efforts are being made to reconcile the various end systems of action. Some churchmen who failed to give consideration to the interests of traditional Christians while pursuing the normative principle have begun to re-examine their position; they are considering the effect of their former attitudes of ignorement upon the church. Hence a few concessions are being made to traditional worshippers. A few leaders are attempting to regard the interests of various types in the religious system, and hence there is alteration of former positions in order to produce salutary results in the Protestant system of action. Irrespective of imperfect integration, there is a degree of coordination in the Protestant collectivity.

CHAPTER XIII

Integration of the Church with the Community

The Ascendancy of Empirical Action with the Diminution of Nonexperimental Action

WITH A decrement of the transcendental in a system of action, experimental ends become important. As change occurs, institutional religion departs slowly from the traditional form of action. As the supernatural further diminishes as a standard for action, the trend toward empirical action is more rapid.

Practical religious action is an outcome of subordination of the supersensory. Therefore it is expected that in the successive stage of religious development (the trend toward experimentalism, being presently considered) practical programs are not as outstanding as the decline in emotionalism. Though nonexperimental and emotional religious actions are closely related and often accompany each other, the change from the former in some respects is not as noticeable as the departure from the latter. As there is further deterioration of nonexperimental beliefs, religious action will increasingly acquire a social quality reflected in group living. Altered religious attitudes indicate a close relationship with the community. Religion is significantly conceived in terms of the principle of group welfare. Religious ideas are directing interests in practical action.

I. LAYMEN'S CONCEPTIONS OF FUNCTIONAL RELIGION

Members' Attitudes Toward Church Functions.—Men's conceptions of religion and the manner in which they desire the church to act exemplify attitudes toward the nonempirical aspects of reality and at the same time reflect a common system of ultimate-values, to which there is a degree of adherence. The supernatural is a determinant of social action; active attitudes toward the Deity influence the nature of religious action.[1] The "social utility" of nonexperimental

[1] Parsons, *op. cit.*, pp. 426–428.

theories is observed in their effect upon action and the type of ends pursued.[1] Being motivated by the belief that religion should prompt one to act for the improvement of community organization, churchmen are directing their religious sentiments toward empirical action. Emphasis is presently being placed upon attainment of the ideal in this world. The teachings of Christ should lead one to consider the interests of fellowmen and to work for establishment of the Kingdom of God on earth.

Informants believe that the church should relate itself to the community. Rural informants are more conscious of traditional religious functions than urban. Nevertheless, rural people are beginning to visualize practical programs of action. Seven rural churchmen think the church should re-affirm religious values by converting and preaching religious sermons. To rural laymen, it is important that the church aid physically and financially incapacitated persons. Twenty South Carolina informants believe that the church should provide opportunities for social intercourse and recreation; it is necessary to expand in this respect in order to attract youths to the church. Ten South Carolina informants believe that the church should facilitate the social adjustment of its members by instructing them and by manifesting interest in the conditions under which members live. (The rural church does little or nothing to relate the church to community life. The primary interest is upon church worship and financial contributions.)

The urban churchman regards it essential that the church coordinate itself with the community. Urban South Carolina informants believe that there should be extension of the church in the community. The church should provide recreational and social centers; it should seek to attract youths by providing a variety of organizations; it should effectively provide charitable aid to sick and aged members who have been faithful to the church, and it should encourage and aid economically depressed groups in the community. It should give attention to the needs of the laborer. It should seek to aid communicants morally, intellectually, and socially. An extensive program of activity should be incorporated in the church. The present program of the church is inadequate.

Seven Boston informants believe that the church should manifest a personal interest in the lives of its followers by contact in the form of visits or correspondence and by providing opportunity for sympathy and understanding.[2] The formal city atmosphere is not satisfy-

1 *Ibid.*, pp. 272, 275, 277.

2 Although some urban pastors visit their members, some of them inform their congregations that they cannot successfully execute the program of their church and

ing to some who feel a need for friendly human association. Most Boston informants believe that the church should integrate itself with the community by giving consideration to the educational, political, and social needs of communicants and others. The church should provide educational and social centers at which people can gather for entertainment, discussion, and instruction.

To rural and urban worshippers, the traditional church program is not feasible. Church members emphasize the importance of local enterprise and missionary work.

In general, informants believe that there should be integration of the church with the community and of religion with life. The deficiency is not only institutional; it is individual also. According to some laymen, members themselves should exemplify the principle of charity in living; churchmen do not sufficiently manifest love and consideration in their social relationships. There should be manifestation of religion in all relations. Members and the church should coordinate religion with life and help to improve the community.

TABLE TWENTY-SEVEN

What the Church Should Do, Provide, Promote, or Sponsor

	Number of Replies	
	S.C.	*Mass.*
Evangelism	7	2
Increase the number of services	3	1
Interesting, effective services	6	0
Encourage and inspire members	0	7
Financial, moral, and religious aid to the sick, the aged, and the poor	17	1
Organizations	6	4
Entertainment and recreation	14	2
Efficient leadership	3	0
Educational and intellectual development (lectures, discussions, clinics, nursery schools, religious and educational centers)	3	10
Encourage voting	1	6
Instruct and teach members how to live	10	0
Employment bureaus and business	0	2
Social work and crime prevention	0	7
Integrate religion with life	1	14
Administer to the physical, moral, spiritual, intellectual, and social needs of man	3	13

visit; therefore members are advised not to waste the pastor's time for insignificant frivolities. They are instructed to notify their pastor regarding illness or important business; otherwise, they should wait for him to make the initial advance.

In regard to functional religion, South Carolina informants are more conscious of a need for recreation than Boston informants. This is understandable since Boston churches have incorporated a more extensive program than South Carolina churches. Observe the responses of informants with respect to recreational activities and social gatherings.

TABLE TWENTY-EIGHT

Sufficient Recreational and Social Activities Sponsored by Churches

	Yes	*No*
Total South Carolina	16	27
Church A	9	3
Church B	2	11
Church C	5	8
City Church	0	5
Total Massachusetts	31	8
Church One	9	3
Church Two	8	4
Church Three	14	1

This table shows greater dissatisfaction in South Carolina than in Massachusetts. City churches, especially those in the North and some sections of the West, have given greater consideration to the social and recreational needs of churchmen by providing a variety of church organizations, by sponsoring community centers, picnics, and camps, and by making arrangements for youths to spend a portion of the summer at resorts. Boston informants who answered in the negative indicated that their respective churches are giving some consideration to social intercourse and recreation. However, informants do not consider this adequate.

By comparing replies regarding organizations and recreation churches should provide as seen in Tables Twenty-Seven and Twenty-Eight, it is evident that churchmen place greater emphasis upon entertainment than the former table indicates. Twenty South Carolina and 6 Boston informants state a belief that churches should provide recreation and organizations; 27 South Carolina informants and 8 Boston informants consider the diversional programs of their churches unsatisfactory or inadequate. The emphasis is upon organized church amusement; that is, members desire a direct rather than an incidental approach to entertainment. They appreciate neighborhood centers in the form of a playground, a park, or a community house. Through church clubs, some recreation is provided in the form of parties, dinners, and games. However, churchmen seek a more coordinated method of supplying opportunities for sport and diversion.

Aside from the consideration that city churches (especially in certain sections of the country) give more attention to pastime activities as seen in a comparison of South Carolina and Boston attitudes, there is another important factor. Metropolitan residents do not rely solely or mainly upon the church to make provision for community services; there are public playgrounds and parks. In the South, Negroes generally have no public facilities for recreation; and welfare agencies do not supply individual, family, and community needs as adequately as in the North.

To religious men, one of the most important programs of action the church should pursue is education. Considerable emphasis is placed upon enlightenment, not simply from the traditional point of view of establishment and maintenance of institutions of learning mainly on the secondary and the college level. Increasingly, members of the religious system believe that the church should stimulate thought and provide opportunities for the group to receive information in the form of speeches by leaders and to exchange ideas in discussion. Attention is being given art appreciation and development of nurseries and kindergartens for pre-school children. The members of the system are giving minor consideration to economic and political channels of action. However, there is not great expectancy with respect to business and politics, as far as lay informants are concerned. Although they believe that the church should sponsor all activity which promotes the well-being of the group, a slight line of demarcation is drawn between religious worship, recreation, education, and welfare on the one hand, and business and politics on the other. Replies of informants indicate this cleavage inasmuch as there was failure to list the latter phases of religious activity as frequently as the former.

Enumerations of 40 college students show a belief that the Negro church should meet various needs. Thirty-five persons believe that the church should satisfy religious (from the point of view of divine worship) needs; 7, emotional; 27, moral; 31, educational; 30, recreational; 12, practical economic; and 6, political. In general, it is believed that the Negro church should act to promote the social advancement of the race.

Changing attitudes toward the transcendental are reflected in members' conceptions of church functions. With diminution of the nonempirical, religion is falling within the category of logical action. The insignificance of nonexperimental ends is seen in the direction of interest to the social midst. The decline of traditional value attitudes is seen in the fact that most Boston informants join the church for social needs to a greater extent than for truly or traditionally religious. Changing religious attitudes are revealed in the importance members attach to recreation, education, and social intercourse. Although there is a degree of retention of traditional values, there is decreasing significance of the religion which prevailed during the stage of static equilibrium. In spite of the decline of the Supernatural as a source of authority for personal moral action, religion is regarded as a means of strengthening community organization.

To maintain influence over its followers, the church must increasingly modify its program so as to provide the type of religion important to its constituents. Since an empirical religion is regarded essential by men in the collectivity, further integration of the church with various phases of community life is necessary. Church members are no longer satisfied with contemplation of the Day of Reckoning.

II. EMPIRICAL RELIGIOUS ACTION

Past and Present Functions of Churches.—As emotional action diminished during the twentieth century, there was increasing integration of the church with the community. During the stage of static equilibrium, the church manifested some interest in improving social conditions. Nevertheless, the chief endeavor of the church consisted of missionary work in this country and abroad. The essential interest of the church was in establishing institutions of learning and christianizing people who were unfamiliar with the Christian religion. Considerable emphasis was placed upon education; many schools and churches were established and maintained by the church. And today the church continues to spend millions of dollars to propagate religion and education in and outside of the United States. However, it is unnecessary to enter an extensive discussion of the promotion of religion and secular education and the establishment of missions consisting of vast tracts of land, schools, and hospitals in foreign countries. To do this would involve a lengthy presentation of facts, which could provide the basis of a study of one phase of interest of the American church. The important point of consideration is that the church has manifested some actions of a practical nature in past centuries, and it has made efforts to promote physical and intellectual freedom and development. To a certain extent, the church has exhibited concern for the welfare of those whose advantages were restricted. Nevertheless, the church has tended to limit itself to the old type of philanthropic endeavor; it has tended to emphasize religious worship and transcendental values. There has tended to be ignorement of the practical benefits of religion in the community.

During the twentieth century, the church has progressively manifested a greater interest in improving community life and local conditions under which communicants live. Therefore, the church became more social and inclusive. It tended to extend into the community as it embraced a religion of social helpfulness. Instead of standing in ineffectual seclusion and drawing a line between religious and secular life, the church has been inclined to coordinate itself with the community. Thus a phase of activity previously neglected—recreation—was promoted by some churches. Community centers and neighborhood houses were established by some churches. Playgrounds and camps were sponsored and promoted by some churches. The church became interested in family life, juvenile delinquency, crime, and psychiatric care. Thereupon, a few churches created social agencies as one phase of the church program and employed social workers to aid handicapped and maladjusted groups in the community. This new phase of church activity accompanied the trend from concentrating upon the supersensory.

Churches in metropolitan areas, such as New York, Cleveland, Detroit, Chicago, have entered the field of social work and give consideration to recreation, labor, employment, housing, politics, and education. The Mt. Olivet Baptist church in Chicago conducts 42 departments and auxiliaries, with 512 officers, 5 assistant pastors, and 24 paid workers. A Baptist church in Jacksonville, Florida, provides a nursery, a kindergarten, a gymnasium, a school of music, a Bible school, and an employment bureau.[1] A Congregational church in Springfield, Massachusetts, conducts a resort, a dormitory for women, classes in music and handicraft, and provides employment and a women's welfare organization. Abyssinian Baptist church in New York is significant for its activity in the fields of labor, politics, recreation, and housing. The National Baptist Convention, U.S.A., disseminates information on business, citizenship, the armed forces, government, juvenile delinquency, health, child care, migration, and labor. These are some noteworthy examples of practical programs of churches in specific areas. Other churches and denominations sponsor projects of an empirical nature. Nevertheless, many churches primarily pursue the traditional form of action.

A. Church Programs in South Carolina

The Role of the Negro Clergyman with Respect to Practical Action.—The clergyman today assumes a more active role in directing

1 Owens, Richard, "Progress Among Negro Baptists," paper read at the Massachusetts Baptist Convention, Holyoke, Mass., October, 1940.

the religious interests of the Negro in practical action than formerly. Considerable attention has been given the influence of the leader upon religious action. It was shown that the ideas and actions of the leader are generally more advanced than those of laymen, and the group tends to pursue action in harmony with the attitudes of ministerial leaders. It was also demonstrated that action involves a reciprocal relationship; the leader is urged and restrained by laymen as he seeks to relate transcendental value attitudes to empirical action. The Negro preacher has held an influential position in the Negro system of action as interests of this racial group are related to religion. All important programs which pertain to the particular interest of the Negro are significantly influenced by the ministerial leader. And at the same time, the leader has sought to coordinate Negro religion with general Protestant Christianity as the Negro group manifested catholic actions. In other words, in addition to general efforts to improve social life through religion is the factor of promoting the aspirations of this particular group. This statement is tantamount to that of certain types of Christians and churches seeking to attain their religious ends as they tend to relate action to the body as a unit and to conform to the normative principle of the Protestant collectivity.

Aside from traditional empirical action, leaders in metropolitan areas (especially in the North) have generally manifested more practical action than leaders in small cities or rural areas. There has been a tendency to maintain the established religion, with respect to experimental action, in the North and the South. A few churches inaugurated broad programs which included various phases of social living. Other churches began slowly to follow the empirical pattern. And it was within the past twelve years that southern Negro clergymen began to pursue certain programs of action to any appreciable extent. And even yet some ministers hesitate to seek to modify certain features of action. In general, southern clergymen are more hesitant to depart from the traditional than northern. The presence of others motivated by different beliefs in the system of action is an obstacle to the realization of religious ends of some leaders. Fear of the threat of application of sanctions to the disadvantage of the person or group which seeks to institute change restrains action. This consideration is important with reference to a comparison of church programs of southern and northern clerical leaders. There are certain underlying features (for example, the reluctance of favorably situated socio-economic groups actively to exert effort to transform the social midst of economically depressed groups) which are similar. Nevertheless, religious differences between the North and the South do exist, partly because of differences in cultural patterns of the two areas. Recently, however, distinctions have diminished.

Empirical action is increasingly prevalent with the deterioration of nonexperimental beliefs.

The Negro Preacher in South Carolina.—In South Carolina, clergymen tend to act in harmony with the system of ends of the Protestant collectivity. It is important to think in terms of leaders because there are many actions which are individually pursued by pastors although certain features of action are shared in common by the pastor and his congregation. Even though there has been a little sporadic practical action other than the traditional, there is a more concerted effort to attain empirical ends at present.

Churches are functioning in various capacities as follows: religious, social, charitable, educational, recreational, economic, and political. The extent to which leaders and followers promote various aspects of these programs varies.

Some churches, cities, and sections place more emphasis upon one phase of action than upon others. For example, Church One concentrates upon recreation and community programs. It is unnecessary lengthily to elaborate upon practical church programs because the most significant part of this religious analysis pertains to the diminution of nonexperimental and emotional action in the Protestant collectivity. At the same time, some consideration is given the ascension of empirical action with the decline in supernaturalism. A condensed statement of present functions of churches is as follows.

Churches seek to give some attention to man's inclination to manifest reverent attitudes in communion with the Deity in religious worship. And some ministers believe that this phase of religion should not be overwhelmed by secular action. In other words, divine worship is primary although religion should prompt man to transform the social environment in harmony with the Christian ideal.

Some clergymen are constructing churches and improving buildings in which groups worship by making repairs and beautifying exterior surroundings with grass and shrubbery. Nevertheless, few improvements are being made in rural sections. The rural church is a neglected area.

Aside from the regular incidental penny or nickel collection for the poor, a few churches are seeking more adequately to provide for the needs of infirm members and destitute persons in the community. A few churches are presenting substantial contributions and a few are attempting to administer to charitable needs through organization. Some advanced churchmen believe that more attention should be given physically incapacitated and economically deficient groups in the community. Some clergymen are instrumental in securing old-age benefits and pensions from the state for the impoverished aged. Some encourage the handicapped and make it possible for them to attend the church by providing a means of transportation. Neither considerable nor adequate attention is given the retarded group in the community, however. Some clergymen manifest humanitarian attitudes and actions while others are indifferent. This applies to church members also. The church, especially in the country, is inclined to ignore the welfare of its communicants.

To proceed with community work which churches sponsor, some churchmen through coordinated effort establish playgrounds, infirmaries, etc. The trend now is toward interdenominational cooperation. Denominational lines are becoming insignificant as pastors seek to act in unison with or without interdenominational ministerial organizations to improve community life. For example, in Newberry, South Carolina, churchmen under the leadership of a physician and pastors of various churches in the community established a hospital, canvassed the county to solicit funds for a playground, to raise money for the National Association for the Advancement of Colored People (N.A.A.C.P.), to create favorable sentiment for an increase of public school teachers' salaries, and to raise money for local public schools, the Red Cross, and the Tuberculosis Association. Cooperation extended across county lines; Negro churchmen of various denominations in Aiken, South Carolina, sent substantial contributions for the Newberry hospital. Aiken clergymen also sought to improve community life in some of the other respects designated above. It is not always the educated or highly trained minister who acts to improve community standards; for instance, some of the most assiduous organizers in Newberry County are men of very modest education who are imbued with the principle of charity. The Negro minister, more so than any other professional in the South, actively seeks to help the people. (This is a general statement and it refers to consolidated groups; there are exceptions, of course. Individuals in some other groups exhibit the principle of love; and on the other hand, some ministers, as well as educators and business men, are exploitative and utilitarian. However, as a unified group the Negro ministers excel by far other professions in the degree of community activity.)

Some Negro ministers in South Carolina are manifesting interest in juvenile delinquents, are visiting jails, and are raising contributions for the defense of minors. This is a hitherto unexplored field; it was very recent that any coordinated group effort was manifested in this respect. Formerly, some clergymen as individuals sought release of members and supplied bond. Now the group is beginning to exert unified action with respect to the individual and not the church member. This field of endeavor is not as advanced as in Boston.

Some ministers are acting to improve family relationships, to secure travel accommodations, and to provide recreational workers in the community. In various counties of South Carolina, ministers combine efforts through interdenominational alliances to strengthen community organization. The center of activity is towns and cities. Organized community work is a recent field of endeavor in the state. Therefore, the opportunity for development is considerable.

With respect to community life, some denominations have had for a long time organizations designed to meet local missionary needs. Nothing significant except for the traditional form of missionary work was done. Some advance is being made through church organizations; yet these organizations have not penetrated the community. However, objectives of youth fellowship councils and women's societies for Christian service are to improve health and civic life, to provide spiritual, moral, and social guidance for youths, and to coordinate the home, the church, and the community. The objective of laymen's clubs is to cultivate the spiritual, moral, and intellectual proclivities of men in relation to institutional life. In some urban churches, especially in the North, these organizations (brotherhoods) are primarily discussion groups which cut across denominational boundaries. Sometimes renowned leaders speak to the group in assemblage, and sometimes financial contributions are made to promote a particular interest. Sometimes these groups bring talented artists before the public.

There has been organization of vacation Bible schools in the South and the North. The purpose of these schools is to offer religious instruction to youths, to provide wholesome leisure pursuits, and to circumvent loitering and delinquency by giving some consideration to recreation. In connection with youth programs, some southern and northern churches sponsor boy scout and girl scout clubs.

South Carolina churches, as well as others elsewhere in the South, contribute money to improve local public schools, maintain high schools and colleges in the state, contribute to regional schools, and maintain and contribute to institutions in foreign countries. (This is the traditional form of missionary endeavor.) Some churches are establishing missions in various foreign areas for which they previously made no provision.

With respect to recreation, effort is being made to provide supervised play activity. A few churches employ recreational workers, provide volunteer supervisors, and establish playgrounds, some of which are adequately and inadequately equipped. The trend from the old toward a new emphasis is seen in the conversion of camp grounds into recreational and training centers, and the formation of plans to establish community projects on camp meeting areas since people are not interested in camp meetings.[1] Some city churches have religious and recreational centers (community houses). And the general Methodist church has made plans to construct a clinic and a recreational community house in one of the retarded sections of isolation in South Carolina. A little is being done in physical education; and the possibilities in this phase of activity are outstanding since most areas are not provided for in any respect.

Economic aid by a few ministers consists mainly of advising members not to spend money for inconsequential things, encouraging thrift in order to maintain one's obligations and to purchase a home, and making small loans.

Many ministers have their congregations contribute to the Red Cross, the Tuberculosis Association, and the N.A.A.C.P. Through the N.A.A.C.P., legal aid is secured for people in the state.

For the past seven years South Carolina clergy have been very active in the N.A.A.C.P. by holding executive positions, making individual contributions, urging their congregations to contribute to this organization, and by carrying the organization directly into the church in spite of opposition from many members. The Negro minister in South Carolina is the leader of the progressive movement among Negroes. Preachers were active in actually executing the increase of teachers' salaries, in educating Negroes for citizenship by conducting classes and speeches, and in urging them to qualify to vote. In 1947 and 1948, ministerial action was conspicuously tremendous. Some laymen have been leaders and followers in this phase of activity.

Preachers have sought to promote harmonious racial relations in their communities and have often promoted tolerance and cooperation between the races.

The following table shows the number of churches out of thirty which sponsor certain phases of religious action, according to clerical informants.

Religion is being related to the community with decrescent supernaturalism. However, coalescence of the church with the community is not general irrespective of advance; many churches still operate under the old program.

[1] Some traditionalists attempted to revive a discontinued outdoor meeting at one camp in 1947 but were forced to abandon efforts for resurrection because of lack of attendance. Few people support the camp meeting, a decaying religious manifestation sometimes retained by some localities.

TABLE TWENTY-NINE

Programs South Carolina Clergymen and Churches Promote

	Rural	*Urban*
Churches providing mainly needs for religious worship	2	2
Welfare work (health, employment, old-age assistance, etc.)	6	2
Recreation	3	5
Literary programs	4	0
N.A.A.C.P. and politics	2	4
Multiple functions	2	4

Factors in the Delay of Practical Action in South Carolina.—There are various reasons for the retardation of practical action in southern churches. Briefly, these reasons are as follows: fear of reprisal, opposition from constituents, apathy of educated or advantaged groups in the Negro collectivity, inertia, and lack of foresight and perspective of some leaders of various occupations. Some clergy fail to promote community programs and local missionary endeavors partly because of fear that controlling individuals and groups will alter the situation to the disadvantage of the local leader. To avoid disapproval, censure, and pressure, some who are motivated by altruistic principles with respect to people in the local community fail to execute their ends. Some have made efforts to inaugurate change, but they modified their course of action after finding it personally disastrous. For example, some persons who sought to improve community life by organizing domestic and agricultural laborers and by giving advice to investors were reported in the outer community (sometimes by persons in the economic group they sought to aid and sometimes by professional people who desired to obtain or retain a position) as promoting unrest and dissatisfaction in the community. After a few experiences, these ministerial leaders considered it inexpedient to advocate change. Other leaders who sought to interest some of the advantaged citizens in the community in constructing hospitals and aiding unskilled laborers were discouraged or ridiculed. Another important point of consideration is the hierarchical relationship in the church (especially some denominations).

Some clergymen believe that a portion of the Crusades for Christ money contributed by Negro Methodists in South Carolina should be specifically designated for education and recreation in South Carolina. (Some of the white South Carolina Methodist churches do this; some white clergymen suggested to Negro clergymen that this procedure be followed.) A few ministers believed that this method would be beneficial to the local community since practically all of this money left the state and still churchmen had to support their local college, which requested $50,000, had to pay fees for their children to attend state and church colleges, and it was necessary for rural people to pay a fee to send their children to the public city high school. Furthermore, churchmen were requested to make special contributions to a recreational center in the Midwest. South Carolina Negro Methodists had already paid $50,000 to this special project which would be of no practical benefit to them.[1] Nine thousand dollars was paid by them for world service in 1947, and $99,000 was contributed to the Crusades for Christ endeavor for the period 1944–1948; $50,000 was provided for maintenance and improvement of the local college in 1946, and contributions were made for the regional theological seminary. The few ministers who suggested that a part of the money which was being sent outside of the state be retained to help establish local recreational centers and to improve educational conditions in South Carolina were reprimanded by superiors and told that they were opposing the program of the church. Those who advocated alteration of policy did not oppose contributions to other areas since they realize that it is desirable to cooperate and consider the welfare of distant people; but they were also motivated by the belief that *the church should act to improve living conditions of economically submerged groups in South Carolina*. Since the chief standard of success is the ability to raise money and to hold the membership intact, many clergymen ignore practical approaches to community problems.

Distance between the rural preacher and his parishioners is another element in retardation. Another is the attitude that other institutions should assume their responsibility for direction, guidance, and provision. The church cannot cover all phases of community life. Some clergy state that it is not within the scope of the church to advise farmers concerning production, marketing, and the formation of cooperatives or organizations to produce and distribute commodities, etc., efficiently and effectively. They maintain that the church is a religious institution and not an instrument of advice in business matters. The essential thing is to persuade people to become Christians; a living Christianity would solve all social problems, they affirm. Furthermore, people do not appreciate the benefit of the knowledge of others. Advising churchmen to invest their money in business or industry would produce antagonism. And if the minister admonishes against spending money for certain secular pleasures (alcoholic con-

[1] This refers only to Methodists of the denomination formerly known as the Methodist Episcopal church. It has no reference to A.M.E.'s, A.M.E.Z.'s, and C.M.E.'s who promote projects of their own.

sumption, for instance), he had just as well begin looking for another charge. Since people spend considerable money for frivolous things or temporal pastimes, the church should seek to get large contributions for the traditional form of missionary work. And the preacher would jeopardize his position in the church and the community by attempting to improve social conditions; therefore it is better to let these matters evolve to an eventual haphazard solution, it is believed by those whose experiences have led them to follow the traditional pattern. Fear of disapprobation is a deterrent of practical action.

Another reason for inactivity is the necessity of study, planning, and energy to institute community programs.

Irrespective of the diverse attitudes toward practical action, some rural churchmen are expressing a desire for instruction and information. Some indicate that they have no knowledge of methods to strengthen rural organization and means of promoting effective community living. Eagerness for instruction is obvious among informants in Churches A and D, who have not had the rudiments of education and who live on the poverty level. These farmers express a need for guidance in the principles of citizenship.

Some churchmen of various sections believe that the church should make more adequate provision for local members. This is one reason that laymen formed a Young Men and Young Women's Christian Association (really a misnomer since this religious organization consists of adults of various ages) among various denominations in counties of the state. Leaders of this organization state that they are doing for people what the church has failed to do. Provision is made for aid to the sick and burial of the dead. This form of group insurance was initiated because impecunious people in the community needed help in illness and death. This society, a religious organization of fifty-six chapters which urges support of institutional religion, originated in 1923 and has extended to various sections of the state. Although this association developed around churches, it is not a part of the organized church.

Observations show that rural people do feel a need for assistance, which they do not receive from various agencies and institutions. This deficiency is an important point of consideration for all groups which touch rural life and all institutions which are related to rural organization. Although rural churchmen seem to be grasping for that which they do not have, and although the urban worshipper more dexterously expresses his religious aspirations and has a more comprehensive view of religion than the rural worshipper, churchmen in all areas anticipate a more practical religion.

Irrespective of delay in empirical religious action, the southern church is beginning to manifest more interest in the local environment. The center of interest and activity is the town and the city, however. Rural needs continue to be greatly disregarded.

The Attitude of the Pastor of Churches A-D.—The importance of empirical ends to this rural pastor is seen in his conception of church functions. Briefly, his attitude is as follows. The church should seek to coordinate religion with life by urging its membership to manifest the principles of Christianity in daily living, by administering to the infirm spiritually and financially, by advising its subjects in personal and business matters, by giving political advice and instruction and urging members to vote and manifest an active interest in civic developments, by urging them to participate in democratic group life and to promote activities which are of benefit to the people in the community, by encouraging economically insecure groups, by seeking to improve conditions under which people live, by urging prudence, economy, and wise investment of money, by indicating the necessity of an active instead of a passive religion, and by emphasizing the importance of the Christian doctrine in its relation to harmonious group life. The church should not lose sight of vast opportunities for service in areas surrounding the local church as it seeks to extend its influence to distant places. While moving toward a rational standard, there should not be submergence of the spiritual in the church. To be a vital institution, the church must regard the attitudes of traditional and conservative Christians in the system of action and it must be aware of its responsibility in the local community. A remote church distantly related to its communicants will become ineffectual in the system of action. This pastor regards it essential that all groups be reminded of the potentialities of the Christian religion; there should be conscious re-enforcement of the necessity of applying the principle of brotherhood in all phases of life.[1]

In observing the relationship between the ideas and actions of this leader, it is noted that there is an effort to conform practice with theory. Nevertheless, constraint and the effect of the actions of others previously referred to have tended to restrain and delay the pursuit of action according to his empirical standard. Since some persons impede departure from a traditional form of religion as far as church programs are concerned, and since some misrepresent motives in the outer community and are indifferent to the conditions under which persons not of their social status live, this leader found it practicable

[1] Interview, The Reverend S. A Funchess, Orangeburg, South Carolina, August 10, 1947.

to delay empirical action. However, he is again embarking, at a moderate rate of speed, upon an active religion irrespective of past experiences. And he is giving advice and urging action in some matters which there was reticence to discuss except sometimes in private conversation. Nevertheless, there are yet some features of action which he refrains from presenting to his congregations, consisting of 600 members. As in the past, his church program tends to be of a personal and business nature. He votes, promotes ministerial, interracial, and community cooperation, and has considerable influence in the outer community.

He is one of the rural pastors who manifest interest (aside from financial contributions to the church) in his communicants. That is, there is an attempt to be of practical aid to parishioners, as well as rural people in other areas. He gives guidance in moral, family, and business relationships. He helps to adjust marital problems; he intercedes in matters of family education on the high school and college levels; he gives advice concerning mortgages; he makes arrangements with banks to provide loans for farmers; he endorses notes, acts as bondsman, helps to adjust legal difficulties and matters, and urges farmers not to throw away their income by taking chances at fairs and being deceived by conniving showmen. He provides transportation for those who have no means of conveyance to church; he visits his members; he renovates and improves churches; he cooperates with extra-religious charitable and benevolent institutions through the church; he gives some instruction regarding qualifications for voting, and he promotes interracial understanding and cooperation. This is considerably more than the average rural preacher does; however, Pastor A-D refrains from presenting certain problems of rural education and farming conditions in relation to his local community because he regards it inadvisable to do so.

B. Church Programs in Boston

Boston Clergymen's Conceptions of Programs Churches Should Sponsor.—Although clergymen's attitudes toward emotionalism, their conceptions of ideas ministers should impart to their congregations during sermons, and sermons indicate the nature of beliefs and actions with respect to programs churches should promulgate, additional information in this respect is conveyed by making specific reference to leaders' attitudes toward services churches should perform.

Clergymen believe that religion is not isolated from life; therefore the church should advocate and promulgate any program which aids adjustment and contributes to the well-being of the individual and the community. Correspondingly, the church should act with respect to poverty, employment, working conditions, housing, delinquency and crime, education, health, recreation, politics, intolerance, and distance between social groups. Since pathological conditions, such as unemployment, inadequate or substandard housing, exploitation, physical and mental disorders, family disorganization, etc., affect the entire community and impair salutary group living, the church should actively seek to correct inadequacies and to promote programs which facilitate an effective social order. There should be conscious effort to influence and to direct action and to encourage policies and procedures which further social adjustment. Each segment of the community is affected by conditions under which other groups live. The church should relate itself to individual and group welfare. By giving adequate consideration to the individual and sponsoring programs which prompt and lead him to pursue a productive life, the church will promote happiness, satisfaction, and social harmony.

The church should act to advance spiritual, moral, intellectual, and social development.

The following excerpts concretely convey conceptions of church functions. (Each paragraph represents a different quotation.)

Aside from religious worship, the primary function should be the spiritual development of man. The church should christianize and crystallize society. The church should preach, teach, and evangelize as Christ promulgated religion. . . . I would not only preach to a man to save his soul, but I would try to satisfy any need (other than subjective evil ends) of this man, such as finding a job for him or lending him money. The church should be interested in and should help to promote individual advancement. The church should serve mankind. The clergyman should advocate and support political and social measures which are for the general good. He should guide members to support programs which accelerate action in the direction of social betterment. Spiritual, intellectual, and social advancement are functions of the church. Our church acts in these various respects.[1]

Religion is related to empirical action. The church should meet community needs, and it should be interested in all phases of social life. In our church, we endeavor to influence all phases of group living.

The church should act to meet spiritual, industrial, and social needs. For me, the objective of the church is steering adjustment to life. The church should be the answer to any unsatisfactory conditions or circumstances. The church should penetrate the community. It should help people; and it should provide employment and establish businesses. It should encourage individual and group saving and investment. The church should be inter-

[1] Interview, Pastor Two, The Reverend Richard M. Owens, January 14, 1947.

ested in the welfare of people in and outside of the immediate community. It should protect the weak from exploitation; it should train men to act judiciously; and it should promote self-reliance and independence of disadvantaged groups. Laymen and public leaders should not form alliances with the strong to defraud the weak. The church should not be dominated by any social group nor serve the interests of one class or aggregate at the expense of another. The church should exist for the benefit of all groups in society, and there should be adequate recognition of the rights of all worshippers. The church has a moral responsibility in the community. Its duty is to improve individual and group life.[1]

Any humanitarian organization, whether labor unions or social agencies, should be supported by the church. The gospel of Jesus should be related to life, with the full realization that man shall not live by bread alone. I do not separate man's spiritual and social needs.

Empirical Action in the North and the South.—Repeated reference has been made to the role of the leader in religious action. A comparison of empirical programs of southern and northern churches has been made. It was indicated that the southern church departs more slowly from established procedures than the northern. Sectionalism influences religion; consequently, the rate of religious and social change in the North and the South is not identical. Since this is true, there has been impairment of practical religious action in the South. And, as a result, the southern church has tended to conserve the traditional form of empirical action and to advance somewhat slowly toward the local community. In other words, the northern church has been more active in relating religion to the various spheres of life than the southern church, which is in the midst of a society which impedes change. Notwithstanding, some city churches in the South have been active in education, employment, recreation, and business. Nevertheless, these churches tended to restrict themselves to certain phases of activity and did not effectively relate themselves to broad aspects of social living. Albeit, distinctions are growing weaker, and the southern church is tending to act in the direction of the community.

The above discussion does not convey the idea that all northern churches are more practical than southern; in the North and the South, there are churches which do not as yet actively identify themselves with community living. With respect to empirical action, the three types of churches are found in both regions. The essential idea is to compare religious action and to note that the collectivity as a unit is moving in the direction of the normative system of ends. The transcendental emphasis is being succeeded by a religion which retains some supernatural values and acquires empirical qualities. Since

[1] Interview, The Director, The Reverend W. Frederic Fisher, Boston, June 2, 1947.

churchmen believe that through the Christian religion man should seek to establish the Kingdom of God on earth, religion is being more actively related to life.

Churches vary in the degree of emphasis upon aspects of group life. Some churches act in some way to relate religion to all phases of institutional life; some select a special field of interest, while others perform only traditional religious functions.

Through things of the spirit, the church is attempting to inspire loyalty to other institutions and is working with the home, the school, and the court to foster character development. A part of this character-building program is sponsored by the church, which is providing educational and recreational facilities as a means of physical, mental, and spiritual growth.

Functions of Boston Clergymen and Churches.—Boston clergy seek to facilitate community organization. Thus churches in Boston sponsor or promote crime prevention and rehabilitation programs, education, recreation, housing, business, and interracial cooperation. It is believed that these phases of group living can be furthered or retarded by government; therefore clergymen participate in the election of governmental officials and seek to influence legislation.

Boston pastors direct welfare and participate in community programs. For example, one pastor, whose church is active in various phases of group life, is a member of the board of directors of the Red Cross, of a community center, and of the Boy Scouts. He has served on the steering committee of the Fair Employment Practices Commission (FEPC) and has held executive office in the Greater Boston National Association for the Advancement of Colored People, and he is a member of the Progressive Citizens of America.

Members of church organizations visit hospitals and homes for the aged, and junior choirs sing for persons in these institutions.

Evidence of institutional cooperation is seen in the relationship between the court and the church. Boston clergymen cooperate with the Juvenile Court, with the objective of promoting the reconstruction and adjustment of delinquents. The Roxbury Ministers' Alliance, and the Greater Boston Interdenominational Alliance appoint representatives to be present at sessions of the Juvenile Court. By a revolving procedure, ministers have assignments to serve as religious representatives for a definite period. The intermediary serves as counsellor to Protestant families of deviators and establishes connection between the defendant and his pastor. After notification, the pastor is present at court proceedings and intercedes in behalf of the defendant. The representative acts in an advisory capacity for unchurched delinquents. Through the consent of the judge, the pastor may become a "big brother" to the deviator, and thus the clergyman seeks to solve family problems and to promote the spiritual growth of the transgressor through guidance. In some instances, boys are placed under probationary direction of clergymen.

With respect to education, Boston churches contribute to the traditional form of missionary enterprise, as well as the new phase of activity. By cooperating with the general church, they sponsor foreign missionary programs in various parts of the world; and they make contributions to religious institutions of learning in the United States. Churches make contributions to individuals and organizations. A few local scholarships are offered. Student-aid is also given in the form of part-time positions in churches as pastoral assistants, musicians, and social workers. Churches also cooperate with public schools while promoting the religious education of youths, who are given instruction in churches during a part of one school day each week. Churches make donations to teachers of religious education whom they employ. Some of the Boston churches have kindergartens and nurseries. Men of information constantly speak in the various churches of the metropolis.

Some churches do not neglect the physical, manual, artistic, and mental development of communicants. Some of the recreational centers have gymnasiums. Some centers provide classes in handicraft, art, and music appreciation. Some provide organizations for youths, and some serve as a focus of community life. The youth center in one of the Cambridge churches began an interracial project among junior boys. There is an equal ratio of white and Negro members.

Some of the Boston churches which have community centers receive financial assistance from their general church, since they cannot support a recreational center unaided. Community centers and nurseries are found among the established churches (Congregational, Baptist, Methodist, A.M.E., A.M.E.Z., etc.). Nevertheless, it is seldom that more than one church of each denomination has more than one community project of this nature. Although most Boston churches have no community or educational centers, most of them sponsor some form of recreation. During vacation months, churches make arrangements for youths to go to summer resorts, and one Boston church sponsors and conducts a camp.

Interest of Boston churches in health and surroundings which are conducive to pleasant, happy, wholesome living extends to the field of housing. Clergymen urge local and national passage of housing legislation, attend hearings on vital public issues, study housing conditions with respect to the people in their community, and conduct meetings in the interest of housing in their communities. Ministerial alliances try to arouse public interest in rental policies, and insurance zoning in their districts, and try to restrain real estate men and rental agencies which seek to speculate and to exploit poor persons in the community by forming restrictive covenants.

In regard to business, this field is not generally developed by Boston churches. The primary interest is in urging sound investments and arranging business transactions for members.

In regard to government, most of the pastors of Boston churches manifest some form of political action. The extent of activity varies as in other phases of group life. Some churches act in a passive capacity, while others actively campaign and support certain candidates for public office. Most ministers impress upon audiences the importance of voting, making wise use of the ballot, and taking advantage of the opportunity to vote. Some present information on candidates for office and discuss various platforms in relation to the community. Some tell their congregations whom to support, while others do not. Some clergymen permit candidates for office to speak in their churches.

Some clergymen seek to be elected to public office. Within the past three years, two Cambridge clergymen have sought to be elected to municipal positions, and they plan to continue to be active in politics.[1] The essence of the platform of one candidate is as follows: "Prime consideration for the individual rather than property, no segregation or discrimination in housing, passage of a municipal FEPC, provision of standard recreational facilities, and establishment of a minimum wage of sixty-five cents an hour." Members of the candidates' churches were the nucleus of political organization for these office seekers who were urged to seek office by their congregations after members had become active in politics as a result of the interest of these churches in passage of national FEPC legislation and abolition of poll taxes. These clergymen had asked their congregations to sign petitions, to write letters to congressmen, and to influence their acquaintances to act in the interest of this legislation; and these leaders had made trips to Washington in an effort to influence congressmen. Other Negro Cambridge churches cooperated in this activity. A Negro Roman Catholic was campaign manager, and white and Negro citizens worked in behalf of these candidates.

Other Negro churches in metropolitan Boston support the N.A.A.C.P. and send telegrams to congressmen urging passage of FEPC

[1] Although Cambridge has an independent municipal government, this city is really a part of the metropolitan Boston area. Residents of Boston and Cambridge manifest interest in the government of both cities; many Cambridge residents work in Boston, and some are heads of departments of the municipal government of Boston. Cambridge clergymen are members and officers of greater Boston ministerial alliances and of other organizations in which residents of the two cities share mutual interest.

and anti-poll tax legislation, rental control and housing bills. In addition to urging members to vote, this form of political activity is the most common among Boston clergymen. Otherwise, there is no consolidated political community strength in or outside of the Boston Negro church. Some clergymen state that they have attempted to unite the community but have not had any success in this respect. In some other metropolitan areas, Negro leaders and churches are more influential in this respect.

Boston Negro ministers are members of interracial ministerial alliances; they exchange pulpits with white clergymen, and they attend interracial meetings. Interracial cooperation is also seen in regard to recreational programs. In order to promote association and understanding, pastors participate in a project which is designed to bring the races together at play and in the home. Believing that racial relations programs should extend beyond speeches, conferences, and books, the Reverend Ritchie Low, a white Congregational minister of Vermont, initiated a plan by which brotherhood could be manifested in action. Believing that contact would be an effective means of promoting good will, he made arrangements through churches in various sections of the country for Negro and white children to visit each other's homes and to attend recreational and social gatherings together. In the interest of this interdenominational national project, this leader has travelled extensively, addressed groups, made plans for persons unfamiliar with the project to cooperate, and has made a study of Negro housing and education in New York. Ministers and laymen have cooperated to the extent that the program has been successful in Massachusetts, Vermont, New Hampshire, Maine, Connecticut, Rhode Island, New York, Illinois, Indiana, Minnesota, Kansas, and California. This race relations program is conceived as "the church of Christ in action for brotherhood."[1]

In order to show the features of action which are emphasized by ten Boston churches, the following table is included.

To a certain extent, eight of these churches are very active in community work. However, only four of them are included under "multiple functions" because of the outstanding position of these churches in relating religion with associational and institutional life. These four not only participate in the general type of empirical action in Boston; they have incorporated organized social work in their churches. And the church program does not rest principally upon the leader, although he is an important factor. The practical work of some

[1] Address, The Reverend Ritchie Low, St. Mark Congregational Church, Roxbury, Mass., May 25, 1947.

churches is pursued mainly by the pastor; were his activity withdrawn, the church would become unimportant with respect to experimental action.

TABLE THIRTY

Programs Boston Clergymen and Churches Promote

Churches providing mainly needs for religious worship	1
Welfare work	5
Education (kindergartens, or other class work)	4
Recreation (community centers)	4
Business and employment	2
Politics	7
Multiple functions	4

Empirical Actions of Pastors One-Three.—Pastors One, Two, and Three seek to relate religion to life. Pastor One encourages and promotes art, education, recreation, employment, and welfare. He is interested in community and social work. He urges passage of legislation which will benefit all groups in the community, and he advocates and promotes legislative enactment which affects the particular group he leads. He acts as adviser to his group and acts to advance harmonious social relationships. He conceives broad religious objectives and believes in a religion directly related to life, a religion which will advance the Kingdom of God in this world. He seeks to impress upon others the importance of living the principle of brotherhood. In Church One, there is advancement of local and foreign missionary endeavor.

Pastor Two seeks to facilitate the spiritual, moral, intellectual, and social growth of his adherents. He provides a variety of organizations for the various types of churchmen in his congregation. He supplies abundant opportunities for fellowship and religious association, gives some consideration to recreation and expects to provide facilities for physical education in the near future. He sponsors art, music, and dramatic productions and engages in local and foreign humanitarian projects. He emphasizes the importance of registration and voting and sometimes advises support of certain candidates. Through his church, he supports the N.A.A.C.P. and urges sentiment and action favorable to passage of national legislation in regard to his group. He, as well as Pastor One, cooperates with other institutions (as the school and the court) in the community. Both leaders give some consideration to the needs of the physically handicapped and the aged. Clubs and special programs to consider these groups are provided.

The Director (leader of Church Three) acts as mediator, and counsellor for the persons he leads. He promotes family solidarity, discourages divorce, disfavors remarriage of divorced persons. He relieves the physically and the mentally ill by making arrangements for them to enter hospitals, by making financial contributions to them, and by guaranteeing the payment of bills, and by providing jobs to hasten recovery. He takes an interest in court cases, he helps to make provision for some aged persons in the community, he gives recognition to the aspirations of all men and seeks to promote adjustment of submerged elements in the community. He sponsors religious education in his church and elsewhere, trains missionaries, and offers scholarships for religious study. He makes contributions to educational institutions. He provides opportunities for leadership and fellowship by having various types of organizations, such as Boosting Jesus clubs, youth congresses, brotherhoods, etc. He participates in and sponsors interdenominational and interracial programs locally and sectionally. The Director and the other pastor of the church urge economy and investment. They promote and establish businesses for people in the community. They sponsor employment, give information on available jobs, and recommend persons for positions in industry. They relate health and sanitation to the church, and cooperate with community health agencies. They bring speakers before the congregation and participate in programs which promote the religious, moral, intellectual, and social advancement of man. And they plan to expand various activities, such as employment, business, and education, which they sponsor. Because of the quality of leadership, there has been coordination of Church Three with the community.

* * * *

Anticipation of Victory of the Higher Principle.—The Deity as a source of authority is significant in action. Man seeks to relate those teachings of Christ which are effective in promoting harmonious social relations to group life. Men extract those elements which they regard pragmatic and seek to achieve the principle of brotherhood in social living.

There is a relationship between social equilibrium and religion. Religion expresses the collective aspirations of men to achieve a harmonious society. It integrates individual ends into a system of action. And men seek to subordinate individual ends to social. There is integration of diverse ends in a system of action. There is operation of the principle of common welfare or "the greatest good for the greatest number." However, there is imperfect integration of individual and group systems of action in the social system. Nevertheless, a degree of harmony exists.

Believing that through religion an effective social order will be realized, men strive to conform their actions to a religious system of norms.

Though not confident that men really live by the principle of charity, men seek and exert effort to realize the ideal in life. There is faith in the social prescriptions of Jesus. Men can, it is believed, attain supremacy of the superior principle over the inferior in society. Actually following the Social Message as a guide for living will impede disintegrating factors, advance elevating and coordinating elements, and hasten realization of the Kingdom of God on earth.

Being motivated by these beliefs, men strive effectively to relate the church to other social institutions. They hope to retard or subdue factors which contribute to nullification of the abundant in this world. Consequently, churchmen are trying to offset pathological social conditions. And they are seeking to reincarnate the principle of charity and to readjust antithetical elements. They are trying to adapt religion to present social needs. They are seeking to strengthen community organization through Christian action. There is ascension of empirical religious elements. And there is a degree of correspondence between belief and action. Practical aspects of religion are becoming ascendant as churchmen relate religion to life, with diminution of the supernatural. And the social character of religious beliefs is obvious. Through religion, man pursues the ideal in social action.

* * * * *

The Movement for United Protestantism.—While taking cognizance of some religious changes, the Protestant faiths are seeking to counteract division and functional ineffectiveness through unification of the various branches of Protestant Christianity in America. By presenting a united front (with or without denominational demarcation) it is believed that consolidation of effort and facilities will facilitate more effective religious organization, which will ensure coordination and unification of church buildings according to need and population change and which will provide a means of effective labor, recreational and racial programs. It is thought that concentrated effort and organization will vitalize Protestant Christianity. The church is now more conscious of a need for general social programs and is interested in passage of legislation which will influence labor conditions. There is formation of broad outlines for Protestant Christianity.

Although realization of the designated objectives would minimize some present deficiencies, other underlying features of action would not be relieved. A pertinent concrete program which directly pertains to areas of conflict is essential.

Summary and Analysis

This analysis of the beliefs and actions of men with respect to the divine is based upon a study of the Protestant church, with particular reference to South Carolina and Boston, Massachusetts. There was measurement of the religious attitudes of Negro churchmen in rural and urban areas, through interview and observation. There was an attempt to determine the nature of attitudes and whether or not attitudes and practices correspond. An objective was to ascertain the extent of modification of religious action with social change. Another objective was to determine the nature of religious motivation today as men seek to realize the ideal. Also, there was an attempt to estimate the effect of present religious attitudes and practices upon the Protestant system of action and to calculate the probable future effects of the course of action upon the Protestant collectivity.

For purposes of this study, it was feasible to employ the type-concept inasmuch as it facilitated an analysis of individual and group end-systems of action in relation to the religious body as a unit. That is, people conceive reality differently; they are motivated by diverse attitudes as they seek to attain the sublime in life. There is not uniformity of thought and practice; there is a variety of attitudes toward the Supreme. Since this is true, the type-concept provides an effective means of condensing facts by classifying those whose attitudes are similar to a significant degree in the same group and by relating these types to the religious system of action. Although the religious conceptions of Christians are not identical, there are some beliefs which are held in common; hence there is a degree of integration of the individual and group end-systems of action. The religious body pursues action according to a normative standard, which expresses the collective sentiments of the group.

Men strive to attain certain goals of action. And they go through certain operations or make use of certain methods (means) to achieve the desired state of things (end). In the pursuit of ends action is regulated by a normative standard of rules, which limit and restrict action by defining appropriate action and by regulating the manner in which goals are to be sought. This normative principle or guiding system of rules accelerates harmony of action and facilitates peaceful operations among men. There is an attitude of respect toward the normative system, which provides the basis of an effective social order. It regulates distributive relations of groups as men seek to provide the maximum of utility for the collectivity. Society pursues common ends.

As men seek to attain aspirations shared in common and as they seek to comprehend the mysterious and the unknown, they relate themselves to a deity, the source of cognition and authority. Religion, which is influenced by men's individual attitudes and collective sentiments, is an expression of the common goals of men. Religion expresses and directs the interests of men.

Society is influenced by men's religious ideas. And social action is understandable in terms of men's active attitudes toward the supernatural.

In the past there was a greater degree of integration in the Protestant system than there is today. There was a striking similarity in attitudes toward the Supreme Being. The Omnipotent was an irrefutable source of authority for moral action. Men accepted the Ten Commandments and sought to regulate action according to the sacred norm. There was great reliance upon the Deity, who sustained life.

Through God one was strengthened to assume and to perform daily arduous tasks. One was reanimated to pursue action regardless of irksome circumstances. By concentrating upon the Divine, recompense for social dissatisfaction was provided. To a considerable degree, men related themselves to the nonempirical aspects of existence.

With the element of awe and reverence, there was outstanding manifestation of emotions of joy and sorrow. Religious emotions were forcibly expressed in action as men confidently anticipated the final triumph of good in Heaven. Emotional fervor was a characteristic religious feature.

Accompanying the manifestation of sentiments in nonexperimental and emotional action was another significant form of action of an empirical nature. Men considered it their Christian duty to propagate the principles of God by converting and teaching. Thus missionary endeavor took the form of promoting the Christian religion through the establishment of institutions of learning. Also, there was effort to make men conscious of the merits of the Christian religion and to induce them to live by the Sermon on the Mount. Christians promoted physical and intellectual freedom.

As time passed, attitudes toward the Supreme Being gradually changed. There was increasing education, scientific discovery, and urbanization. There was transformation of men's religious actions. Men began to take various attitudes toward the Omnipotent. And differences in attitudes eventually became conspicuous, far more striking than formerly.

By the twentieth century there was outstanding alteration of religious practices. And those whose religious interests continued to be conceived in terms of the static form of equilibrium found their position impaired in the Protestant system of action. Men were progressively seeking new religious ends; and as forces moved in a different direction, new elements introduced in the action system increasingly overbalanced and outweighed former elements. The position of those who tend to retain traditional religion is comparable in many respects with that of the masses during the former equilibrium.

The popular Protestant churches (Methodist and Baptist) have altered and are modifying procedures and actions to a considerable extent.

As a result of changes which are occurring in the Protestant church, clearly defined types are apparent. The three main types of Christians whose attitudes toward the supersensory are different irrespective of common beliefs are as follows. The traditional type of Christian tends to retain established religious practices. The authority of the Deity is incontrovertible. Action is regulated according to the system of sacred norms. There is overt manifestation of religious emotions. And empirical action is of the former form of missionary enterprise. The conservative type or "moderate religionist" gradually departs from customary practices, expresses his religious emotions in a semi-subdued manner, and regards the spiritual superior to the empirical as action is related to the local and the distant community. The empirical type of Christian is not particularly interested in attainment of a nonexperimental ideal. He seeks actively to coordinate religion with the various aspects of social life as he expresses his religious emotions in a subdued manner. The three types have a common characteristic: Man should seek realization of the ideal, should try to conform action with the teachings of Christ, and should direct others to the attainment of an abundant life.

Churches emerge according to type and there is a preponderance of certain types of Christians in certain churches.

The presence of three types of Christians in a church has provoked disturbance. Disharmony of action has resulted from various motivations. There is conflict of end-systems of types in the Protestant collectivity.

This analysis of the attitudes of churchmen shows the social nature of religious beliefs. As values in society change, religious beliefs and actions are altered. This is seen in regard to the sacred norms as regulators of conduct, in regard to the diminution of transcendental value-attitudes, in regard to the form of empirical action, and in regard to the position of the church in the social system.

As a unit, churchmen believe that religion should prompt man to act to attain the ideal in society as there is regulation of action in correspondence with the Christian norm. Man should integrate religion with life and coordinate the church with other social institutions as he seeks to act in compliance with a standard of rationality. There should be extirpation of extreme emotional manifestations from religious action. Emotionalism is a barrier to rational action. Man should actively identify himself with society and cease contemplating the Day of Reckoning. However, man must not lose sight of spiritual values in the pursuit of empirical ends.

This normative system of rules enjoys institutional authority. There is application of sanctions against nonconformers. Though there is a degree of integration of ends in the system of action, men take various attitudes toward the norm. Some accept and adhere; some adhere unwillingly, while others do not comply with "the unemotional norm." The last group combats and resists the guiding principle of action.

The presence of others motivated by different beliefs in the system of action is a barrier to the attainment of the religious objectives of some men.

The application of sanctions has outstanding effects upon the Protestant church. Traditionalists are maladjusted to the progressive form of equilibrium. As a result of unfulfillment of religious aspirations there is withdrawal from the established Protestant church. During the twentieth century there has been a tremendous growth of the cult movement. Cultism provides satisfaction for those to whom emotional expression of religious sentiments is important. It gives recognition to submerged social groups in the system of action. Some cult leaders include practical economic elements in their religion—this is an attractive feature to economically depressed groups.

As there is an increase of rationality, education, and urbanization, division on the basis of social status proceeds in the established church. Social stratification, an index of division in the community, is seen in the Protestant church. Some churchmen in churches consisting of professional and business groups, in addition to some wage-earners, regard themselves as being of an elevated status and hence manifest supercilious attitudes toward more conservative or traditional churches. At the same time, a conservative church consisting of persons of varying background and attainment has division within its membership. Cleavage is seen in church organizations; there are affiliations of certain types of persons in certain clubs. Church members tend to identify themselves with clubs whose membership comprises persons of common interest, attainment, or attribute. In the empirical type of church heretofore described affinity is seen in the formation of associations of persons of education and money. Internal division in the structure of the church promotes relegation of traditional Christians or economically insecure groups to an obscure position. Thus men seek new religions.

As change proceeds in the Negro Protestant collectivity there is departure from the church in two directions. Some unsatisfied laymen seek religions which emphasize nonexperimental action and which include other attractive features. Increasingly, Negroes are becoming Catholics, as well as cultists.

Some members who remain in the Protestant church are unsatisfied. Some desire a more effective form of practical action irrespective of the trend to relate religion with life. *The rural churchman desires recognition and consideration of the social conditions under which he lives;* and he is grasping for a religion which has far more significance than a semi-monthly or monthly Sunday service. *He feels a need for local missionary endeavor.*

Some ministerial leaders who take cognizance of denominational trends and of the submergence of traditionalists in the Protestant church are altering their policy and are seeking a more mild application of the unemotional norm inasmuch as effects of former attitudes are not now regarded salutary. Thus there are efforts to reintegrate the traditional type in the religious system. Some leaders reversed their policy because competition with cults of the metropolis became acute. In addition, there was consideration of the religious aspirations of various types of Christians; and there was regard of the individual prerogative to worship with a degree of freedom. Some Protestant denominations (Baptist, for example) have churches for various types of Christians. There is some adjustment in the religious system.

Action proceeds in harmony with the normative system of ends in spite of some concessions.

Irrespective of differences in attitudes of Protestants, there is integration of the end-systems of churchmen in the Protestant collectivity, so that in general there is a degree of convergence of ends about one point.

In order for the church to retain a position of eminence it is essential that leaders make important considerations. A religion which fails to regard certain factors will disintegrate.

Since changes in a system of action affect various groups differently, it is important to compare the utilities of diverse groups to facilitate further synthesis and integration of the ultimate end-systems of the individuals in the collectivity. By regulating the distributive relations of groups of men there is provision for the maximum of utility for the aggregate. Leaders of the action system must seek increasingly to render the utilities or ends homogeneous, or more nearly so, in order to lessen friction, competition, and withdrawal. *Concession and cooperation are essential.*

Finally, there is diminution of nonexperimental action in the religious system with the decrement of transcendental value attitudes. There is elevation of an ethical or a socio-religious code with the diminution of the sacred norm as a standard for conduct. The social character of religious beliefs is evident as men seek to relate the teachings of Christ to actual life situations. The church is more actively relating itself with associational and institutional life. And clergymen are more actively interested in retarding pathological developments in society. Religious actions are acquiring an empirical quality as the church exerts effort to adjust itself to social change.

Traditional religion has significantly declined in the collectivity as a body. However, nonexperimental religious manifestations are longest retained by rural groups and by socially depressed or isolated groups as action progresses according to the normative principle.

Bibliography

GENERAL REFERENCE WORKS

Bureau of the Census, Negroes in the United States, 1920–1932, U.S. Government Printing Office, Washington, 1935.

Bureau of the Census, Religious Bodies: 1916, U.S. Government Printing Office, Washington, 1919.

Bureau of the Census, Religious Bodies: 1936, U.S. Government Printing Office, Washington, 1941.

Eastman, Irvine E., *The World Almanac 1947,* New York World-Telegram, New York, 1947.

Guzman, Jessie Parkhurst, ed., *Negro Year Book 1941–1946,* Tuskegee Institute, Tuskegee, Ala., 1947.

Landis, Benson Y., ed., *The Year Book of American Churches, 1945 Edition,* Sowers Printing Company, Lebanon, Pa., 1945.

Murray, Florence, *The Negro Handbook, 1946–1947,* Current Books, Inc., New York, 1947.

Statistical Abstract of the United States, Fifty-Fourth, Sixty-Seventh, and Sixty-Eighth Editions (1932, 1946, and 1947), U.S. Government Printing Office, Washington, D.C.

Work, Monroe N., *The Negro Year Book 1937–1938,* Negro Year Book Publishing Company, Tuskegee Institute, Ala., 1937.

BOOKS

Brawley, Benjamin, *A Short History of the American Negro,* The Macmillan Company, New York, 1919.

Burkhardt, Roy A., *How the Church Grows,* Harper and Brothers, New York, 1947.

Discipline of the Methodist Episcopal Church, 1932, John W. Langdale, Editor.

Discipline of the Methodist Episcopal Church, 1940, John W. Langdale, Alfred F. Smith, and Nolan B. Harmon, Jr., Editors.

Discipline of the Methodist Church, 1944, Nolan B. Harmon, Jr., Editor.

Doctrines and Discipline of the Methodist Church, 1944, Nolan B. Harmon, Jr., Editor, The Methodist Publishing House.

Durkheim, Émile, *The Elementary Forms of the Religious Life,* 1926 edition, translated by Joseph Ward Swain, The Macmillan Company, New York, 1926.

Fauset, Arthur Huff, *Black Gods of the Metropolis,* University of Pennsylvania Press, Philadelphia, 1944.

Greene, Harry W., *Holders of Doctorates Among American Negroes,* Meador Publishing Company, Boston, 1946.
Homans, George C., and Charles P. Curtis, Jr., *An Introduction to Pareto,* Alfred A. Knopf, New York, 1934.
James, William, *The Varieties of Religious Experience,* Longmans Green and Company, New York, 1902.
Mays, Benjamin E., *The Negro's God,* Chapman and Grimes, Inc., Mount Vernon Press, Boston, 1938.
Mays, B. E., and J. W. Nicholson, *The Negro's Church,* Institute of Social and Religious Research, New York, 1933.
Parsons, Talcott, *The Structure of Social Action,* McGraw-Hill Book Company, Inc., New York, 1937.
Washington, Booker T., *The Story of the Negro,* Doubleday Page and Company, New York, 1909.

UNPUBLISHED MANUSCRIPTS

Allport, Gordon, *Lowell Lectures,* 1947.
Breul, Henry Hurd, *An Enquiry Into The Beliefs in God and Immortality in Modern Society,* Harvard College thesis, Harvard University, Cambridge, Mass., 1947.
Funchess, Ruby P., *The Social Significance of the Rural Negro Methodist Episcopal Church,* Master of Arts thesis, Atlanta University, Atlanta, Ga., 1937.
Owens, Richard, "Progress Among Negro Baptists," paper, Massachusetts Baptist Convention, Holyoke, Mass., 1940.

REPORTS OF CHURCHES AND DENOMINATIONS

Christ Temple Church of Personal Experience, 30 Kenilworth Street, Boston, Mass., and *International Gospel Party Boosting Jesus Groups,* Inc., 1946.
Official Journal Seventh Annual Session South Carolina Conference of the Methodist Church, Central Jurisdiction, Marion, South Carolina, 1945.
Proceedings of the Sixty-Third Annual Session of the National Baptist Convention U.S.A., Inc., Chicago, Ill., 1943.
Souvenir Fiftieth Anniversary The St. Mark Congregational Church of Boston, Incorporated, Boston, 1945.
Souvenir Program of Peoples Baptist Church, Boston.

MAGAZINES AND PUBLICATIONS OF CHURCHES

Alpenfels, Ethel J., "Our Racial Superiority," *The Reader's Digest,* Vol. 49, No. 293, pp. 79–82, (September, 1946).
The Asburyan, weekly newspaper of Asbury Methodist Church, Washington, D.C., (August 10 and 17, 1947).
"Religion," *Newsweek,* Vol. XIX, No. 21, p. 56, (May 25, 1942); Vol. XXIX, No. 3, p. 78, (January 20, 1947).

The Voice of the Temple, Vol. III, Nos. 138–141, p. 1, (January 26, February 2, 9, 16, 1947); Vol. III, No. 153, p. 1, (May 11, 1947); and Vol. IV, No. 160, p. 1, (June 29, 1947).

Wintjen, Carolyn, "Interracial Conference," *The Central Christian Advocate,* Vol. 123, No. 5, p. 73, (January 29, 1948).

SUPPLEMENTARY BIBLIOGRAPHY[1]

Caldwell, Erskine, and Margaret Bourke-White, *You Have Seen Their Faces,* Modern Age Books, Inc., New York, 1937.

Cooper, Charles C., *Religion and the Modern Mind,* Harper and Brothers, New York, 1929.

Daniel, W. A., *The Education of Negro Ministers,* George H. Doran Company, New York, 1925.

Daniels, John, *In Freedom's Birthplace,* a Study of Boston Negroes, Houghton Mifflin Company, Boston, 1914.

Dowd, Jerome, *The Negro in American Life,* The Century Company, New York, 1926.

Drake, St. Clair, and Horace R. Cayton, *Black Metropolis,* Harcourt, Brace and Company, New York, 1945.

Du Bois, William E. B., *The Negro,* Henry Holt and Company, New York, 1915.

Du Bois, W. E. B., *The Negro Church,* Atlanta University Publication, The Atlanta University Press, Atlanta, Ga., 1903.

Du Bois, W. E. B., *The Philadelphia Negro,* Ginn and Company, Boston, 1889.

Ferm, Vergilius, *Religion in Transition,* The Macmillan Company, New York, 1937.

God Struck Me Dead, Fisk University, Nashville, Tenn., 1945.

Kennedy, Stetson, *Southern Exposure,* Doubleday and Company, Inc., Garden City, N.Y., 1946.

Kincheloe, Samuel C., *The American City and Its Church,* Friendship Press, New York, 1938.

Kirkpatrick, Clifford, *Religion in Human Affairs,* John Wiley and Sons, Inc., New York, 1939.

Koos, Earl Lomon, *Families in Trouble,* King's Crown Press, Morningside Heights, N.Y., 1946.

Mathews, Shailer, *The Gospel and the Modern Man,* Macmillan Company, New York, 1910.

Miller, Randolph, and H. H. Shires, *Christianity and the Contemporary Scene,* Morehouse-Gorham Company, New York, 1943.

Montagu, M. F. Ashley, *Man's Most Dangerous Myth: The Fallacy of Race,* Columbia University Press, New York, 1945.

Montizambert, Eric, *Christianity in Crisis,* The Cloister Press, Louisville, 1945.

[1] This list of sources consulted includes books only. In the main bibliography, "supplementary sources" were included under all sub-headings except "general reference works" and "books" in order to avoid needless classifications.

Moreno, J. L., *Psychodrama,* Beacon House, New York, 1946.
Myrdal, Gunnar, *An American Dilemma,* Harper and Brothers Publishers, New York, 1944.
Richardson, Harry V., *Dark Glory,* A Picture of the Church Among Negroes in the Rural South, Friendship Press, New York, 1947.
Silver, Abba H., *Religion in a Changing World,* Richard R. Smith, Inc., New York, 1930.
Sorokin, Pitirim, *Contemporary Sociological Theories,* Harper and Brothers, New York, 1928.
Sorokin, Pitirim, *The Crisis of Our Age,* E. P. Dutton and Company, Inc., New York, 1945.
Stroup, Herbert H., *The Jehovah's Witnesses,* Columbia University Press, New York, 1945.
Sweet, William W., *Religion on the American Frontier 1783–1840,* The University of Chicago Press, Chicago, Ill., 1946.
Swift, Arthur L., Jr., *Religion Today,* Whittlesey House, McGraw-Hill Book Company, Inc., New York, 1933.
Vogt, Paul L., *The Church and Country Life,* Missionary Education Movement of the United States and Canada, New York, 1916.
Washington, Booker T., and W. E. B. Du Bois, *The Negro in the South,* George W. Jacobs and Company, Philadelphia, 1907.
Weatherford, W. D., *The Negro From Africa to America,* George H. Doran Company, New York, 1924.
Zimmerman, Carle C., *Family and Civilization,* Harper and Brothers, New York, 1947.

Index